What People
Chicken Soup

"I loved *Chicken Soup for th*　　　　　　　　what
they are likely to experience　　　　　　　　book
will touch the lives of many girls and at the same time, one of
the most important lessons in life—to be yourself."

Aubrey Caswell, 13

"Real. Relevant and 'Right on!' Finally, a book just for girls that
truly supports and inspires at the most important time in a girl's life!"

Tami Walsh, M.A.
President
TeenWisdom.com

"All of the stories were great. Each one was unique in its own way.
Some of them made me think about how good my life really is. For
the people that wrote these stories—you rock!"

Linnea Whisman, 11

"This book really nails it! *Chicken Soup for the Girl's Soul* reflects all
the complexities, joys and challenges of a real girl's life, and provides
peer support during a time when peer pressure is a strong force. The
message is loud and clear—stay true to yourself and know that
others are experiencing many of the same issues."

MJ Reale
President/Founder
www.girlzone.com

"*Chicken Soup for the Girl's Soul* is uplifting and comforting. It made
me feel that other girls were going through the same thing that I was.
I think that girls all over the world will love and appreciate this book."

Wynden Rogers, 14

"*Chicken Soup for the Girl's Soul* is a wonderful compilation of stories
that inspires girls to reach new heights, and soothes those who may
feel left out, or different, as they take on the challenges of growing up!
As both a mother and the founder of Girls on the Run International, I
appreciate this book for its impact on me (as a grown-up girl) and the
support it has had on my own precious daughter."

Molly Barker, Founder and Vision Keeper
Girls on the Run International

"I thought that these stories were very powerful and they made
me laugh. Some of the stories gave good advice to girls and some
made me feel like I was right there in the story."

Jazz Brandon, 12

"The joys and strains associated with this phase of life create an exciting and challenging emotional period for all young women. When I think of my own daughter reaching this stage, I am comforted to know that *Chicken Soup for the Girl's Soul* will be there to help guide her through the tough subjects that she would most likely prefer not to discuss with her mom or dad."

Jonathan Graff
President
www.Kaboose.com

"These stories are very different and exciting. Every story had problems that real girls go through. Every girl should read *Chicken Soup for the Girl's Soul*."

Morgan Conklin, 11

"There are few resources I would recommend to teachers and parents that can build character like the *Chicken Soup* series. With the *Chicken Soup for the Girl's Soul* we have a timely resource for equipping today's young women with meaningful stories of character—I wholeheartedly recommend it as a professor, writer, and father of three girls!"

Jeff Keuss, Ph.D.
Educational Specialist and Author, *Character in Action!*

"I found all of the stories unique and empowering. I loved how all of them taught me a different lesson about life."

Ying Johnstone, 12

"*Chicken Soup for the Girls' Soul* has a message that every young girl should hear, and one that can, unfortunately, be hard to come by. It lets girls know that trouble and hardship can come their way, but that intelligence, courage and wit will help them rise above it, and take them far! Any girl who needs a little inspiration, and any parent looking for a fun, spunky read for their daughters should take a look at this book!"

Rachel Muir
Founder
Girlstart.org

"I like how open and truthful the authors of *Chicken Soup for the Girl's Soul* are."

Riley Fleet, 11

"Most of the stories in *Chicken Soup for the Girl's Soul* just wind you into them and you get stuck until the story is over. You really feel your emotions. The stories make you laugh and cry. They really are for your soul."

Elise Greiner, 12

CHICKEN SOUP
FOR THE
GIRL'S SOUL

Chicken Soup for the Girl's Soul
Real Stories by Real Girls About Real Stuff
Jack Canfield, Mark Victor Hansen, Patty Hansen, Irene Dunlap

Published by Backlist, LLC,
a unit of Chicken Soup for the Soul Publishing, LLC. www.chickensoup.com

Front cover photo by Al Nomura
Front cover models: Jenny Aguilar, Elizabeth Geocaris and Gabby Romanello
Front cover design by Kevin Stawieray
Originally published in 2005 by Health Communications, Inc.

Back cover and spine redesign by Pneuma Books, LLC

Distributed to the booktrade by Simon & Schuster. SAN: 200-2442

Publisher's Cataloging-in-Publication Data
(Prepared by The Donohue Group)

Chicken soup for the girl's soul : real stories by real girls about real stuff / [compiled by] Jack Canfield ... [et al.].

p. : ill. ; cm.

Originally published: Deerfield Beach, FL : Health Communications, c2005.
ISBN: 978-1-62361-031-9

1. Girls--Psychology--Anecdotes. 2. Girls--Conduct of life--Anecdotes. 3. Anecdotes. I. Canfield, Jack, 1944-

HQ777 .C54 2012
305.23/082   2012944280

PRINTED IN THE UNITED STATES OF AMERICA
on acid free paper

21 20   11 12 13 14 15 16 17 18 19 20

CHICKEN SOUP
FOR THE
GIRL'S SOUL

Real Stories by Real Girls
About Real Stuff

Jack Canfield
Mark Victor Hansen
Patty Hansen
Irene Dunlap

Backlist, LLC, a unit of
Chicken Soup for the Soul Publishing, LLC
Cos Cob, CT
www.chickensoup.com

All around the world
With all kinds of faces
Are all kinds of girls
Of all kinds of races.

All colors of eyes
And their own body size
Many different ages
At many different stages
Many kinds of names
And all sorts of fame.

Whether rich or poor
Red, tan, black or white
We are all in this world
And we all unite.

Meredith Brown, 13

Contents

3. FRIENDSHIP AND BFFS

4. FAMILY MATTERS

5. SISTER SISTER

6. TOUGH STUFF

7. THE PRESSURE'S ON

8. CRUSHIN' HARD

9. CHANGES, CHANGES AND MORE CHANGES

10. FREE TO BE ME

Foreword

It isn't easy being a girl today—I know from experience! As the publisher of *Discovery Girls*, I read mail from the thousands of preteens who write to the magazine each issue. These letters have given me a window into what concerns girls most, as well as what energizes them as they strive for success. What I love about *Chicken Soup for the Girl's Soul* is that it's all here. There's the pain of being rejected by friends, the confusion of a crush that doesn't work out, the sadness of losing someone you love. And these stories capture the excitement of being a girl, too: of making true friends, conquering fears and knowing that *you* write your own destiny.

But the best part is that this book is written "girl to girl"! What better way to show girls that they are not alone? You'll find a friend in every chapter—and a ton of inspiration, too. I wish I would have had this book when I was growing up!

So whether you are in need of some extra support or a boost of confidence, or you just want to soak in all the wonder of being alive, you'll know where to go—straight to these pages! And remember, you can do anything! After all, you're a girl!

Catherine Lee
Publisher, Discovery Girls

xii

NO RODEO®

NO RODEO. ©Robert Berardi. Used by permission.

Introduction

Who would ever think that so much went on in the soul of a young girl?

Anne Frank

What exactly is a soul? Is it as light as air, as beautiful as an angel? Is your soul what keeps you alive? Are you your soul? I think if we just keep feeding our souls with stories of encouragement, we'll find out what a soul really is.

Vivian Ling, 11

For a girl growing up, life is an experience rich in swirling emotions and adjustments. You're sorting out who you are and who you want to become; what role family, friends and that special crush play in your life— and all of this happens during a few short years that include more changes than any other time of life.

When you were younger, you spent your time playing with Barbie dolls—but now, you and your girlfriends find yourselves trying on makeup and looking at bras in the Victoria's Secret catalog. But life for a preteen girl is far more than exchanging Barbies for bras. One minute you're edgy with excitement, the next, you are immobilized by your fears—only to be overcome with hysterical laughter, and then betrayed by your tears. Chicken Soup fan twelve-year-old Lindsey Appleton has this to say:

> *Hormones, well, that is something everybody deals with. Like crying for no apparent reason and being happy—just because.*

And preteen reader Paige Rasmussen puts it this way:

> *Right now is a time in our lives when we are dealing with peer pressure, boys and puberty. And it is really nice to know that in a rough time like this in our lives, there is actually someone else in the world who is going through the same things! Most of us have our mothers and sisters, but sometimes that is not enough.*

The preteen years, between nine and thirteen, carry with them so much to sort out. We want to share examples with you that can guide you and to let you know that you aren't alone in what you are going through. We want you to see that these years can be a roller-coaster ride where sometimes you have to hang on for dear life—but you will come through it. Each of you will have your own unique experiences at your own timing. At the end, you will be ready for the next chapter in your life—your teen years.

This book was created to be your companion to help you move through the maze of your sometimes confusing and challenging experiences as a preteen girl. Each contributing author, whether a preteen or an adult, gives you a glimpse of her life and that pivotal experience that helped shape the person she is. The stories shared in *Chicken Soup for the Girl's Soul* are meant to be empowering to a growing preteen girl—and they are as incredibly diverse as are the changes and emotions you are feeling.

Another one of our readers, Devoreaux Walton, explains:

> Going through the preteen years can be really tough. Your parents pressure you about your grades, and your teachers are really starting to pile on the homework. High school seems so far away, like it's hard to visualize. Deep down inside, you know you're not ready for high school yet. At night, you wonder when you'll be ready or if you ever will be.

Your preteen years just might be the most important years of your life. You are taking shape in every imaginable way—body, mind and soul. As you navigate through, remember that this time is unique and very significant. You are becoming a woman, so be in the moment. Embrace every day as you journey through the unknown in the company of millions of other girls like you, who are also making their way through this time of life. It's your life—love it and live it. Grab on to the adventure! Dream and plan. Take the good with the bad. Most of all, stay true to yourself and be good to others along the way. And while you do, hold close the words of Karen Ravn:

> Only as high as I reach can I grow, only as far as I seek can I go, only as deep as I look can I see, only as much as I dream can I be.

We love you, and we hope you will love this book. As you grow into the woman you are meant to be, we hope you are blessed with joy, love, fulfillment, peace and wisdom. We want you to celebrate just how fantastic it is to be the gender that has so much complexity—and, without a doubt, so much power!

Patty Hansen and Irene Dunlap

1

STRAIGHT UP GIRL STUFF

When we stand together
  We all hold the key
  Once we open the door,
  Everyone will see
  Pride is what we have
  And pride is what we'll keep
  Being girls forever . . .
  You and me.

Courtney Bullock, 11

A Perfect Fit

Risk! Risk anything! Care no more for the opinions of others, for those voices. Do the hardest thing on earth for you. Act for yourself. Face the truth.

Katherine Mansfield

When I was twelve, my summer consisted of getting into trouble on my family's farm. I spent hours on end swimming in a make-do livestock tank and climbing oak trees, getting my knees and elbows all skinned up. Thoughts of clothes, makeup or boys were far from my mind. I was a tomboy.

I grew up in a rural Texas town. The only movie theater was forty miles away, and my parents didn't travel unless it was to go to the grocery store and back. I was fortunate to have the daily company of two sisters close to my age, which meant I could easily go an entire summer off from school without getting lonely and needing to see any of my girl-friends. So, I was basically out of touch with anyone but my family for two entire months. That is how the first day of sixth grade almost turned into the worst day of my preteen life.

Two weeks before school started, my mother took me shopping for the usual school clothes, just like she did every year. As usual, I had to be dragged to the bright, fluorescent-lit department store in the next county, and then practically forced to try on clothes. I never once glanced at the dresses on the circular silver racks or showed the slightest interest in any shoes other than those that could be tied with laces. I quickly learned to regret my lack of attention and enthusiasm for this particular back-to-school shopping trip.

The first day of school began like any other school year. I left the house dressed in my new clothes, carrying my purple notebook under one arm, eager to see my friends after two months apart. I couldn't wait to tell them about the new baby calf we were bottle-feeding or that I had nearly broken my arm in July climbing the tallest tree I'd ever conquered.

But from the moment I walked up those concrete steps to the junior high school, I knew something was horribly wrong . . . with ME.

My friends were huddled together in a circle, and the first thing I noticed was that most of them were carrying purses—some white, some hot pink, some brown leather. I didn't even own a purse. Four of them were wearing sandals with heels—we're talking lime green—with the tips of their pink-painted toenails peeking out! I immediately looked down at my plain white sneakers and felt out of place.

A boy we'd all known since kindergarten walked up and tapped my friend Morgan on the shoulder. She tossed her blond hair to the side just as he grabbed the back of her thin, frilly blouse. Then he popped the elastic on the back strap of her bra and ran away laughing. Morgan pretended to be mad, but I could tell she was somehow pleased. The other girls started laughing and teasing Morgan by saying that he liked her.

Somehow, without my even knowing it, over the summer our whole class had graduated from grade school to junior high—complete with new wardrobes, crushes on boys and bra-popping. I no longer knew what planet I was on.

I hadn't given the idea of needing a bra a single thought. I looked down at the front of my shirt. It looked no different than it had this time the previous year. There was nothing there that needed support, for sure. I think the phrase "flat as a pancake" was one my mother had used to describe me.

The bell for first period rang before I could ponder this further. But already I was feeling like my whole world had changed overnight, and no one had bothered to clue me in.

My first class was PE, but not the PE of my previous years. The gym of the junior high included locker rooms and showers, and we were issued polyester shorts and T-shirts to wear. The teacher informed us that from here on out, we'd be wearing these during gym class. In absolute horror, I clutched the uniform tightly to my body and numbly made my way to the locker rooms to change. I looked around me as all of my friends took off their shirts, gabbing about stuff the whole time like, "How cute is Devin this year?!" and "Did you know that he's going out with Chelsey?" All I could do was stare at the forty or so bras glaring at me from every angle. I was obviously the *only* girl in the *entire* sixth grade, perhaps the Entire World of Sixth Graders, who hadn't gotten the memo: *Sixth grade meant girls wore bras.*

I huddled next to a locker, hoping to get my shirt off and the uniform on without drawing attention to the fact that I wasn't wearing a bra. It didn't work, of course.

Morgan saw it first. "Where on earth is your bra?"

I swallowed and looked up as a group of six girls gathered around me.

"I . . . I . . ." was all I could muster.

Whispers rushed around the room and echoed off the tall ceilings, and I could feel my heart beating so hard against my chest I was sure everyone could see it, right there where my bra should have been.

"I forgot it," I said. *Yep, I could really think on my feet.*

"How could you forget a *bra?*" one of the girls asked, snickering over her shoulder at the others.

I didn't know the answer. All I knew is that I was now blushing in places I never thought possible.

As the day wore on, so did the rumors about what I *didn't* have on. Boys ran up to me and brushed their hands across my back in the hall between classes, shouting to each other that it was true. Nothing there to snap.

My so-called circle of friends closed their circle, and I was quickly on the outside looking in. I hung my head and hunched my shoulders as best I could to make viewing my chest as difficult as possible. And I secretly vowed to get even with my mother for not knowing about all this and for not preparing me like the other girls' mothers obviously had done. I had never felt this alone—or this foolish. I had missed the boat that carried the rest of my class to the shores of sixth grade, leaving me behind; me and my braless, boobless, purseless, high-heeled-sandal-less self.

Last period could not have come soon enough. I took a seat in the back and prayed the math teacher would not call on me for anything or draw attention to me in any way. I made marks on my spiral notebook, indicating to myself the number of people who had actually spoken to me since PE—and behind my back certainly didn't count. I was up to three, and one of those was the janitor.

That's when a redheaded girl named Maureen picked up a pencil that had rolled off my desk and handed it to me. I nodded my thanks without looking up or even really moving. In fact, I was beginning to master the ability of breathing without even the slightest rise and fall of my upper body.

"Listen, I heard what happened this morning."

So even Maureen had heard. She was the least popular girl in the whole class. She was taller than everyone else, weighed more than most eighth graders and had probably been wearing a bra since she was a toddler for all I knew. Her face was already covered in zits, something most of us girls hadn't begun to deal with yet. Most of the kids were either afraid of her or ignored her. I had always tried to be nice to her, but not in an overly friendly way that would get me cast out of the in crowd. A lot of good that had done me. One underwear mistake, and I was now on my own.

I allowed myself to slightly turn toward her. "I just forgot it, that's all." I was sticking to my story—it was all I had.

Maureen smiled at me. "Some people can be really mean." She probably knew that better than anyone.

"Yeah," I said, fully realizing that by now, some of the other girls had noticed I was carrying on a conversation with Maureen.

"I've got an extra one in my gym bag if you need it," she said.

I thought it was the nicest thing anyone had said to me in years.

Then we exchanged glances, each of us looking at our own chests, then at the other's. Let's just say Maureen's C cup wouldn't have been the best fit for me. My body wasn't even in training bra mode yet.

We began to laugh. In fact, we couldn't stop. Classmates around me rolled their eyes. The teacher gave us the look that said, "Quiet down or else," but we couldn't stop.

Sitting there, I realized I loved the way Maureen's

laugh sounded, full and real. I liked her smile and the way she was far beyond caring about what others thought of her. I liked that nothing about her was fancy and that she carried a backpack. I liked that she wore jeans and sneakers like mine, and that her T-shirt was just like the ones I'd seen at Wal-Mart on the clearance rack. Her bra might not have been the right size for me, but everything else about her suddenly seemed like a perfect fit.

By the end of last period, I finally let the stress of the day fade away. I no longer cared what everyone else thought I *should* be wearing. I didn't really need a bra, so why should I be forced to put one on everyday until I was ready?

After class, Maureen and I walked down those junior high concrete steps, and I stood with her as she waited for the bus, our chests out and heads high.

And frankly, I didn't care who noticed—anything.

Kathy Lynn Harris

NO RODEO®

NO RODEO. ©Robert Berardi. Used by permission.

Not Just for Girls Anymore!

Learn to laugh at your troubles and you'll never run out of things to laugh at.

Lyn Karol

"Mom, I'm sick again!" I shouted from the bathroom. My mother appeared in the doorway.

"Did you start this morning, Sweetie?" she asked sympathetically. "Your periods sure are awful for you." She wasn't kidding. It wasn't just the cramps, although those were bad enough. My stomach got so upset that I would throw up for the whole first day, every month. It was completely miserable.

"Why don't you crawl back into bed? It's obvious that you can't go to school today," Mom said. "I'll bring you some Sprite and a piece of toast for your stomach."

I did as she suggested. When she came to my room a few minutes later, she looked distracted. "Honey, the radio just announced that the school district called a fog delay. Tim's bus is going to be coming two hours late, and I have to be at work soon. Can you help him catch the bus?" Tim is my brother, who was six at the time.

"Sure, Mom, I'll make sure he gets to school. Thanks for the toast."

My mother left thirty minutes later. I was responsible for making sure that Tim got on the bus for school. *No problem,* I thought, until my stomach decided it didn't want the toast I'd eaten. I was resting on the bathroom floor when Tim walked by and asked me why I wasn't at school. He was still wearing his pajamas. "I had to stay home today," I explained. "My stomach is really sick because I have my period." Tim nodded, although he clearly didn't understand.

"It was foggy this morning, so your bus is going to be late. Mom asked me to make sure you get to school. Your bus should be here soon." It was then that we heard the distinct sounds of a school bus horn. *Had two whole hours gone by already?* I'd been so sick that I'd forgotten to wake Tim up and get him ready for school! My mom was going to kill me!

I racked my brain and decided to call a neighbor and beg her to drive Tim to school. She agreed, and the situation was resolved. I was able to relax with my heating pad for the remainder of the day.

The following week, Tim ate too much sugar and ended up with a stomachache. He was holding his belly when my mom saw him and asked him what was wrong.

"Oh, Mom, my stomach is killing me," he moaned. "I feel awful! I think I have my period!"

Growing up is tough, and sometimes, you have to laugh to keep from crying. The next time you're doubled over with cramps, just think of little Timmy holding his belly, complaining about having his period!

Diane Sonntag

The Bust Developer

Self-esteem isn't everything; it's just that there's nothing without it.

Gloria Steinem

I was sure that there was something wrong with me because I was thirteen and still flat. Ann Tompkins, my best friend, was six months younger than me, and she was already in a B cup. She had started wearing bras while I was still in undershirts, and my envy grew, even though nothing else did.

Every morning I wrapped a measuring tape around my chest, and every morning it was the same pathetic thirty-one inches. I examined my breasts for changes, however small. My nipples were beginning to get puffy, but I looked like a little girl compared to Ann Tompkins. Each day at school, the outline of a bra under Ann's blouse was a constant reminder of my inadequacy.

I thought the answer to my problem was a bra of my own, so I badgered my mother to buy me a pretty one from the Victoria's Secret catalog. I dwelled on the satiny, lacy bras, while my mother talked only of the need for "support."

"I don't know why you're in such a hurry to grow up," she said. She finally promised that she'd look in the cedar chest for my older sister's outgrown training bras. Training bras! When I heard them described that way, I expected them to train my breasts somehow and pull them out of my chest like magic.

When Mom opened the lid of the chest, the scent of cedar radiated from it. Beside the baby quilt, a first communion dress and my mother's wedding dress, there were three slender bras. I gladly traded them for my undershirts, certain that I was entering a new stage of my life. I ran to the bathroom and clasped the hooks on the smallest setting, then spun the bra around and put my arms through the cotton straps.

To my dismay, the cups weren't padded. They were made of some kind of stretchy material.

"That's why they're called training bras," Mom said. "They expand as you grow." But I wasn't growing, so the stretchy stuff just drew in the little nipple swellings that I did have. They actually bound me in a way that made me look flatter than ever! The tag said AA, which was the smallest size in the Victoria's Secret catalog and a far cry from Ann's B.

A few days later, I noticed an ad in the back of a magazine for something called a Bust Developer. It showed a picture of a woman in a bikini with huge breasts. She'd grown from a 34-inch A cup to a 38-inch C cup in just six months using this thing. According to the ad, any woman could improve her bust line to whatever size she wanted by doing simple exercises with the developer. It cost only $19.99, plus $4.00 shipping and handling. I quickly tore out the ad. It was time to take matters into my own hands.

There was twenty-five dollars stashed in the honey bear jar on my dresser; money I'd earned baby-sitting my cousins on my aunt and uncle's bowling nights. I'd been saving for a new bike, but this was more important. I gave the money to my mother and asked her to write a check. She tried to convince me to wait (my breasts would grow on their own, she assured me) and not to order it, but I broke her down and she finally wrote the check. I plopped it into an envelope and mailed it off that day.

Every afternoon, I jumped off the steps of the school bus and rushed inside. "Did anything come in the mail for me?" I'd ask, out of breath.

"Not today, Mary," my mother would say.

Finally, when I'd almost given up all hope of it ever coming and had begun to compose nasty letters to the company, there it was, sitting on the kitchen table when I got home one day—a small package in a plain brown wrapper with my name on the address label. I grabbed the box and raced up the stairs.

Once inside my bedroom, I quickly ripped open the box. The gadget was pink and plastic, with two paddles connected at the top by a hinge and in the middle by a thick metal spring. This couldn't be all! The only thing left in the box was a little booklet of instructions. On the first page, it had the same picture of the woman from the original advertisement. Seeing her boasting again about how she grew to thirty-eight inches reassured me. I didn't even want to be that big. Thirty-six would be plenty big for me.

The directions were filled with diagrams showing the correct way to hold the paddles in front of you and push them together. It looked simple. Push, hold the spring closed for five seconds, then release. Push. Hold. Release. I was supposed to repeat this ten times, then ten more, gradually increasing the sets of ten pushes each day until I was doing fifty sets. What could be easier? With a little persistence, I'd grow and grow and grow!

Eager to get started, I placed my hands on the paddles and pushed, straining to contract the thick coils of the spring. It took all my strength to squeeze those paddles together. I held that position and counted: one, two, three, four. On five, the spring suddenly sprang open, and the contraption slipped out of my hands, flipping onto the floor. I picked it up and tried again, breathing in deeply with each release. The muscles in my upper arms felt tight, and somewhere deep in my chest there were tingles of dull sensation.

For the next few days, I used the Bust Developer faithfully. Morning and night, I stood in front of the bathroom mirror with the paddles, working my way up to ten sets. The weekend came, and I had more time, so I did twenty sets a day. It was excruciating, but I knew it was for a good cause.

Two weeks later, I measured myself, and I was still thirty-one inches. I wasn't getting any bigger; I was just getting sore. My arms ached and felt heavy. They hurt when I carried schoolbooks. Disillusioned, I shoved the developer under my bed, where it collected dust.

Summer came, and I went through a growth spurt. By the end of August, I was an inch and a half taller and my training bras were too tight. Mom took me shopping for new school clothes, and she bought me some new bras, size 32A. I guess I was a late bloomer. But the difference between the size of my bra cup and the size of Ann Tompkins's somehow didn't matter as much anymore. In fact, one day Ann confided to me that she didn't like being busty, that boys made fun of how her breasts bounced when she ran. She was even afraid of how big she might be by the time she stopped growing. I doubted they made a Bust Reducer, and even if they did, it probably wouldn't work anyway. So I just listened sympathetically and actually felt a little sorry for her.

But only just a little.

Mary Laufer

"One Day You'll Look Back on This . . ."

I've learned to take time for myself and to treat myself with a great deal of love and respect 'cause I like me. . . . I think I'm kind of cool.

Whoopi Goldberg

"I can't go to school like this!" I wailed as I stared into my mirror, hating my face, my body and life in general. A river of salty tears traced a path down my cheeks. Summoned from the kitchen by my shrieking, my mother appeared at my side a second later.

"What's the problem?" she asked patiently.

"Everything . . . just everything!" I complained and continued to stare horrified into the mirror.

At almost thirteen, the problems that I felt I had were overwhelming. I had a hideous new crop of angry, red pimples that had erupted on my forehead and chin overnight—every night. My hair suddenly looked greasy all the time, even though I washed it every second day. My aching tummy signaled that my newfound "friend" was about to visit once again, causing my jeans to fit too snugly and make me appear as though I had been eating nothing but hot fudge sundaes. And to top it off, my chewed-up fingernails were torn and bloody, since biting them seemed to go along with the way I worried about how other people perceived me. But everything that was bothering me wasn't just on the surface—I also had a broken heart. The guy I had been going out with had recently dumped me in favor of an older, more developed girl. Everything combined, I was a physical and emotional wreck.

"Come on, now, Honey. Try not to cry," my mother said with a smile. "I remember what it was like to be your age. It was awkward and frustrating, and I got my heart stomped on, too, but I came through it—and so will you! It's not as bad as you think, and once you get to school with all your friends, you'll forget all about your pimples and what's-his-name, and one day you'll look back on this and wonder why you were ever so upset."

Convinced that she didn't know what she was talking about, I gave her a dirty look and headed off for school, greeting my girlfriends on the sidewalk while my mother waved encouragingly from the front door. Later, as much as I hated to admit it, I found out that my mother was right. As I spent time with my friends who were going through the same things that I was, my mind wasn't on my troubles anymore, and soon I was laughing.

When I returned home later that day, I was in a much better mood and because I had put my best foot forward, my mother rewarded me with a bag of goodies she had purchased from the drugstore. On my bed was a bag that included shampoo and conditioner, some acne medication, a gift certificate to a hair salon and, surprisingly, some hot, new shades of nail polish.

"What on earth is this?" I asked bewildered, thinking that my mother had to be out of her mind if she thought I was going to flaunt my gnarled nails.

As it turned out, she had a plan. I thought that it was

cruel at the time, yet it turned out to be highly effective. I wasn't allowed to have any of the stuff in the bag, nor was I allowed to keep my ever-so-important stick of concealer. The deal was that for each week that I didn't bite my fingernails, one item of my choice would be returned to me. Desperate to retrieve my makeup and to get my hands on everything in the drugstore bag, I concentrated heavily on my schoolwork, instead of biting my nails and worrying about what people thought of me. Over the next few weeks, I was thrilled to watch my nails grow. By the time I earned the certificate to have my hair cut and restyled, my nails were so long that my mother also treated me to a manicure while we were at the salon. And as time wore on, I began to see that I was getting through the rough spot, just as she had promised I would.

I liked that I received so many compliments on my hands and hair, but more than that, I was proud of myself for sticking with the deal and improving myself in the process—so proud, as a matter of fact, that I failed to notice my acne slowly clearing up. And I couldn't have cared less about what's-his-name. He quickly became a distant memory as I began to date many different boys, some of whom broke my heart and others whose hearts I broke.

Though it certainly wasn't my last acne outbreak, bad hair day or crushed spirit, I did learn something. I will hold with me forever my mother's words of wisdom: "One day you'll look back on this and wonder why you were ever so upset."

Years later, after several ups and downs in my life, I look back and realize that I did come through it all and I am the better for it. I only hope that if one day I have a daughter who is experiencing the struggles of adolescence, I will be as understanding, helpful and creative as my mother was with me.

Laurie Lonsdale

The Day I Gave My Panties Away

One loses many laughs by not laughing at oneself.

Sara Jeannette Duncan

"Oh," I groaned, frustrated. "Where is that stupid bathing cap?"

My sixth-grade class was going swimming this morning, and we were all required to wear a bathing cap at the pool we were going to. I'd left the packing of my swimwear until two minutes before I had to leave for school, and now I was in a panic. I had torn apart almost every drawer of my dresser trying to uncover a bathing cap. So far I had found nothing.

Finally, stuffing my hand into the far left corner of my top drawer, I felt something that resembled the missing cap. I pulled my hand out hopefully. In my grip was more than I had bargained for. In my hand were *two* bathing caps and a couple of pairs of panties. I let out an audible sigh of relief as I hastily flung one of each item into my bag. The remainder of my find I dropped on top of one of the many mountains of clothes that rose from my bedroom floor.

"Okay, class," my teacher, Mr. Smith, began enthusiastically. "The bus will be here in about five minutes, so I would like you all to go out to your lockers and get your equipment. But before you go, I want you to know that I will expect to see your best behavior. . . ."

I knew that I should be listening to this lecture on expectations, but I was too engrossed in my excitement and daydreams to care. I was imagining all the fun I was going to have with my friends on inflatable pool toys and jumping off diving boards. Perhaps I would even have enough guts to take the plunge from the high dive.

A timid knock at the classroom door roused me from my dreams and transported me back to the classroom. Mr. Smith answered the door. Though the conversation between my teacher and the mysterious visitor was hushed, I was almost certain that I could hear my mother's voice. *What in heaven's name is she doing here?* I thought confusedly. Within a few minutes, the conversation at the door had ceased and the visitor was gone. Mr. Smith returned to his former place at the front of the classroom, carrying a brown paper bag in his hands. "Your mother brought you your bathing cap, Katherine," he called casually.

"But . . . ," I looked up at him quizzically. "I already have my bathing cap."

"Then why don't you lend it to someone who *did* forget theirs," he replied as he handed me the bag.

I shrugged. "Sure. Anybody want it?" Kris, the boy who sits behind me, shot up his hand. I turned and tossed him the bag.

By the time we returned to school, it was lunchtime. I usually went home for lunch, and today was no exception. On my way home, all I could think of was the field trip. It had been awesome. My friends and I had spent our time trying to steal the inflatable boats from the boys and leaping from the diving boards. I was a bit disappointed in myself for not having the courage to conquer the high dive, but I could attempt it again later.

As I stepped into the porch of my house, the soft aroma of batter filled my nostrils. My mother was at the stove flipping pancakes. She glanced at me as I skipped happily into the kitchen and then remarked proudly, "Aren't you glad that I brought you your panties and ba ..."

"What!?!" I wailed, mortified. Instant tears gushed down my burning face. Was she telling me that the brown paper bag I had so kindly given to Kris contained my bathing cap as well as ... MY PANTIES? I had a horrifying vision of Kris sitting on a damp bench in the boy's locker room, the brown paper bag in hand, expecting to dump my bathing cap onto his lap and having my panties tumble out along with it.

"You put my *panties* in that bag?" I cried again despairingly. "I gave it to the boy who sits behind me." I collapsed to the floor in anguish and embarrassment.

My mother stared at my stricken face, dumbstruck.

"How could you have done this to me?" I prattled on, sobbing. My voice was husky with emotion. "I already had a bathing cap and panties. Why didn't you tell Mr. Smith that my panties were in the bag too? I'm so embarrassed! I'm never going to school again."

"I'm sorry, Katherine. I thought I was doing you a favor," my mother apologized. "After you left for school this morning, I went up to your bedroom and saw a bathing cap and a pair of panties on the top of that monstrous pile of clothes on your floor. I thought that you must have dropped them in your rush out the door. And *what* exactly did you want me to tell your male teacher? Something along the lines of ... 'Uh, Mr. Smith, I have Katherine's panties and bathing cap in this bag ... ah ... I was wondering if you could give them to her'?"

I couldn't help chuckling at her little drama through my tears, but in a few moments I was lamenting again. "But, Mom, how am I ever going to be able to show my face at school again? Kris has probably told everyone, and the entire class will make fun of me!"

This time it was my mother's turn to laugh. "I'll bet that he hasn't told anyone, and I doubt that he ever will. He's probably more embarrassed than you are."

I remember it taking every bit of my mother's strength to get me out the door after lunch that day. It was later on in the afternoon when I felt the small soggy bundle of the brown bag containing the panties and bathing cap roll over my shoulder and tumble into my lap. I sneaked a quick glimpse behind me. Kris was staring straight ahead, unsuccessfully pretending to pay attention to the math lesson. My mother was right. He must have been just as embarrassed as I was, because he never said thank-you for the bathing cap, and he hasn't ever even mentioned the trip to the pool in my presence.

Katherine Anne Magee, 14

Unidentified Floating Object

Total absence of humor renders life impossible.

Colette

I couldn't believe my eyes as I peaked above the water, desperately hoping to become invisible at the public pool. I had never felt so humiliated in my entire life! If I could have become a tiny fish and exited out through the filtration system, I would have been gone in a flash!

My sixteen-year-old sister and I had been enjoying another Saturday afternoon sunbathing, diving, chatting with friends and flirting with boys. At fifteen, I felt awkward-looking and definitely not pretty. My hair was too curly and unmanageable, my face was covered with huge pimples and I was shorter than most other girls my age. But worst of all, nothing had developed up top.

That spring, my aunt had flown in from Idaho for her annual visit with our family and had taken me shopping. She bought me the most beautiful bathing suit ever. The problem was that I did not fill out the top of it. My aunt had been very, very blessed in the bust area and found the situation to be humorous. I didn't find it funny at all, but I felt a little better when she bought some white foam inserts for me that could be slipped under the thin mesh lining of the suit. Once I got them in place, the suit looked much better on me.

I couldn't wait for summer so that I could wear my new suit to the pool and show off my fake figure. When the day finally came, I carefully placed the foam inserts under the mesh lining and went to the pool feeling more confident in myself than I ever had. I soon noticed that I was getting more attention from the boys than before. It was a great Saturday of fun and sun—until I took a plunge off the diving board.

When I swam back up to the top of the water, at first I didn't realize what had happened. I had swum over to the shallow end and was standing up to talk with some of my friends when my sister swam over with a look of panic on her face, grabbed me and spun me around to face her. She told me that one of my inserts was missing and my chest was lopsided. I looked down in disbelief, but she was right! I quickly ducked under the water, removed the remaining foam insert and squeezed it tightly in my hand so that it could not be seen. At least now my body was even on both sides, but where was the missing one?

My sister and I looked around the pool frantically for several minutes before we discovered its whereabouts. It had floated to the top of the pool while I was finishing my dive and several boys had discovered it. They were tossing it back and forth to each other, laughing loudly and making crude comments. I wanted to die! Absolutely die! If the boys figured out where the foam insert had come from, I would become the object of horrible jokes. I would never want to swim at the pool again!

My sister, who was always my protector when other kids were doing something to hurt me, sped into action.

She got out of the pool, grabbed our towels and stood by the edge of the pool. I quickly got out and wrapped the towel around myself as fast as possible. She then grabbed our belongings and made a fast break to the pool office, where she called our dad to pick us up. As we waited outside for our dad to get there, a cute boy that I had been making friends with that day came out to see why we were leaving so soon. I bunched the towel up in front of me and acted like I was cold so he wouldn't notice that I was much flatter than the last time he had seen me. I was so relieved when our dad showed up to take us home.

My sister and I never did know what ended up happening to the wayward insert. Maybe it became a souvenir for some boy. What I do know is that was the first and last time I ever wore that beautiful new swimsuit!

Sandra Wallace

NO RODEO®

NO RODEO. ©Robert Berardi. Used by permission.

Girl to Girl

Ever felt happy one minute and sad the next? Experienced moments when you were awed by the beauty of love, friendship and family, and a few minutes later you found yourself screaming at your mom, hitting your brother and swearing at your friends? Wanted to fit in very much but still wanted your own identity? Scared to stand up for yourself, yet you know you were right? Trembled when your crush stood next to you? Then welcome to the preteen years of a girl! Enjoy your journey through these words of advice that might help.

Zainab Mahmood, 13; Rosephine Fernandes, 12

I wanted to be in the "in crowd," but I was never good enough, skinny enough or pretty enough. What I learned through that whole experience is that it is better to be yourself than someone you are not. Your true friends are the ones who are always there for you, although they may not be "in." People are not your real friends if they say you can't do this or you can't do that. True friends will let you be you. So to save yourself a lot of heartbreak and tears— be true to yourself!

Rebekah, 11

If you have a crush on a boy, some of the ways to tell that he likes you are:

(1) He is sweet to you. (2) He sits next to you or in front of you. (3) He starts avoiding you for about three weeks and starts acting strange around you. (4) He asks you out.

Christie, 12

Never write a letter to your crush saying you like him if you don't really know him.

Daria, 13

Don't worry about looking fat or whether or not your favorite music is "in." Don't ever worry about what other people think. I know it's hard, but you have to try.

Emily, 12

When you have a crush on a person, take it easy. Usually our crushes in our preteen and teen years don't last very long. It's not worth changing your whole personality and who you are just for a person who might not be your mate forever.

Before you say something about somebody, keep it to yourself first, until you know the whole situation. You never know when your words are going to hurt someone. Right? Try hard not to gossip!

Remember to keep your friends' secrets private and confidential!

Hannah, 13

1. Never eat spinach on a date.
2. Soda + fast car = messed up shoes.
3. Be true to your friends, b4 ya boyfriend!
4. Everyone is cool inside.
5. Laugh when peeps tease ya!
6. Sometimes you cannot even trust buds.
7. Do your science fair report in advance.
8. Play with you lil' sib sometimes.
9. Once a month, be little again and play out a story with Barbies, Beanie Babies, My Little Ponies, etc.
10. Respect your 'rents, but also speak up for what is right.
11. Popular girls can be insecure too.
12. Do not run in the store, cuz you might run into an old lady.
13. Don't stuff your bra; you can always tell!
14. Be the first to apologize when you have an argument with your bud.

Fabiola, 11

It is so hard to tell a boy that you love him. Nobody likes to admit it, but everyone is afraid of rejection. The only way a boy can like you is for you to be yourself and think your own thoughts. Don't underestimate your smarts or do anything stupid to make him think you're dumb.

Sharnelle, 11

At times you may feel like no one cares or you have no friends. I have felt that way many times before, and I am sure plenty of other girls have. But that is not always the case. Someone cares about you. Have you ever heard the quote, "When everyone walks out, a friend walks in?" Instead of worrying about yourself, try to be a better person and step in where somebody else needs a friend. You never know, you could be meeting your next best friend!

Angie, 14

A zit cannot make the difference that a smile can.

Just because you have the rap CD that costs twenty bucks and has all the latest songs, it doesn't mean you are cool.

The things you want to be, you already are. Be unique. Be yourself. Believe in your ideals.

Makeup doesn't change who you are inside.

Don't grow up too fast. You can never be a preteen again. Live these years to the fullest. There's more to life than boys, kissing, clothes, CDs . . . and you, you, you. The world does not revolve around you.

Stand up for yourself. A strong "no" is something you can be proud of. Only weaklings agree to do drugs, smoke and lose their virginity at a young age. You are smart and cool if you are a nonsmoker and still a virgin.

Being popular doesn't necessarily mean having boyfriends or being on the cheerleading squad. Don't pressure yourself.

Your moms were preteens once, no matter how weird that seems. They know what you are going through.

Always carry an extra pad or tampon to school. You never know when you'll get your period!

Your grades do matter, not how many parties you've attended. In the course of a lifetime, who cares if you've been invited to nineteen birthday parties in a month?

There is a world out there that needs your help. Every little idea counts. You can make a difference.

Zainab, 13, and Rosephine, 12

If a boy says that you are ugly, he is wrong. A boy has to know you to like you. And it is not about looking good—it is about what is inside. Everyone is unique.

Katheryne, 10

If your boyfriend wants to make you do something you are not ready to do, then he isn't your true love. Your true love will wait until you are ready.

Tierra, 13

If you have a crush on someone, don't tell anyone except your best friend—or just keep it to yourself, because if you tell three people, they will tell everybody.

Valeria, 10

Everything will work out okay in the end, so don't worry. You might have some embarrassing moments (SOME???), but you should know that it happens to everyone.

Don't let people put you down; stand tall.

Sara, 13

Tell people what you want them to know before it's too late.

Charlotte, 10

When you are in a fight with your friend and she asks, "Why are you mad at me?" don't say, "You know why I'm mad at you!" because she might not know and she can't fix it if she doesn't know what she did.

Kristen, 11

NO RODEO®

NO RODEO. ©*Robert Berardi. Used by permission.*

Never go out with a boy who is a flirt. He will probably end up liking one of your best friends.

Alana, 13

No matter how mean people are to you, don't try to fight back—it only makes matters worse. Just try to be friends.

Bryttan, 9

When your mom and dad are yelling at you, don't yell back. You'll just get in more trouble. Talk in a nice low voice or just call your boyfriend and complain about it to him after it is all over.

Kelly, 13

When things aren't going too good for you or you are stressed out with family, school or guy issues, listening to music helps out a lot—or learn to play an instrument or sport.

Ann, 9

If you like someone, don't try and keep it a secret, because when you do, you will feel all unwanted. Just tell him that you like him and see where it goes.

Kathryn, 10

Most boys think it is cute when you blush!! They try to make you blush for a reason and that reason is that they probably like you. If you like what he says that makes you blush, let him know you like it and that it means something to you.

Lyndsay (a.k.a. Blushes a Lot), 12

Seventh-grade guys aren't too interested in romance.
Always put on deodorant after the gym.
Never stuff your cat in a backpack.
Don't stay mad at your best bud—there is no one else like her.
Be happy that you have a family.

Mysticats, 12

If you like a boy, don't change. If he doesn't like you for you, you're too good for him!

Marschae, 13

Boys can be really immature—but if you like one, don't be nervous. Just go up to him and tell him. If he doesn't like you, just move on—there will be another one around the corner.

School can be rough sometimes, but it's better than staying at home with your little brother, ain't it?

People who pester you are jealous of you or of things you have.

Becca, 11

Do Girls Belong?

If you want a place in the sun, you've got to put up with a few blisters.

Abigail Van Buren

I couldn't pee in the woods. All the other scouts could just unzip their pants and go, but life doesn't work that way for girls. We need more privacy than turning away can provide, as well as small comforts like toilet paper. *I can do anything they can do*, I thought, *except pee in the woods.*

When I joined Scouts Canada with my friend Brittany, we expected to be shunned because we were the first girls who had ever joined the 57th Scout Troop. Standing in the horseshoe the first night opposite each other, I saw fear in her eyes. I'm sure she saw the same in mine. One of the leaders, Scouter Mike (who also happens to be my dad), greeted all of us.

"Welcome to a brand new year of scouting! We are undergoing some changes this year. As you can see, we have a few new leaders and a few new scouts," he said. All eyes turned to Brittany and me. "Let's welcome Angelica and Brittany to our scout troop. I hope you will make them feel comfortable."

When it came time to split into patrols, Brittany and I clung to each other. But I was put in one patrol, and she was put in the other. The other scouts in my patrol asked me questions like why I wanted to join scouting and why guys couldn't join Girl Guides. My replies were simple. "I like camping," and "Do you really want to learn how to paint your fingernails?"

The next few months followed the same pattern. Halfway through the year, another friend of mine named Christina joined. The three of us girls stayed together for a week. Then Brittany left the group. Not too long after that, Christina left the group as well, so I was left as the only girl in the scout troop. But by then I had solid friendships with most of the guys. I went to camps and watched the boys wrestle each other, while I sat on a nearby picnic table. When we went swimming, I wore a T-shirt and shorts over my bathing suit because I was afraid of being teased. A couple of the boys who I was really good friends with came up under water and flipped me.

In my second year of scouting, I was still the only girl. Just me and a few of the guys I had known from the previous year stayed in the group, and there were a bunch of new guys. But I was relaxed now and didn't care quite so much about being accepted, as long I wasn't disliked. A couple of the guys gave me a nice welcome. I was picked first for soccer, and I got to be APL—Assistant Patrol Leader—for my patrol. My dad wasn't a leader for my troop that year, and that was fine with me. I wanted to be independent, to make friends and expand relationships on my own.

Then at one of the weekend campouts, we were down by the river, ready to go tubing. I was scared of the rapids, so I was trying to see the river and figure out which spot would be the safest and easiest to launch from.

"Whatcha looking for, Ang?" a guy named Ray asked.

"A spot where I can get out, going around the rapids," I replied.

"Why? You can do those rapids. I've seen you rock climb, and that's more dangerous than this!" Ray said.

"Um, I don't know," I told him.

"Hey! I'll stay with you, okay?" Ray offered.

"I guess," I hesitated. "You're sure I won't flip?"

"Positive!" laughed Ray, and he got into his tube. I looked around at the many friends I seemed to have accumulated.

"Hey, Angi! Come see this cool cave!" Tim called.

I looked over in amazement. *Was he talking to me?*

"Ain't it cool? It's slippery in some spots, so be careful," he warned.

"You actually know my name?" I asked hesitantly. Tim was one of the new guys this year, and he had never started up a conversation with me before.

"Yeah."

"I'm impressed," I replied.

"Everyone knows your name. It's not like we all hate you or something. You're a really cool person. You've just got to be a little louder. You're so quiet!"

"Thanks, Tim." I muttered.

"Hey, just telling the truth!" he laughed. We floated off into rapids and rocks, and I didn't fall out at all!

In the past two years, I've climbed walls and rocks, taken part in canoe trips and winter camps. I've snow-shoed and hiked and cycled and floated down a river on a tube. It's been a great time, and I've gotten to do a lot of things that a lot of girls haven't had the chance to do. And so far, it hasn't even been necessary to pee in the woods.

But if I had to . . . I probably could.

Angelica Haggert, 13

2

I'VE GOT THE POWER

Life is short
  Don't ever waste it.
Life is sweet
  Take time to taste it.
Life is a journey
  Find the right path.
Life is entertaining
  Don't be afraid to laugh.
Life is for good times
  Make them last.
Life has its bad times
  Put them in the past.
Life is a chance
  Make sure you take it.
But most importantly
Life is what you make it.

Kelsey Lyn Carone, 12

Big Things

Challenges make you discover things about yourself that you never really knew. They're what make the instrument stretch, what make you go beyond the norm.

Cicely Tyson

It is an old photo. Sixteen years old this past May 29th, to be precise. The Kodak colors have faded slightly. It shows a baby, only a week old, in an incubator and hooked up to an array of wires and tubes and medical gadgets.

There is also a brown teddy bear with a bright red bow around its neck lying next to the sickly infant in the picture—my first gift from my dad. The teddy bear looks huge—nearly the same size as the baby. In reality, the teddy bear is very small, measuring only about eight inches long. Now you realize how incredibly tiny and fragile the baby in the photo is.

It is hard to believe I am the baby in the picture.

Toxemia, a terrible collection of syllables, is what caused me to be born prematurely. When my mother was stricken with the condition, it was considered life-threatening to both of us, and suddenly I had to be delivered by an emergency cesarean section three months before the due date.

I weighed just two pounds, six ounces!

What was even scarier was that the hospital where I was born didn't have a neonatal intensive care unit, so a medical team of specialists had to fly in from the nearest biggest city to deliver me. Then hours later, they flew me back with them to their NICU while my dad stayed behind, because my mom had to remain in the intensive care unit for another three days.

When I was born, the chances that I would survive were small—as small as I was—but one of the doctors who delivered me told my dad that night, "Your daughter is a fighter."

I guess he was right. I guess I am. Indeed, sometimes when I'm facing a challenge, I think about those words, "Your daughter is a fighter," and it gives me strength. My personal mantra when things get tough, like in the late stages of a cross-country, or when I climbed Mount Whitney this past summer, has become "PAST"— Preemies Are So Tough. Indeed, I am proud to be a "preemie." It makes me feel special.

Not that it has always been easy. It's funny now, but until I was about ten, having my toenails clipped was so traumatizing it would bring me to tears. I still don't like anyone touching my feet. A NICU nurse recently told me it is common for preemies to subconsciously remember having their heels constantly used as pincushions to draw blood samples, so it makes sense.

There were also IV needles stuck into my scalp, feeding tubes forced down my nose and monitors attached to my chest. I even had to be on a respirator while my tiny lungs completed forming.

The first month was especially touch-and-go. I owe my life to the dedicated doctors and nurses who cared for me during that precarious period, and I will always be grateful to them.

After spending ten weeks in the hospital, I finally got to come home. I was still so small and frail—not quite five pounds yet—that my parents had to buy Cabbage Patch doll clothes to dress me, because no company made baby clothes tiny enough to fit me.

It took a long time for me to catch up. I didn't grow any hair until I was over a year old. My parents say that even when I was wearing pink, people always thought I was a boy. I'm happy to say that doesn't happen any longer, and I have school dance pictures to prove it.

More seriously, my little lungs remained susceptible to bronchitis. Even when I started kindergarten, I still seemed to always have a bad cough and asthma.

But wait, my story isn't over. The miracle didn't end with just my survival. Hit the fast-forward button.

That tiny sickly baby in the picture has accomplished big things. People can hardly believe that I was a preemie when I tell them. You see, I am a perfectly healthy sixteen-year-old high school junior with no lasting effects of my precarious start in life. In addition to lettering in basketball, cross-country running and track, I am a straight-A student. I'm involved in the student body, and I even wrote the play my school's drama department put on this past year. And, this is the part most people can't believe: I am now five feet, ten inches tall! Yes, I have come a long way from the teddy bear-sized baby in the picture.

My dad says I was a preemie because I couldn't wait to get started doing all the things I want to do in my life. Maybe he's right. After all, I have already written, self-published and sold more than 700 copies of a book. While both the *Los Angeles Times* and *Girl's Life Magazine* gave it good reviews, I am the first to admit it can't compare to my real storybook life to date.

I try to use my frightening premature birth as an inspiration and benefit. Every year on my birthday, my dad and I visit the neonatal intensive care unit. It not only makes me appreciate how wonderfully blessed I have been, but it gives the tearful mothers and fathers of preemies who I am visiting hope that words from a doctor can't. Hope that their tiny, sickly babies can grow up to be the tallest in their classes, that their tiny lungs can someday be strong enough to win a ribbon in a 400-meter dash or finish a 5K race, that their fragile legs may one day carry them to the top of Mount Whitney, or that their GI Joe or Barbie doll-sized hands will one day be able to hold a pencil, shoot a basketball and swing a bat. Hope that their little tiny baby will grow up like I did and accomplish big things.

My personal hope for them is that PAST will become their child's mantra too as they grow up to have a big, bright future of rainbows and roses, ice cream cones and Ferris wheels, four-leaf clovers and proms, just like the teddy bear-sized girl in the picture—the girl who is now a young woman and not sickly anymore.

Dallas Nicole Woodburn, 16

Call Me

Reputation is what other people know about you. Honor is what you know about yourself.

Lois McMaster Bujold

"I know it's here somewhere."

I dropped my book bag to dig through my coat pockets. When I dumped my purse out onto the table, everyone waiting in line behind me groaned. I glanced up at the lunchroom clock. Only three minutes until the bell, and it was the last day to order a class memory book if you wanted your name printed on the front. I did, but for some reason, I couldn't find my wallet. The line began to move around me.

"Come on, Cindy!" Darcy might as well have stamped her foot, she sounded so impatient. "We'll be late for class."

"Darcy, please!" I snapped back. Even though we were best friends, Darcy and I often frustrated each other. We were just so different. Darcy had "budgeted" for her memory book and ordered it the first day of school, while

I had almost forgotten . . . again.

"Darcy, my wallet's gone." I threw my things back into my purse. "My memory book money was in it."

"Someone took it." Darcy, as usual, was quick to point away from the bright side of things.

"Oh, I'm sure I just misplaced it," I hoped.

We rushed into class just before the second bell. Darcy took center stage to my problem and happily spread the news about the theft. By last period in gym class, I was tired of being stopped and having to say over and over again, "I'm sure I just left it at home." Rushing late into the locker room, I changed then ran to catch up with my soccer team.

The game was a close one, and our team was the last one back into the locker room. Darcy was waiting for me as impatiently as always. She brushed past the new girl, Juanita, to hurry me along.

I turned my back on her to open my locker. "Darcy, I know, I know, we have to go."

There was a gasp behind me, and when I looked back at Darcy, her face was white with shock. There, at her feet, was my wallet.

"It fell out of her locker!" Darcy pointed at Juanita. "She stole it."

Everyone took up the accusation at once.

"That new girl stole it."

"Darcy caught her red-handed."

"I knew there was something about her."

"Report her!"

I looked over at Juanita. I had never really noticed her before, beyond her "new girl" label. Juanita picked up the wallet and held it out to me. Her hands were trembling. "I found it in the parking lot. I was going to give it to you before gym, but you were late."

Darcy practically spit the words "I'm so sure!" at her.

"Really, it's true." Juanita's eyes began to fill with tears.

I reached for my wallet. I didn't know what to think, but when I looked over at Darcy, her smugness made me feel sick inside. I looked at Juanita. She was scared but looked sincere. I knew I held her reputation in my hands.

"I am so glad you found it," I smiled. "Thanks, Juanita." The tension around us broke.

"Good thing she found it," everyone but Darcy agreed.

I changed quickly. "Come on, Darcy, there's just enough time to order my book."

"If there is any money left in your wallet."

"Not now, Darcy!"

"You are so naive!"

It wasn't until we were standing in line that I opened my wallet.

"It's all here." I couldn't help but feel relieved. A folded piece of paper fluttered from my wallet. Darcy bent down to pick it up and handed it to me. I opened it to see what it was.

"She just didn't have time to empty it yet," Darcy scoffed. "I know her type. I had her number the first day she came."

"You had her number, all right. Well, I have it now, too."

"It's about time," Darcy huffed.

"Maybe that's the problem, Darcy. Maybe you spend too much time numbering people."

Darcy grabbed the note, read it and threw it back at me.

"Whatever!" she said and stomped off. I knew that something had broken between us.

I read the note again.

> Cindy,
>
> I found your wallet in the parking lot. Hope nothing is missing.
>
> Juanita

P.S. My phone number is 555-3218. Maybe you could call me sometime.

And I did.

Cynthia M. Hamond

NO RODEO®

NO RODEO. ©Robert Berardi. Used by permission.

The Slam Book

When you have decided what you believe, what you feel must be done, have the courage to stand alone and be counted.

Eleanor Roosevelt

I stared at the page so hard I thought my eyes would pop out. There was my name, and scrawled right underneath it the words "The Mop." My heart pounded, my face and ears burned red hot. I wanted to run, hide, anything to get away from the destructive words of this cruel creation by some of my classmates. They called it the "Slam" book.

I couldn't imagine anything worse than being thirteen, living in a new town, going to a new school, trying to make new friends and then having some unknown person write this in a book for everybody to read.

I'd watched during math class as the black book circulated from desk to desk. Each time the teacher turned toward the blackboard, the book was swiftly passed to the next person and hidden until it could be opened, read and written in. When it landed on my desk, I opened it and saw the vicious anonymous comments scribbled across each page.

Who are these people? Why would someone say these things? "Barbara—The Mop." I'd only been at the school a month. I didn't even know them. My fragile confidence was shattered. I'd tried to make new friends, but it hadn't been easy. It was a small town, and they'd all known each other for years. I wondered, *Will I ever fit in?*

I turned the pages to other names. Amanda, "conceited, big lips, hairy eyebrows." I thought she was nice and even pretty. Courtney, "witch's pointed nose, thick glasses." I was just getting to know Courtney. She lived around the corner from me, and we walked to school some mornings. She was kind to me and had a good sense of humor.

I hated school for the next few days and did whatever I could to not be noticed. But that didn't last long. It couldn't. The vicious book kept circulating and gathering more anonymous slander. Somehow I knew the cycle had to be stopped—but how? Determining right from wrong is usually not all that difficult. The scary part is doing it, and I had to dig deep to muster my courage. I wasn't all that brave.

I didn't tell the teachers or rant and rave at the students, although I wanted to scream at a few. Instead, I did the only thing I could do—I refused to participate.

"No," I stammered, pulse racing. "I won't read it, and I won't write in it," I said the next time the book came my way. The boys mocked anyone, especially a newcomer, who refused to participate. Standing alone against them took all the courage I had, at a time when I needed friends.

Suddenly, I noticed other girls saying no, and one even ripped out the page with her name on it. Finally, when all the girls refused and there wasn't an audience, the book faded away into oblivion. The old saying, "If you extinguish the reward, you extinguish the behavior" proved true. We eliminated the reward.

There was, however, another lesson I learned from this experience—one that proved more valuable than just affirming right from wrong. I learned to make up my own mind about people. I learned to understand and welcome their differences, to not accept someone else's shallow criticisms or petty observations, but to see people for who they really are.

Amanda was proud of her full mouth, thick dark eyebrows and olive skin, all of which were beautiful attributes of her Italian heritage. Courtney's poor vision didn't diminish her wit and intelligence. She made me laugh, and eventually we became best friends.

And as for me; I learned to laugh when "The Mop" stayed with me as a nickname. I looked at my tangle of naturally curly hair that wanted to go its own way and eventually came to love it. It wasn't going to be tamed, and neither was I.

The "Slam" book showed up another year, but its history was short lived, and its impact minimal. The girls refused to be intimidated, refused to participate, and the reward was once again extinguished.

Barbara J. Ragsdale

Compassion for a Bully

There is always time to make right what is wrong.

Susan Griffin

My sixth-grade year was one of confusion, intimidation, strength and friendship. There was a girl in my class named Krista. She was taller than me and very skinny, with bony arms and legs. I remember her beady brown eyes and the hard look on her face. Krista didn't like me. In fact, I think she hated me. I was always the smallest in the class and maybe that made me easy to pick on. She would say, "C'mon, little girl, show me what you got! Or are you scared? No one likes you, little girl."

I tried to act like it didn't bother me and walk away. Sometimes it would just get to me, and I would say, "Stop it!" I definitely didn't want her to see me crying in the bathroom. As the year went on, Krista began to get more aggressive. She started coming up to me and punching me in the arm with her bony knuckles. My friends told me to ignore her as we walked away. But those punches hurt. *Why me? What did she have against me?* I had never done anything to invite this kind of behavior.

One day at recess, I decided to face the bully. I had been imagining this moment for weeks. Oh, how good it would feel to punch her back. I wanted to show her that I wasn't scared. So right as the bell was about to ring, I went up to Krista and kicked her in the leg, and then ran as fast as I could into the classroom. I was safe with the teacher in the room. But Krista beamed an evil look my way and said, "Be scared. I'll get you later."

I worked hard at avoiding her the rest of the year. I remember telling my mom about it, and her consoling me with open arms and kind words. She said, "Nobody can tell you how little you are—you decide how big you will be." I really liked that saying. I would say it in my head often and find strength in these words. Krista continued to punch my arm periodically, but eventually it slowed down. But the thought of Krista and her torment didn't die so quickly in my mind.

A year later, in seventh grade, I received a letter from my temple letting me know the date of my Bat Mitzvah, the biggest day of my youth. Then I read who my partner would be for this special occasion. KRISTA. How could this be? I would stand in front of family and friends and read from the Torah, become a woman and share this moment on the pulpit with *Krista*? She was the source of all my anxiety and insecurity and yet this day was supposed to show my strength, pride and wisdom. I was supposed to become an adult. And she would be there, waiting to belittle me. It wasn't fair.

I practiced my portion for months and planned a wonderful reception. I tried to put the thought of Krista out of my head. When the day came that Krista and I saw each other for the first time in a year, we both acted civil. I could tell she wasn't pleased either. Of course, she couldn't punch me in the temple.

I was all dressed up, standing before a huge audience, wanting so much for things to go smoothly, especially in front of Krista. I would have died if I messed up in front of all these people and then had to deal with the laughing and teasing of this bully. I imagined all the names she would call me.

When I read my Torah portion and my speech, I read loudly and confidently. I knew it well. I had practiced long and hard. I saw my friends and family smiling to me, and I focused just on them.

Then Krista came up. She was shaking. I was shocked at how nervous and scared the bully seemed. I had never seen that side of Krista. She was always so strong. But as I watched her fumble through words and chants, I saw this tough girl become weak, flawed and human. I hadn't thought of Krista as human and emotional. As she sat back down in her seat, she quietly cried in her hands. I suddenly felt something that I never imagined feeling toward Krista—compassion. I had always dreamed of the day I could laugh in her face and make her feel as little as she made me feel. But now that the day was really here, I didn't want to anymore. I sat down next to the sad girl, as her hands remained over her eyes.

"I know I messed up; you don't need to gloat. Go away!" she said.

"You were nervous. Everyone understands. No one remembers the mistakes. They love you and will focus on all the good. That's what family and friends do," I told her.

"Not my family. They love to tell me my mistakes," she answered. And then it made sense to me. This is why she was a bully. This is all she knew.

I put my hand on her shoulder and told her again that she did great. She could barely look me in the eyes, and then she whispered, "Thank you. I don't know why you are being so nice; I was never nice to you."

"I know. But it is in the past; it's over."

"I'm sorry," she finally said. I smiled and gave her my forgiveness. I told her what my mom had told me the year before, "Nobody can tell you how little you are—you decide how big you will be." Hopefully, those words gave her the strength that they gave me.

I truly believe I became an adult that day.

Melanie Pastor

The Most Important Lesson

*The externals are simply so many props; every-
thing we need is within us.*

Etty Hillesum

During my elementary school years, I began to compare my mother with all the mothers of my friends. Most
often, I would compare her with the mother of my best
friend, Tiffany Sherman.

Tiffany always came to school with the most fashion-
able clothes, the most beautiful makeup and the most in-
style hairdo. Her weekly allowance could feed a family of
five in Cuba for a year, and she had more jewelry than I
had grass in my backyard. She coordinated her shoes
with her outfit and her outfit with her purse. She constantly had a glamorous group of people following her,
and more or less, she always got her own way.

All of the boys in school would have killed to have her
for their girlfriend. Tiffany was allowed to go to rock concerts, to go places alone with a boy and to have two sleepovers in a row—three things that my mom had *never* let
me do. Her mom showered her with money for things she

did that *my* mother took for granted, such as getting good grades and making the bed. Whenever I went to the mall with Tiffany, she would whip out a crisp $100 bill, and I would be standing there with two fives and a handful of quarters.

Whenever I didn't get what I wanted, *when* I wanted it, I would scream out the classic, *"Tiffany's* mother would let her! I wish *she* was my mother."* My mom would calmly say—every time—"Poor Tiffany."

Tiffany got to buy that $200 outfit. "Poor Tiffany."

Tiffany got to hire an interior decorator to redo her room. "Poor Tiffany."

Tiffany had a television in her room—complete with a DVD player and surround-sound system. "Poor Tiffany."

I never understood my mom. *She shouldn't be feeling sorry for Tiffany!* I thought. *She should be feeling sorry for me!* Tiffany had everything, and as far as I was concerned, I had nothing.

One day, I had heard it one too many times. I cracked.

"Poor Tiffany?! *Lucky Tiffany!* She gets *everything* she wants! She practically has the world at her feet, and you're feeling *sorry* for her?!" I burst into tears and flopped down onto the sofa.

My mother sat down next to me and said softly, "Yes, I do feel sorry for her. I have been teaching you a lesson, Hope, that she will never be taught."

I sniffled and looked up at her. "What are you talking about?"

My mom looked at me with sad eyes. "One day she will want something, *really* want something, and she'll find out she can't have it. Life doesn't work like that, you know. You don't get every little thing you want. Her mother won't always be around to hand out cash, and what's more—money can't buy everything.

"But you! I have taught you valuable lessons by not tossing you every dollar you desire. You'll know how to look for bargains and save money—she won't. You'll understand that you need to work hard to get the things that you want and need—she won't. When Tiffany is a grown woman, she'll wake up one day and her mother's money will be gone and she will be wishing she had a mom like the one you've got. Life lessons, Hope, are more important and necessary than rock concerts and Gucci clothes."

I understood my mother's lesson. It took some time, but I eventually understood it. I look forward to the days when I am a smart woman and know how to fend for myself. And I will truly pity those who won't.

Poor Tiffany.

Hope Rollins, 13

Lost and Found Dream

*Have faith in tomorrow for it can bring better
days.
Never wish for yesterday for it has gone its separate way.
Believe in today for it's what you're living now.
And dare to dream all your dreams for it's not
why, but how!*

Tonya K. Grant

From the time I was in the third grade, I knew I wanted
to be a writer. After winning an award for my story that
was chosen to be hung on a board for Open House, I
spent much of my free time writing wild stories of strange
creatures, kids' fun adventures and poems of how I felt
about my world. I dreamed of seeing my stories in magazines and books. I wrote all through school that year. In
the fourth grade, I continued to write, and I put them all
into a notebook so I could carry them around and write
whenever I felt like it.

When I started the fifth grade, my English teacher was

Mrs. Foster. She was the best teacher I'd ever had. She always had something nice to say about everyone, and she never failed to say it out loud. I loved her so much that I showed her my notebook and what I had been writing ever since the third grade. When she returned my stories to me, she had written encouraging notes on them praising my imagination and skill, which made me feel really great.

One day during class, a classmate found my notebook of stories and hid it from me. A friend in my class told me that she'd seen a boy pick up my notebook while I was on the other side of the room working on a group report. I confronted him, but he pretended like he didn't have any idea what I was talking about. No matter how much I pleaded, he claimed he hadn't seen it. I looked everywhere and couldn't find my notebook. All of my stories were handwritten, and I had no other copies. I was completely devastated. I finally gave up on ever seeing my stories again, until one Friday a few weeks before the school year ended.

"Kathy, I wonder if we could talk," Mrs. Foster asked. As my friends went to wait for me in the hall, I walked over to Mrs. Foster's desk. She smiled at me and then pulled out a binder labeled, "Second Period Class." Inside, she browsed through dividers. On each divider, I could see the names of my classmates. Finally, she stopped at one. When she turned the divider, I saw my name. Inside of my section were my stories.

Astonished, I asked, "How did you find my notebook?"

She shook her head. "I didn't find it. These are my copies of your stories. I keep all the wonderful stories my students write. They remind me of each of you and your imaginations." She opened the binder rings and pulled out all my stories. Then she took me down the hall to the teacher's lounge, where she made copies of each one and placed them in my hands. They even had her notes on them.

"Don't give up your dream, Kathy," she said. "I didn't give up on mine. I always wanted to be a teacher, and here I am."

I was so happy! I held my stories tightly, thanked her and ran to find my friends.

I did what Mrs. Foster encouraged me to do. I never gave up on my dream. I won contests throughout school, and now I have had hundreds of my stories published in books and magazines.

It takes strength and persistence to follow a dream. And sometimes, it takes other dreamers to help keep our dreams alive. I'm glad Mrs. Foster was a dreamer too.

Kathryn Lay

A Cheer of Triumph

Holding on to anger, resentment and hurt only gives you tense muscles, a headache and a sore jaw from clenching your teeth. Forgiveness gives you back the laughter and the lightness in your life.

Joan Lunden

As I sat in the bleachers surrounded by fifty girls, butterflies did back flips in my stomach. We waited anxiously for the judges to give the final results of the cheerleading tryouts. One by one, each girl leaped from her seat, jumping up and down, ponytail wagging as her number was called out.

Would I be one of them? I wondered.

I was getting more nervous and excited by the second, and each second felt like an eternity.

"Number seventeen," the judge announced. I leaped from my seat and ran over to stand next to the bouncing girls.

We hugged each other and giggled with joy as we each realized we were part of the ten-girl junior high cheerleading team. Little did I know my happiness wouldn't last long.

It all began when I showed up to the practice before the pep rally in the wrong uniform. I felt silly. I must have misunderstood. And I was co-captain of the team!

All the other girls on the squad were practicing in their white tops and skirts. There I stood in my blue uniform. It felt like everyone was laughing at me.

"I'll give my mom a call," said Tammy, one of the girls in white. "She doesn't work, and she'll drive you home so you can change."

When we reached my house, I couldn't find my uniform. I looked everywhere. Finally, I opened the hamper, and there at the bottom of a smelly heap of my brother's clothes was my dingy white uniform crumpled into a ball. I quickly put it on and ran out the door to Tammy's mom's car. We had just fifteen minutes until the pep rally started. We barely made it there in time.

"I can't thank you enough," I told Tammy's mom as I bolted from the car. She smiled and waved good-bye.

Humiliated, I ran toward the gym and joined the other girls in front of the school for the opening cheer. I heard waves of laughter ring out from the bleachers as we did the first cheer sequence. We did the cheer again, and the laughter grew even louder.

They must be laughing at my uniform. I felt a sickening feeling growing in the pit of my stomach. But it wasn't the uniform they were laughing at at all.

The next day, my friend Jay was the one who clued me in.

"Kim, at one point you were doing the cheer with your arms opposite of everyone else. That's why they were laughing."

"I couldn't have been doing it wrong," I said, feeling

confused. "The cheer captain taught me herself and said that I was doing it perfectly."

I didn't want to believe that the team captain had done this on purpose. I couldn't imagine why anyone would be so mean in the first place. But the denial that was keeping me from feeling hurt quickly faded away after the next thing happened.

The team captain told me to meet everyone at her house that morning before driving to the away football game. When my mom and I drove up to her house, we noticed no cars in the driveway. When I rang the doorbell, her dad answered.

"They're not here," he said in a gruff tone.

"What! We were all supposed to meet here at nine o'clock."

I knew he could tell by the expression on my face that I was very upset. Anger was sweeping over me as I walked back toward the car. Now I knew for sure that this time it was intentional—and that probably all the other times were too.

Why don't those girls like me? What did I do? The heavy weight of pain hit me like a sledgehammer. I felt like crying. I felt like throwing up.

In those few moments, I gave up on believing in the kindness of people. I felt like the world was against me. I wanted to quit the cheer team.

"Wait a minute, Kim."

I've never met this man before and he knows MY name.

Her dad had been watching me as I walked toward the car. "They're at the McDonald's on Main Street," he whispered, as his eyes caught mine.

I knew he wasn't supposed to be telling me this. To my surprise, there was kindness in the way he was looking at me. It was as if he was saying he was sorry for what they were doing to me. I was deeply touched in the most extra-ordinary way.

Mom and I went to the McDonald's and joined the other girls. They told us we must have misunderstood where to meet, and they laughed it off, but I knew that it wasn't true.

For the rest of the season, I cheered my heart out on that cheer team and tried my hardest not to let the mean girls get me down. A year later, I learned from another girl that it had been the captain and her mother who caused all the turmoil against me. They believed I was their competition and were trying to get me to quit by leaving me out and being mean. I was shocked because I never thought I was that good. Most of the other girls hadn't had a clue about what was really going on.

It was over the next few years of cheerleading that I began to feel sorry for the team captain and her mom for treating me so cruelly. They continued to act this way until high school graduation.

I had almost lost hope that there were any nice people left in the world until that day I stood in the cheer captain's front yard. The smallest gesture of kindness that had come from my rival's own dad had put a spark of hope into my hurting heart.

A few years later, I did something that surprised me even more. I decided to forgive them.

Kim Rogers

3

FRIENDSHIP AND BFFS

Tight as a knot we are bound together
Although we're still young we'll be friends for-
*   ever.*
So many memories, even more to be made
The tears and the laughter . . . may they
*   never fade.*
From birthdays and Barbies to boyfriends
*   and bras*
We've made it this far like Dorothy to Oz.
The parties, the fun, the jokes played at school
The times when we agreed what was and
*   wasn't cool.*
I hope I'll never lose you; you're my very best
*   friend*
I know that we'll always stick together 'til the end.

Chloe Scott, 13

Soul Sisters

I suppose there is one friend in the life of each of us who seems not a separate person, however dear and beloved, but an expansion, an interpretation, of one's self.

Edith Wharton

Ku'ulei and I were the best of friends. In school, you would never see one of us without the other. It was like we were Siamese twins, going everywhere with each other, stuck together. Even if we ran out of things to talk about, which was hardly ever, it still seemed like we were talking, just not verbally. It was almost like a silent conversation. She always knew what was going on in my head without being told. To me, that's what I call a "true friend." As an example, one time for some reason when I was feeling down Ku'u came over to my house, and I was acting like nothing was wrong. I thought that I didn't show it, but she already knew.

It was like we were meant to be best friends. "Soul sisters" is what I would call us. Since we knew that we were going to be friends forever, we had a saying—*Ku'ulei and*

Kayla, Best Friends Forever! Nothing can tear us apart! Not years, boys, parents, distance or fights! In our world, friendship is #1! In every letter we would write to each other, this was our "P.S." It was true then, and it still is.

I always thought to myself, *What would I do without her?* Now I know—I am living in pain, grief and sorrow. My life seems like it has ended. But I have to know that this is better than having her live in pain from the accident. God did the right thing and took her back home to heaven so she could live a happier life.

It was July 8th. I was visiting Hilo, a town on the other side of the Big Island of Hawaii, where I live. I was staying at my grandpa's house, and Ku'ulei was at her house, back home where we live in Kona. I woke up that morning and jumped on my golf cart with my cousins to ride around the ranch. As we were coming up the hill, my mom was in the garage talking on her cell phone with a terrible, worried look on her face. My cousins were on the back of the cart screaming, laughing and being silly. I was driving but suddenly felt numb when I saw my mother. I was worried that something bad had happened to my dad back home in Kona. I parked the golf cart and asked my mom what was wrong.

"Kayla, there has been a really bad accident in Kona," she replied.

"Was it Dad?" I asked.

"No."

Since it wasn't him, I wasn't too worried.

"It was at Ku'ulei's," she responded.

I panicked and hoped with all my heart that it was not something that involved her.

"I'm not sure, but either Ku'ulei or Charley (Ku'ulei's older sister) was run over by their truck and killed. One of the twins, Pua or Anela (Ku'ulei's younger twin sisters) was also killed. I think you should call Ku'u's house."

Even as my eyes filled with tears, my heart filled with hope. I was praying as I dialed their number that nothing had happened to my best friend. A girl answered the phone, and I started to breathe a sigh of relief. I thought it was Ku'ulei.

"Hello? Ku'ulei?"

"No, Kayla . . . this is Charley."

Hearing Charley's voice, I immediately knew. I knew that it was Ku'ulei who had been killed. I started to cry.

"Charley . . . is Ku'ulei there?" I asked with hope in my voice.

"No . . . Kayla . . . didn't you hear?"

"What?" I asked.

"My sisters are dead."

When I heard those words, I choked and fell to the ground. It was as if the world had stopped and my life had crumbled into bits and pieces. For a moment, I thought I was the one who was dead.

"Kayla! Kayla!?! Are you okay? I'm so sorry . . ." said Charley.

"Yeah, Charley . . . I'm okay. No, I'm sorry, too. . . ."

"Well, I'll talk to you later," she said in a sad voice.

We hung up, and I walked outside to my mom. As I got closer to her, she asked me who had had the accident. "Was it Ku'u?"

I was speechless. All I could do was nod my head. She grabbed me and hugged me tight. "I'm so sorry."

As I hugged her back, confusion ran through my head. I didn't know how to act. I couldn't handle it anymore. I took a walk down the road. I thought of our memories and wondered, *Why did this happen to me? . . . to her? . . . to us?*

It was like she was perfect. She did rodeo, sports, volunteered at gardens and took great care of her sisters. She was sweet, optimistic, loving and fun to be around. She was EVERYTHING!

I walked back and told my mom that I wanted to go back home so I could go to Ku'ulei's house to see her family. When we got there, everybody was there; they were digging a hole for her ashes and bringing in a special rock to place on top. I went to her parents and gave them my love. I sat next to her dad, looking at everything.

"No more your buddy," he said to me.

I looked up at him and replied, "Yeah."

Tears rolled down my face, but I knew she was up there doing better than she would be down here, where she might have been suffering. I just wished that it could have been different—that it wouldn't have happened to her.

The funeral came, and hundreds of people showed up to honor my friend, who had been such a special girl, and her little sister. Then it was over, and the days went by. It has been very hard for me. At times, I still can't believe it, and I often think that she's just in another state but that I can't call or write. It's as if she will come home any day.

Two years have gone by now, and I still go to her grave and visit her and her sister. When I sit on the bench and stare at the rock on the grave with the beautiful flowers that are always fresh, I feel that Ku'ulei is with me. It's like our "silent conversations" from the past, but without her body there. I now understand that my soul sister had to go back home.

Now I go through school without my pal, my best friend, my soul sister, my buddy, my everything. Her spirit is always by my side, in my heart and in my mind.

So hang on to the friends that you know are good and true and give them what they deserve. You never know when God will decide to take them back home.

My poem to you, Ku'ulei:

It's been two years since you went away
I still remember that very day.

I remember that moment, that time and place
I remember trying to picture your sweet gentle face.
My whole body sank to the ground
And my world was dead, all around.
I couldn't believe how fast this all came
I couldn't deal with all of the pain.
We were so young, childish and carefree.
We lived our lives with joy and glee
This didn't come into our heads
It wasn't what was being talked about or said.
I wish we could go back to how it was
Writing each other letters, "Just Because."
Now I am here, sad and lonely
You were my trusted friend, my one and only.
Whenever I was down and blue
I would always turn to you.
I wished this hadn't happened, from the start.
Now the only way I can keep you is here in my heart.
I can only wait 'til it is my day to see you again
As for now . . . take care, my friend.
I LOVE YOU! GOD BLESS! R.I.P.

Ku'ulei Kauhaihao
1990–2002

Kayla K. Kurashige, 13

[EDITORS' NOTE: *For more information about how to deal with death and grief, log on to* www.kidshealth.org/teen/ *(keyword search: "death and grief").*]

The Five Flavors

*The most beautiful discovery true friends make
is that they can grow separately without growing
apart.*

Elisabeth Foley

In fourth grade I had four best friends. We were all as
different as we could possibly be, yet we got along perfectly. One day we decided that we should be an official
group. Since I love food, I thought we should be "The Five
Flavors," kind of like Baskin Robbins's thirty-one flavors.
We were all unique individuals, but together we were one
sweet mix. We all came up with names for one another. I
was Vanilla Bean, Samantha was Mix 'n' Match, Leah was
Shaky Sherbet, Lily was Chilly Lily and Jessica topped it
all off with Sweet Sorbet. And so The Five Flavors were
born. We never really told anyone else about it. Just a little something we kept to ourselves.

That year Leah decided that she wanted to have The
Five Flavors sleep over for her ninth birthday party. We
slept outside in a huge tent. We had a blast staying up
late, eating junk food and laughing at all the stupid things

we did. It was that night that we decided this should be something we do at least once a year. We decided to call it our "Tradition."

Between fourth and sixth grade, we had Tradition more than once a year. We were all so close and felt like nothing could ever tear us apart. We would joke about having Tradition when we would be eighty years old and how we would have to put our teeth in a cup rather than brush them. Tradition was a night where we could forget all of our troubles and just have a crazy time.

Then came seventh grade. We had managed to stick by each other through the first year of middle school, but we soon realized that we had all dramatically changed by seventh grade. We weren't the same Five Flavors that we had been three years before. We began hanging out with different groups. Despite our differences, we still had Tradition that year.

But by eighth grade, we were completely separate. We each had our own friends, opinions, teachers . . . everything. Lily's best friend was my worst enemy. Jessica's friends made fun of me. We all were our true selves, and we all liked it that way. However, surprisingly enough, we STILL had Tradition that year.

Next stop, high school. We were now each our own person with completely opposite personalities. We barely saw one another, and if we did, we wouldn't even say, "Hi." No one could have ever guessed that at one point we had been so close. The ninth-grade school year was coming to an end, and we hadn't had Tradition yet. We had basically given up on the idea, but Leah insisted on having one. After multiple attempts to find one weekend that we were all free, Leah finally found one—the weekend of her fifteenth birthday. We all came, expecting it to be just like the first one we had had six years ago, and it was.

It was like we had never changed at all. We were all

exactly the same. We all still laughed at the fact that Lily threw M&Ms in the tent, Jessica and I were still chasing each other around and fighting, Leah still yelled at us to stop screaming and Sam was still the sleeping doormat. The only thing that had changed was how little room we had in the once gigantic tent. That night you would have thought we were all still the best of friends. We were open about everything, as if nothing had changed between us. The past six years had altered the way we dressed, thought and talked, but we were still the original Five Flavors.

That night we all realized that no matter how far apart we grow, we would all have each others' back. I learned that nothing can replace good old friends; people who to this day can make you forget about all your problems and allow you to have nothing but fun. Sure enough, after our last Tradition, we went back to our own friends, our own ways, our own lives. But we all know that we'll be back in a year, laughing together as if we were still in fourth grade. And that's what's so great about a little thing we like to call Tradition.

Roxanne Gowharrizi, 14

My Friend

I'm not quite sure where to begin or where to start
All I really know is that this poem's from my heart.
This may sound confusing—it is for me too
But I'm ready to begin this poem to you.

A tortuous winding path—life is a confusing place to be.
I want to get away from this stress and find the real me.
Why can't I be happier? Today's a brand-new day . . .
Yet I have thoughts and memories that don't go away.

I think of my life, and that my problems aren't so bad
But for some unknown reason I still feel kind of sad.
It's tough being a preteen, sometimes it's just a scare
I wish I had some answers. Life isn't always fair.

Sometimes I'm just really lost and don't know what to do.
I wonder where to go and who I can talk to.
No one really knows which thoughts I choose to share,
But even if I told them they probably wouldn't care.
Sometimes I want to say, "Thanks for all that you've
    done,"
But the words fly from my head as quickly as they come.
I don't know how to talk to you, to tell you how I feel

Now and then it's so complex. Life sometimes is surreal.

You may not always see me when I stumble, trip and fall
When tears are in my eyes and there's no one to call.
You may not hear me when I cry in bed at night
Hoping that my worries will somehow be put right.

You may not always love me when we just don't get along
I may screw up when I just won't admit that I was wrong.
I'm sharing with you because I know that you really care
The friend you are to me is special, precious and rare.

Sometimes I might act joyful to camouflage my fears
But deep down inside, I want to burst right into tears.
All I need sometimes when my heart just wants to break
Is your smile and a hug. That's what I can't fake.

I need you, my friend, to take my hand and try
To help me mend my broken heart and be there when I
     cry.
I want you to be with me and walk with me on this road
To step along beside me and help me with this heavy load.

I want you to feel free—I hope I don't ask too much
Just be there when I need you, and offer me your touch.
Some people are ashamed to cry, but I am not afraid
For crying is the way that I let out all my pain.

A friend walks in when all others walk out.
You knocked on the door when I was full of doubt.
You are an angel. You've helped me do what's right,
When I had no eyes, you saved me—you were my sight.

You helped me through, without you, where would I be?
A blessing and a treasure is what you are to me.
You are a great person with good advice to lend

I just want you to know that you are a wonderful friend.

Have I changed you? You have changed me a great deal
You've let me be who I am and tell you how I feel.
The best thing ever was finding a friend just like you
Who listens and talks to me, you make each day seem
   new.

I hope you liked this poem . . . like I said from the start
This poem was written for you, from deep inside my
   heart.

Anna Vier, 14

NO RODEO®

NO RODEO. ©Robert Berardi. Used by permission.

Forget Him

I have always grown from my problems and challenges, from the things that don't work out. That's when I've really learned.

Carol Burnett

My friend Cristen and I both had a major crush on the same guy, Brennan. Cristen had gone to a different school, where she met him and used to chase him around. During the sixth grade, they both came to my school, and he rode on the same bus that I rode everyday. Brown hair, awesome blue eyes . . . no wonder we both liked him. Everyday at school we would obsess over him; if he looked at us, if we talked to him, whatever. I guess you see my point about the word "obsession."

Pretty soon, I started to get to know him better. We would talk on the bus longer than usual (which meant that we spoke only about four words to each other) and that was okay for me! Finally we began talking almost every day through instant messaging, and he seemed really nice. I started to like him even more.

One day, I found out that Brennan was going out with

a girl named Lisa. I was so mad—although I had no clue as to why I should be so mad. I mean, it was none of my business. Even so, I started obsessing over him even more.

Later, I found out that Lisa had dumped him because she just wanted to be friends with him. I felt like that was some of the best news I ever heard in my life! That night, on instant message, I almost asked him out but decided against it. I was only in sixth grade, and I felt like I was too young to go out with someone. Not only that, but I knew that Cristen liked him too, and I thought it would hurt Cristen if I started going out with Brennan.

One day, Brennan told me that he talked to Cristen on instant message! I decided to call her, but there was no answer. *Dang,* I thought. *I'll call her back later and ask her about it.* About five minutes later, Cristen called me. The first thing she said to me was, "I have a boyfriend!" I laughed, thinking it was a joke, because we had joked about that before. "No seriously," she replied to my laughter.

So I took a chance at asking her who it was. "Mark?" I asked. He was a boy who had moved in across the street from her. I figured it could be him.

"No. Guess again," she said to me. I guessed, already knowing who it really was. I just didn't want it to be true.

"Brennan," I said in a flat tone.

"Yes!" she excitedly replied. I tried to act normal and be positive, but I could barely hide my disappointment.

"That's cool. You have a boyfriend, Cris. Great." I could hardly fake any excitement.

I later asked Brennan about it and found out that it was true—he was going out with her. He and Cristen had instant messaged each other for an hour and forty-five minutes the night before. He told her that he had liked her since kindergarten! I was furious and sad all at the same time. I went up to my room and tried not to cry.

I called Cristen later and we talked, but when she asked if I was okay about her and Brennan, I hung up on her. She didn't call back. I really don't know if the relationship between Brennan and Cristen will last, but meanwhile I'm trying to not have hard feelings toward Cristen since this is the first time we've ever experienced something like this. If Brennan had asked *me* out, I would have said no— because my friend liked him too. I wish that Cristen would have done that; but it was her choice, not mine.

I've read in teen magazines: "If you and your best friend like the same guy, you should BOTH forget him. Otherwise, someone is going to end up getting hurt when the guy you're crushing on goes out with your friend and not you. FORGET HIM."

I totally believe that advice and I have decided that's what I'm going to do if the situation should ever come up again. In the end, friends will be there long after the crush is over, as long as we play by the same rules and respect each other's feelings.

Sarah Hood, 12

Do You Remember When?

Do you remember back when we were little kids
Laughing as our hair flew wildly in the wind?
Playing all day long, talking through the night
Those were the times when everything was right.

Do you remember our very first day of school?
You were the one friend who helped me make it through.
That tough first year you were there to ease my fears
And you've always been there for me through all the years.

Do you remember I told you that you're my best friend?
We promised we'd be there for the other, until the very
    end?
People always used to say that they never saw us apart.
Do you know that you have a special place in my heart?

Do you remember when our bond began to break?
Fights became frequent and our hearts started to ache.
Suddenly our forever friendship came to an abrupt end
When we realized it was something we couldn't mend.

Remember when we decided to go our separate paths?
To be on our own and make friends who can't last?
Did the loss of our friendship ever make you cry?
Feel empty or sad—or have you even wondered why?

We've grown older and we realize that things often change.
They don't need to end, but they cannot stay the same.
Still, in the back of my mind this question won't end . . .
Do you remember, or ever think about . . . when we were
    best friends?

Mina Radman, 11

One Is Silver and the Other Is Gold

Trouble is a sieve through which we sift our acquaintances. Those too big to pass through are our friends.

Arlene Francis

"What? We're moving *AGAIN?*" I asked in disbelief after hearing my mother's "news."

"I'm only in fifth grade, and this is my eighth school! It's not fair! I just finally made some friends!" I ran into my room, threw myself on the bed and cried.

By mid-January I had started yet another school. It wasn't quite so hard moving in the summer, but I hated moving during the school year. By then, everyone had made friends, and it always took a while to be included.

My first day at Mitchell Elementary was hard. Even though Mrs. Allen introduced my classmates, nobody ate lunch with me or said hi at recess. I sat alone, watching everyone on the playground having fun. Boys were running around trying to catch each other; girls huddled together, whispering and giggling. I noticed that everybody was wearing nice clothes and shoes, far nicer than

my hand-me-down dress and tennis shoes that were rip-
ping near my toes. I told myself that everyone here was
rich and snobby, so I didn't care about being friends anyway. Yet I *did* want to make friends. I was already missing
the girls at my old school.

The next morning when my mother left for work, she
reminded me not to be late for school. I decided to wear
my best dress and shoes that day, the ones I usually wore
to church or birthday parties. I figured that not only
would the other girls notice me, they would want to be
friends. I looked in the mirror and decided to add one last
touch for good measure.

I slipped into my mother's bedroom, opened her jewelry box and took out an expensive, beautiful bracelet that
she had promised to give me when I was older. It was
made of sterling silver beads that were hand-carved into
roses. I looked in the mirror again, smiled and felt confident enough to start a conversation with even the most
popular girl in school.

Walking into my classroom, I sensed many eyes on me.
I held my head high, believing that everyone was thinking
how pretty I looked. Instead of sitting by myself again on
the steps during the morning recess, I marched right up to
a group of girls from my class and said hello. I introduced
myself, asked everyone their names again and played with
my hair so they would notice the beautiful bracelet I had
on—the one I wasn't supposed to wear until I was older.
"So, what are you guys talking about?" I asked.

"Just about riding our horses last weekend," Tammy
replied.

I was right! I thought to myself. *They ARE rich!*

The girls kept talking about their horses, their riding
lessons, the new saddle they wanted.

"I have a horse, too," I suddenly blurted out in a lie.

There was silence. I couldn't believe that I'd said such an outright fib, but it was too late now.

"Well . . . I mean, I *used* to have a horse," I continued, trying to undo the lie a little. "But we had to sell him when we moved here."

"What a shame! You must be so sad!" everyone chimed in together. "What was he like?"

Instantly, I had everyone's attention! I told them all about, Red, a stallion that actually belonged to a family friend. I became so caught up in describing "my" horse that I almost started believing the lie myself.

When the bell rang, signaling the end of recess, we headed back to class. "Wanna join us for lunch?" Jan asked with a smile.

"Sure, thanks!" I answered, thrilled that I'd found a way to fit in so quickly. I snuggled into my desk, glancing down to admire my beautiful bracelet that surely impressed those rich girls.

"Oh, no!" I heard myself gasping aloud. *The bracelet was gone!*

"Did you say something, Karen?" my concerned teacher asked. I burst out crying, and everyone turned to stare.

I don't know if I was more upset over losing that beloved bracelet or fearing my mother's reaction after she learned what I had done. "I . . . I lost my silver bracelet," I stammered. "It must have fallen off during recess."

I was so visibly shaken that Mrs. Allen took sympathy on me. She told me not to worry, quickly scribbled a note and told me to take it to the office. The instructions said, "Please read this on the PA system." Within seconds, the secretary's voice boomed over the loudspeakers: "Someone lost a very special bracelet this morning. Mrs. Allen has a Good Citizen Award for whoever finds it during the lunch recess."

I went back to my classroom, feeling relieved that my prized possession would certainly be found. At noon I joined the other girls in the cafeteria. We gobbled down lunch so that we could race outside and start hunting. Within twenty minutes, it seemed that all 300 kids in that school were helping me look, searching every inch of the girls' restrooms, the hallways and the playground. I kept nervously glancing around, waiting for someone to yell, "I found it!" When the school bell rang, alerting everyone to return to the building, the bracelet was still missing.

I sat down at my desk, fighting back the tears. My kind teacher asked the secretary to announce another search. I just couldn't believe that it hadn't been found with all those kids looking for it! I developed a horrible feeling that someone secretly picked it up and decided to keep it. After all, it was the most beautiful bracelet in the world and obviously worth much more than some Good Citizen Award.

Again, during the afternoon recess, it seemed that everyone was looking for my bracelet instead of playing tag or standing around talking. Again, the bell rang, signaling that recess was over. Again, those silver beads were nowhere to be found.

Trying not to cry, I put my hands over my face. Several girls all gathered around me in the yard, and they all promised to help me look again tomorrow. I couldn't believe how caring and supportive they were!

"Thanks, everyone. You are so nice," I said, forcing a smile. "It's just that I shouldn't have even worn that bracelet this morning. It belongs to my mother." Then, without knowing why, I suddenly added, "And I'm sorry. I lied to you guys this morning. I've always wanted a horse, but we've never owned one. Red belongs to a friend of my mother's. I guess I told you that so you'd like me. I even wore my best clothes today so I'd fit in better."

"That's okay!" they all answered reassuringly. "It does-
n't matter whether you own a horse or what kind of
clothes you have!" Rhonda gave me a hug, and two other
girls offered to let me ride their horse sometime.

It felt so good to tell the truth and to learn that I had
misjudged those girls as being snobby! I really did feel like
smiling then . . . even before I happened to glance at the
ground and discover an almost-hidden, sand-covered
bracelet, smack in the middle of my circle of new friends.

Karen Waldman

NO RODEO®

NO RODEO. ©Robert Berardi. Used by permission.

A Friend's Secret

Sometimes being a friend means mastering the art of timing. There is a time for silence. A time to let go and allow people to hurl themselves into their own destiny. And a time to prepare to pick up the pieces when it's all over.

Gloria Naylor

When I was a kid, every Thursday night was my mom's night out (usually she went to choir practice at church) and my dad's night to take the kids to dinner. We'd go to Red Lobster (Dad loved seafood) and order popcorn shrimp and hush puppies.

Suddenly, when I was in the seventh grade, my mom started going out almost every night of the week. After dinner, she'd kiss my sister, brother and me and say, "Good night. See you in the morning."

"But where are you going?" I asked, incensed that she would just leave us, even when my dad wasn't home from work yet. My sister, Carla, was fourteen, but still . . . .

"I'm going to see a friend," Mom would respond vaguely. "Someone who needs my help."

But I could see the signs. She'd put on a skirt, touch up her mascara, add another misting of perfume to her neck, grab her purse and head out the door.

Mom was having an *affair*. On top of that, my own mother had lied to me. A friend who needed her help—ha!

I was furious.

I didn't tell anyone my suspicions, not Carla, who was too busy talking on the phone to her new boyfriend; and not Charlie, my eight-year-old brother, who barely looked up from the TV to tell Mom good-bye. Dad just acted like there was absolutely nothing wrong with his wife leaving the house after dinner to go on a *date*.

Apparently, everyone in my family had gone crazy.

Then, one day after school, Mom came to my room.

"Honey," she said, "there's something I need to talk to you about."

I knew what she was going to tell me. There would be a divorce, then a custody battle, then for the rest of my life I'd be packing up a suitcase to go from Mom's house to Dad's for the weekend. My stomach dropped to my ankles.

"What?" I demanded, surprising even myself by how hostile I sounded.

"It's about Christy."

Christy was one of my best friends. We didn't go to the same school—I went to public school and she went to private. We'd met at church and our parents were friends and we had grown up together. We played tennis on the weekends and then made chocolate chip cookies together. We both knew the recipe by heart.

The year before, Christy's family had moved to a new house on a hillside with a spectacular view. It had a long flight of steps down the back that led to a swimming pool and hot tub. I was jealous when Christy got to live in such a luxurious house. I shouldn't have worried, though, because I got to enjoy the new house too. Now after a hot game of tennis, we could go back to Christy's house for a dip in the pool, followed by lazy sunbathing.

"Well, what about her?" I finally asked.

Mom took a deep breath. "I just want you to be really nice to her for a while."

I rolled my eyes. "I'm always nice to her. She's *my friend.*"

"I know, and you're a good friend. But things might be hard for her for a while, and she'll need your friendship more than ever."

"Mom, what are you talking about?"

"Maybe I'd better just tell you, Bethany. Christy's parents are getting a divorce."

It felt like the time during a soccer game that someone kicked the ball right into my stomach. I couldn't breathe. Then the guilt set in.

"You mean, when you said you were going out to help a friend . . . ?"

"I was seeing Christy's mom. She needed to talk through some things."

I closed my eyes, feeling guilty for my suspicions, feeling even guiltier for the relief that flooded through me once I knew it wasn't my parents getting divorced.

"But, Bethany, you have to promise me you won't say anything to Christy. She doesn't know yet."

"She doesn't know?"

"Her parents still have some things to work out. They're not ready to tell Christy and Robbie yet." Robbie was Christy's little brother. "Promise me?"

"Yes, Mom, I promise."

That was a hard promise to keep. For weeks, I made a special effort to hang out with Christy and do fun things with her. Mostly we did the same old things: played tennis, swam in the pool, made cookies, went to the mall or the movies. It was summer and school was out, so we spent lots of time together. Christy didn't say anything about her parents, so I didn't either.

One day, Christy and I were lying on lounge chairs next to the pool at the beautiful house of which I had once been so jealous. While I read my book, Christy dozed. But she must not have been asleep, because suddenly she spoke. "Bethany?"

"Mm-hmm?"

"I have to tell you something."

My heart skipped a beat. "What?" I lifted my eyes over the edge of my book. Christy lay on the chair, her eyes still closed.

"My mom and dad are getting a divorce."

Knowing this information for weeks should have prepared me to say something profound when this moment came. But it hadn't. I couldn't even figure out how to act surprised.

"Christy, I'm so sorry."

"Thanks." A tear rolled out from underneath one of Christy's closed eyelids.

"That really sucks."

"Yeah." Christy turned her head in the other direction, so that she faced away from me.

"Do you want to talk about it?"

"Not really."

For a few minutes, silence floated between us like sunlight on the surface of the pool. "Christy?"

"Yeah?"

"Want to stay over at my house tonight?" I held my breath. "Mom has choir practice, so Dad's taking us out to eat."

Christy turned her head to face me again and smiled. "I'd like that," she said.

In that moment, I realized something. I couldn't make

things better for Christy. I couldn't keep her parents from splitting up. I couldn't make Christy's pain go away. But if I kept being Christy's friend, even when she had to move to a new house with her mom, a house without a pool or a spectacular view, even when she got angry and threw things across the room, even when she needed to cry but didn't want to talk about it—if I could stick by her through all those things, then she would know that I loved her and cared about her.

And maybe that would help . . . just a little.

Bethany Rogers

A Valentine to My Friends

It's the season of love
(Like we could forget).
Romance is in the air,
And it's making us sick.

Couples are holding hands,
And all through the day,
We walk down the halls
And have to witness PDA.

Then those same girls
Will go home at night
And thank God above
For the man in their life.

But when it comes down to it
We've got something they don't—
Friends who will be there
When a boyfriend won't.

Friends who will be with you
There through it all.
When you're feeling little
They make you feel tall.

Friends understand
When you want to stay home.
No, you're not mad . . .
You just need time alone.

When you're eating with friends,
You can just dig right in.
There's no guys around . . .
So who's trying to stay thin?

Now and then there's an urge
To someday meet a guy
Who'll put a smile on your face
And a spark in your eye.

And "someday" will happen,
But until that time comes
Take advantage of now
And simply have fun.

So while other girls pray
For a love that is true,
When I pray at night
I thank God for you.

Rachel Punches, 18

4

FAMILY MATTERS

*F*or the good times and bad
*A*lways there
*M*ine
*I*nspirational
*L*ink to the past
*Y*ours forever

*M*entors
*A*musement
*T*ears
*T*riumphs
*E*ternal
*R*elationships
*S*piritual

Ashleigh E. Heiple, 16

The Day Our Dad Came Home

*Parents are friends that life gives us; friends are
parents that the heart chooses.*

Comtesse Diane

I remember so clearly the day I found my dad. It was a
few days away from my fourteenth birthday, and Mom
had sent me to the store to buy a few things. As I
approached the front of the store, I saw this man sitting
on a Harley-Davidson motorcycle. He had dark hair, and
he was wearing a black T-shirt and black jeans. I thought
he was so handsome. I decided that I wanted to take him
home to meet my mother. She was divorced with six children, and I was determined they would meet, fall in love
and get married.

I walked up to him and said, "Hi, my name is Pam.
What's your name?"

He smiled, and said, "Well, hello there, Pam! My name is
Duke." I asked him if he was married, and he said, "No,
but I think I'm a little too old for you."

I laughed and said, "Not for me silly! I want you to meet
my mom."

He was so full of life. I thought he would be good for Mom—she needed some excitement in her life. She married my daddy when she was very young, and he was a truck driver who rarely came home. Daddy was an alcoholic so he spent all of his money at the bars, and everything was left up to my mom. She finally divorced him after he came home one day in a drunken rage.

My mother was a conservative and modest woman. She was raised in a Baptist church in a small Southern town. I just knew that today would be her lucky day.

I took Duke to my house, telling him how beautiful Mom was and how I just knew they would fall in love. He smiled at my excitement, but Mom stopped us in our tracks as we walked inside. I said, "Mom, this is Duke, and he is going to take you on a date!" He stood there, snapping his fingers and looking so cool!

Mom quickly asked him to leave and walked to the door to show him the way out. He turned to look at me and said, "Don't worry. I won't give up."

After he left, Mom gave me a lecture for bringing a stranger to our home. "What were you thinking? He looks like some kind of crazy man. I bet he parties all the time."

Well, the crazy man did not give up, just as he promised. He kept coming back and finally, mom gave in to his handsome ways. They went on a date a few days later, and on a beautiful day in April my mother married Duke. He became Dad to Brenda, Denese, Ruth, Johnny, Jody and me. He would never allow anyone to refer to us as his *stepchildren*. We were his *children*, and he was adored by our entire family.

He was such a positive influence for us. I can't recall ever hearing him say anything derogatory about anyone. He encouraged us to believe in ourselves and that we could accomplish anything we desired or dreamed of achieving. "Just set your goals and go for it!" he would tell us. He took real good care of my mom and all of us.

A few years later, Dad started having some problems, so he made a doctor's appointment to have a biopsy done on his throat. The results were not good—Dad had throat cancer. His prognosis was maybe six months. The doctors had to insert a feeding tube into his stomach, and he would never be able to eat or drink again. He would never again be able to have his cup of coffee in the mornings as he sat and watched the birds playing on the many feeders that he'd made for them.

A couple of weeks passed, and we noticed Dad getting weaker—he was sleeping all the time. Dad was giving up, and we had to encourage him to fight. My sisters and I took turns feeding him, and we had to give him morphine around the clock for the pain. Our emotions were like a roller coaster—we wanted to cry, but we couldn't. We had to stay strong for Dad and Mom.

Early one morning, I slipped into Dad's room and sat down beside him. I started singing, "Good morning to you, good morning to you. Good morning, dear Dad, good morning to you."

He smiled weakly and sang, "Good morning, dear daughter."

I took his hand in mine and whispered, "Do you remember singing this song to me when I was a little girl?" And I sang to him the song about the rubber tree and the ant that had high hopes. It was the song he sang to us whenever we were having a difficult time. He nodded and smiled up at me.

In April, my sister and I were giving Dad a bath. Dad turned his head and said, "Pam?"

I whispered through a broken voice, "Yes, Dad. I'm here."

He said, "Thank you for finding me that day. I didn't know I was lost until you found me."

I laid my head on his chest and as tears fell from my

eyes, I said, "Oh, Dad. It was you that found us."

Dad held on until the next morning. His wife and all six of his children were by his bed. I held Dad's hand. The room was crowded as Dad slipped away to heaven.

I will always remember the first day I saw him. He didn't just *happen* to be at that store. I know in my heart that God had placed Duke right where we needed him the most. My dad had seen a woman with six children, and he had fallen in love with all of us. He said, "I'll do whatever it takes to take care of them," and he kept his promise. Dad never thought of himself, only of those he loved. He filled the gap for the children who had always longed to have a loving daddy.

The other day when I was getting a little discouraged, I found myself humming the song about the ant. And when I got to the chorus, I swear I thought I heard Dad singing, "... because, he's got high hopes."

Pamela D. Hamalainen

God on Her Side

God will help you if you try, and you can if you think you can.

Anna Delaney Peale

I was only five years old. People think that children don't remember things from such an early age, but when I live to be 100 I will remember that day as if it were yesterday.

It seemed like we were sitting for hours in the emergency room, waiting for our turn to see the doctor. It has been my mother and me for as long as I can remember. My father and mother separated when I was a baby. I don't like doctors or hospitals much, so my mom did her best to keep me happy and occupied while we waited. She did a good job of hiding how very awful she felt. We sang and played little games. She had called my grandparents, and they were on their way, but they were delayed in traffic.

Finally they called my mother's name, and we were taken to a small bed with curtains all around it. The nurse asked my mother to change into a gown and to lie down. After she lay down, I quickly jumped on her tummy and straddled her with a leg on each side. We continued to sing and play our games while we waited for the doctor. Mom had had pants on before she was asked to change, but now with the hospital gown on, her leg could be seen, but I could not see it because I was looking into her face.

When the doctor finally came, he opened the curtain. I did not see his face; he was not there long enough for me to even turn my head. He said, "Oh my god!" Then he closed the curtain and left. A few moments later, he returned with not one, but five doctors. I will always remember the looks on their faces. It was a look of extreme terror. Then came the next words, "You have a flesh-eating disease, and unless we cut off your leg in the next ten minutes, you will die." Then they closed the curtain and left just as fast as they had appeared.

My mother tried her best to change the subject. She asked me about school, my friends, my cat. I wanted to be brave for Mommy, but I couldn't. The tears started coming faster and faster, and I could not control them.

When my grandparents arrived a few minutes later, they thought at first that something had happened to me, because when they opened the curtain I was crying and my mother was trying her best to comfort me. Now that I am older, I wonder how in the world she managed to comfort me, when her whole world was crashing in around her.

The nurse asked my grandparents to take me away from my mother, and the three of us left her and went to a private waiting area. All I could think about was how the doctor said my mother could die in ten minutes. I know every child thinks his or her mother is special, but mine is especially so. Ever since I had been born, we had spent every moment we could together. My mother has two artificial hips and has a hard time doing things, but that has never stopped her. She just figured out how she can do things in a different way, even if it meant she went to bed in pain. She never wanted to let me down. I know that now—I didn't know that then. She was my rock, my hero, my champion, my best friend, and I was terrified that she was going to die.

The doctors came into the little room where the nurse had put us, to explain the situation to my grandparents and to ask my grandparents to talk to my mother. She had given them permission to take out the part of the leg that was infected, but they were *not* allowed to cut her leg off. The doctors told my grandparents that this would not be enough and that she would die that night if they were not allowed to cut off the entire leg at the hip. This all seemed liked a dream. Again, in front of me, they said the same thing, "Your daughter is going to die if we do not cut off her leg." My grandparents had a lot of questions, but the doctor said there wasn't enough time to answer them. They were already preparing my mother for surgery.

I thought back to the day before, when my mother had been outside with me. We played hide and seek with our duck, Crackers. Crackers loved to hide, and when we found her, she would quack and quack and quack. It was May, and the weather was beautiful in California where we lived. We were in the process of repainting our entire home inside. I helped paint each room with a roller. We wanted to make it our home; a place that the two of us created with love. She had been fine all that day. What had happened? I only knew that she got a high fever, and it did not go away. She had not shown me her leg, swollen all over with bright red spots and one big bump with a big white circle on the top. I only caught sight of it as the nurse was taking me from her lap.

My grandparents told the doctor that they could not help him. My mother was forty-one years old, and they could not make her cut her leg off if she did not want to. I did not understand this as a five year old. They were her parents. Why couldn't they tell her what to do? She always told *me* to do what was right. Why couldn't they tell her what was right? I just wanted her to live. I wanted my mommy.

Before she was taken to the operating room, my mommy insisted she see me. Instead of being worried about herself, she was worried about me. She was angry with the doctors for saying she was going to die while I was right there on her lap. She wanted to see me to tell me something before she went in for the surgery.

So the nurse came to get me but asked my grandparents to stay behind. There I was, holding the hand of a stranger, going down what seemed to be the longest hall in the world. There were no other beds in the hall. Just one. And on it was my mother. She greeted me with a big smile. There were no tears in her eyes or on her face. She asked the nurse to pick me up and put me on her chest. I remember that the nurse said no. But my mother insisted. There I lay, on top of my mother. I could feel her heart beating. I could smell her smell, the one I had always known. It was comforting.

She looked me straight in the eyes and told me these special words. "I have told you before, Ashleigh, that you are my gift from God." She had told me the story since the day I was born. My mother was told that she could never have children. She had had a condition called endometriosis, and she had had many surgeries due to complications from the condition. Her doctor told her she could never have children, but she wanted me so very badly. On the night I was conceived, she said a prayer over and over to God, begging him for the chance to be a mother. When her cycle did not come, she called her doctor and asked for a blood test, but he refused. He said she could not possibly be pregnant and told her it was a "hysterical pregnancy." He explained that he thought it was because she wanted me so badly, she just had the symptoms of being pregnant. Another month went by and my mother took a home pregnancy test. She said it seemed like forever before the results showed in the window of the test stick (she still has the stick, framed on the wall). It said she was pregnant! Again she called her doctor. He still refused to do the blood test. Another month went by and finally the doctor agreed to see her. He did not want to perform a blood test for her though, because he was sure that she was not pregnant. Instead he did an exam. My mother said the look on his face was priceless. He said, "I don't know how you did it, but you are indeed pregnant!" My mother promptly told him she had prayed for me.

So there I was, lying on my mother, feeling calm but not really understanding why. She used to say a prayer to me every night before we said our other prayers together. She said she heard it in the movie *Yentel*, and it had stayed with her. She recited the prayer to me again as we lay there together, in that long hallway with the nurse standing next to us. And then she told me, "Ashleigh, I don't want you to worry. I am not going to have my leg cut off, and I am not going to die."

"But, Mommy," I remember saying, "the doctor said you would die unless he cuts it off."

"He is a doctor, Ashleigh. He is not God. God gave you to me as a special gift. The doctor does not know that. But I know that God is not going to take me away from the special little girl he gave me. He knows you need me here right now. He can wait a little longer for me in heaven."

The nurse was crying, but I wasn't. My mother was right; we had God on our side. So from that very moment on, I was fine.

When, I returned to my grandparents, the doctors were still begging them to "talk some sense" into my mother.

My mother had told my grandparents, too, that God was not going to let her die. When the doctors left the room, you could tell that they were exasperated.

My mom was in surgery for hours, and my grandparents tried their best to keep me busy as we all waited. I know now that they must have been crazy with worry, but they didn't show it to me. We went to the cafeteria where I had some ice cream, and we waited and waited . . . and waited.

Finally, one of the doctors appeared in the little waiting room. He told us that the surgery was over. They did not cut off her leg, although they had to take a lot out of the front of it.

It has been six years now since that day. On the wall in our house is a paper. The paper reads, "We told her we had to cut off her leg or she would die. The patient states that God would not let this happen." My mother and I smile each time she walks past that paper, on her own two legs. We even smile as we look at the scar on the front of her leg that also serves as a reminder. A reminder to us of a gift from God—me—and how important he knew it was for me and my mom to be together a little while longer.

Ashleigh Figler-Ehrlich, 11

Miracle Babies

I know not by what methods rare, but this I know: God answers prayer. I leave my prayer to Him alone whose will is wiser than my own.

Eliza M. Hickok

My Aunt Raquel and I have always had a special connection. Every time I visit her and my Uncle Tony, she has something to talk to me about or to ask my sister and me. When I'm around her, she brings such a glow to my heart. She always has that way of making me smile because she is such a fun-loving person. I have never been around her when she didn't smile or wasn't in a cheerful mood.

After getting married to my mom's brother Tony, my aunt's dream was to start a family together. But then my aunt was diagnosed with cervical cancer at the age of twenty-six, and everyone was devastated by the thought that she might never have a chance of having children.

After some treatments and the doctor's hard work for a couple of months, my Aunt Raquel was cancer free. We were all happy that she would have a chance of having a baby. And before long, she became pregnant with not just one baby, but two!

The months passed quickly, and it was coming to the sixth month of her pregnancy when suddenly, the unthinkable happened! My aunt went into labor. The doctors couldn't stop the delivery from happening, so my first cousin, Brianne, was born weighing one pound, six ounces. My second cousin, Brooke, was born weighing one pound, two ounces. After being delivered, the girls were put in incubators and rushed to the nearest children's hospital.

My mom and grandma were there when my aunt had the girls, but I wasn't. I had to stay home with my dad and wait for their phone calls to find out what was happening. My mom finally called and said she couldn't believe her eyes when she saw Brooke and Brianne in their incubators. She said she had never seen such little babies in her entire life.

Aunt Raquel and Uncle Tony had already been through so much. Now they had to worry about Brooke and Brianne. Brooke was pretty much okay. She really didn't have any problems. But Brianne needed two brain surgeries. She had some bleeding in her brain, and she had holes in her heart. That meant she needed heart surgery.

Over the following three months, both girls remained in the hospital. As they were being cared for, they were pricked and poked at with shots and needles from IVs that left scars. Their stay in the hospital seemed like an eternity. My mom went up to see them about two or three times a month, and I would always beg her to let me go with her. Since I was only eight, there was no chance that I could go into the neonatal intensive care unit where they were. I would have to wait for the girls to come home.

Brooke was the first to get to come home. I can remember going to see her at my aunt and uncle's house where she was still hooked up to the oxygen machine. Brianne came home about a week and a half after Brooke. She was also hooked up to an oxygen machine and had to stay on it longer than Brooke did. It was so scary to see them like that, but the thought of how much they had gone through made me realize that they were strong babies and deserved a chance in life.

There were times when their machines would sound an alarm, indicating that the girls had stopped breathing. Luckily though, they were all false alarms. My aunt and uncle always dreaded those times, but they got through them.

Many people in the community knew about Brooke and Brianne and they prayed and prayed for them. I think the whole town was reaching out to the girls in prayer. So, by the time the girls were home and settled in, they had become celebrities. The newspaper featured a story about them on the front page of the local news section. ABC News even did an interview with my uncle on Father's Day when the girls were in the hospital. The whole time they had their own fan club as well—our family.

Now healthy and full of life, the girls are five years old and are beautiful as can be. Brianne still has some difficulties with mild seizures every once in a while and has a slight case of cerebral palsy. Other than that, Brianne and Brooke act like normal everyday five year olds.

Currently, my aunt is teaching fifth grade, my uncle has his own business and my cousins are going to start kindergarten. They live on a ranch in the country, and the girls love taking care of their animals. With every new day, the girls have something to live for, and they are enjoying it! They will always hold a special place in my life and will always be miracle babies to me and to everyone else.

I once made a goal list when I was eleven. One of the goals was to witness a miracle. I believe I can cross that goal off my list now, because the girls were definitely a miracle as far as I am concerned.

As I mentioned, my aunt is such a special person. She has been an inspiration to me and always will be. Even though she has faced many obstacles in her short thirty-three years, she has an unbelievable faith and constantly reminds everyone of us to live well, laugh often and love much!

Stephanie Marquez, 12

The Perfect Brother

You had better live your best and act your best and think your best today; for today is the sure preparation for tomorrow and all the other tomorrows that follow.

Harriet Martineau

I've never had a very good relationship with my nine-year-old brother, Geoff. We started fighting with each other just about as soon as he could talk. For some reason, we enjoyed tormenting each other, and it wasn't a very good pastime. I still wonder why we fought at all, but I think he has a lot going on that I don't know about. He gets angry very easily, so it's hard to talk to him, much less play with him. It's pretty frustrating sometimes. I used to tell him that I hated him and that I never wanted to see him again, but I stopped doing that after what happened just before Christmas last year.

It was around 8:00 in the morning when my parents woke up to noises coming from Geoff's bedroom. My mom went into his room and discovered that he was having a grand mal epileptic seizure. This had never happened before, and of course she was terrified. She woke me and got Dad up out of bed. Frantically, we rushed around the house to get Geoff in the car. When we got into the car, with Geoff still having the seizure in Mom's arms, she grabbed the phone and called 911. About five minutes before arriving at the emergency room, Geoff's shaking stopped, and he started breathing rapidly and got really cold. We were all so scared. All of a sudden, I felt guilty for everything bad that I had ever said to my brother. All I wanted right at that moment was for him to be all right, so I could apologize for everything.

We got to the hospital at around 8:20, and they took him right in to a room with Dad. I stayed in the waiting room, crying, while Mom filled out some paperwork. Then she called my aunt Katie, who was visiting with a friend of hers, and our family doctor, who is also a friend of Mom's. Then Mom and I went into Geoff's room and cried. It was so hard seeing my little brother hooked up to all the tubes and machines. Minutes after we got into the room, Katie came and then the doctor came. We all hugged and reassured each other that it was all going to be okay.

After a while, Geoff regained consciousness and started throwing up. He kept throwing up until the doctors gave him some medicine to stop it. He was too weak to talk very well, but my dad filled him in on where he was, since of course he had no idea. I eventually started to break down, so Katie took me out into the waiting room. Katie has been like a second mom to me forever, so I felt totally comfortable with her. I just hugged her and cried for about five minutes. Then she took me home, while Mom and Dad stayed with Geoff.

At home, I tried doing everything possible to get my mind off Geoff, but I couldn't. The next morning, we went back to visit him. By then, he had been transferred to a regular room with a TV and all that stuff. I just sat on the bed with him and talked. It was fun listening to him talk to me about all the cool things he got at the hospital, like cable TV. He also had a little monitor that he snapped onto his finger that would alert nurses if he started having another seizure. He thought that was pretty awesome. I was so happy he was enjoying himself. We watched TV and did a puzzle together, and before I knew it, it was time to go home.

The next morning, I snatched a couple of Geoff's Christmas presents from under the tree and took them to the hospital with me. When he opened the one from me, a Palm Pilot, he had the biggest smile on his face. I showed him how to use it, and that's when I realized that he was going to be okay. I lay there and hugged him for so long, and I talked to him about how I was sorry for all the things I had said before. He hugged me back, and I started to cry but forced myself to stop. I was so happy.

The next day was crammed with a bunch of tests. The doctors determined that he had a cyst on his brain, which scared me. It was hard listening to all the talks my parents had with the neurologist and the doctors. Even though they told us that it was nothing serious, I still worried a little. I was happy to hear, though, that Geoff would be released from the hospital that night.

It was so nice to finally be home together again, and Geoffrey was overjoyed to be back for Christmas. We got along really well, and I even started reading up on epilepsy and what to do during seizures. I pulled pages and pages from the Internet and looked at medical books. I even switched my personal research topic at school from computers to epilepsy. I think I know pretty much everything there is to know about seizures, and I feel much more confident about what to do should he ever have another one.

It has now been eight months since Geoff's seizure. He is on medication and has not had another one since. I still worry about him sometimes, but I have gotten a lot better about it. We started fighting again, but I try to avoid phrases like, "I hate you!" or "Get out of my life." Because through it all, I learned that I don't really hate him. I love him. And I have thought about what my life would be like if he wasn't in it. He is such a big part of my life, even if we do fight, and I never want him to leave.

I guess the moral of this story is to love your siblings just the way they are, because you never know when the day might come when they leave your life forever.

Kacy Gilbert-Gard, 12

One Single Egg

The history, the root, the strength of my father is the strength I now rest on.

Carolyn M. Rodgers

I didn't think that I could take much more. I *had* to keep up with the other girls.

The target loomed closer and closer. Only a little further ... ready ... aim ... splat! I let my missile sail through the air. Then the fear set in—I had to get away! Porch lights were being turned on.

"Separate," yelled Ashley. I passed two homes safely. When I reached the third house, I saw a face peer out of a window in a blur of motion as I sped past. I flew past the last house; I was almost home free. PHEW! I made it. My legs trembling, I watched as Sara, Ashley and finally Carrie caught up. We hadn't gotten caught! Still, I didn't feel proud of my first "egging." I was filled with fear that we would still be discovered every second of my stay at Ashley's sleepover. Finally, my mom came to get me, and I was unusually silent on the ride home.

My friend Ashley and I had been born only one week

apart. We were inseparable until the day her mom and dad decided that they would move to a new neighborhood. I lived for the times that my mom would take me over to her house. Everything went okay at first, but gradually Ashley made new friends and started acting like she didn't need me as much. I no longer felt like I belonged. Carrie and Sara would make it a point to talk about things that I couldn't relate to, like when they went to the mall without me. Slowly, I felt the close bond of friendship slipping away. I wanted to fit in, but I didn't know how.

It had been Sara's idea to go egg the house. She brought a brand-new carton of eggs to the sleepover. It didn't seem like a very good idea, but I didn't want to look like a baby, so I decided I had better do it with them.

The day after the sleepover was bright and sunny, and I began helping clean our house, which was a weekend chore for me. My dad was also up, cleaning away. As I polished the furniture, my dad asked me what we had done over at Ashley's house. It must have been the guilt that caused me to tell him.

"You see, Dad," I began, "this is kind of funny, but we went and, uh . . . egged this house." My dad turned pale. Then he turned red. Then purple.

Please understand a few things here. One thing is that my dad is a cop. Two is that he is a juvenile detective, and he works with kids around my age who have broken the law. Three is that he was currently investigating about ten different kids who had just gotten into trouble for doing exactly the same thing that I had just done.

"Do you think that's funny?" he asked softly. "DO YOU THINK THAT'S FUNNY?!!" he roared. And then, he *really* got mad.

Let's just say that it boiled down to him making me get into the car. As I sat there, sobbing, his purpose became clearer. As we got closer to Ashley's house, I pleaded, "No, Dad, no."

But he replied, "If you are adult enough to go throw an egg at someone's home, then you are adult enough to apologize for it." I gasped. This was even worse than I had thought. He wanted me to knock on the front door of the house we had EGGED! I just sat there in a blind panic.

As we pulled closer, he told me to point out the house. "There," I said in a shaky voice as he slowed to a stop.

"I want you to come with me," he said.

As we walked toward the door, I was filled with dread. I rang the doorbell once and waited. It seemed like the longest twenty seconds of my life. A lady answered the door.

"Hi, I, uh, just wanted to tell you that I, umm . . . threw an egg at your house." I watched as her smile of welcome changed to a puzzled look. My dad quickly introduced himself and told her that I would clean up any mess that had been left. As we walked around the side of the house that had been egged, I began searching for damage.

"This had better be the right house," my dad growled. There was nothing visible on the house itself, and I could find no shells on the ground. Desperately, I began poking around in the tall grass. Then I started to wonder if I had been the only one to throw an egg.

Sure enough, I found the remnants of one single egg in the grass. The other girls had all dropped their eggs somewhere else. I picked up the shell of my one egg, but there was no evidence that the egg had ever hit the brick home. I apologized to the poor lady and promised never to do anything like that again.

As my dad and I made our way back home, he explained to me about what he had been putting up with at work from all of the other kids. "You are one of the reasons I can go into work every day and face the problems of others. If it weren't for you, I wouldn't be able to go in and see the children who are hurting and the ones who need guidance. When you make a choice like this, I wonder how I failed as a parent in guiding you the right way. It makes me wonder how anything I do out *there* could ever make any difference."

With that profound speech, there ended my life of crime. I understood why what I had done had disappointed him so much. More important, I knew that my dad still would love me, unconditionally, no matter what.

I apologized to him for disappointing him and for making a bad choice. I tried to become an example of the good that my dad fights for.

My friendship with Ashley was never quite the same after that, but I learned a valuable lesson and I grew up a little bit. Throughout the years, there were many situations with my friends where I had to make a choice that didn't make me the most popular, but I knew that my dad would be proud of me for making the right decision. That was enough.

I later followed in my dad's footsteps and became a police officer myself. When I first caught a group of kids "egging" a house, I was faced with bringing them home to their parents. One of the boys begged me to let him go . . . just that one time. He told me that I didn't know what he was in for from his dad. I told him that it wouldn't be as bad as he thought. He scoffed at me, until I said, "Listen, do I have a story to tell you. . . ."

Cheryl L. Goede

Raining Memories

*Please teach me to appreciate what I have,
before time forces me to appreciate what I had.*
                                                    Susan L. Lenzkes

Time: The world revolves around it, and mortals are always attempting to beat it. I don't generally run with the pack, and I am usually not concerned with time. However, on this one particular day, I was, in fact, running with the pack to *beat* time.

A surly gray sky thundered above, while light raindrops splattered upon my stone-cold fingers. Captured in my nine-year-old hands were the first raindrops of the morning. The cold rain trickled down my slick warm-ups and into my shoes that stood perpendicular to the white starting line of the 200-meter dash. A distant sound of the warning whistle flowed into my ears through the cold breeze. The race was soon to begin.

I removed my warm-ups, as did my competitors, none of whom seemed to be as cold as I was. All the same, the race would begin whether my tight muscles were ready for it or not.

"On your mark . . ." a man's voice sounded.

I readied myself at the line, situated comfortably in my blocks.

"Get set . . ."

I thrust my backside into the air, my legs ready to spring forward into motion.

BANG! The gun sounded, and I shot into my lane, rain stinging my face as I ran against the wind. Nearly midway through the race, I wished that I had thought to put on some glasses to protect my eyes from the tormenting downpour. However, this was not a possibility, so I turned my head slightly to the left to keep the rain from going straight into my eyes. Much to my surprise, I saw a familiar face in the crowd. Standing apart from the others stood a man in a hooded green windbreaker, light blue jeans, and a pair of white, blue, and yellow-green running shoes. Though the rain was falling quite heavily now, he ignored his hood, revealing a full head of light-brown hair. Behind his strawberry-blond goatee, a smile was evident upon my father's face.

Why was he here? He never comes to any of my sporting events. Why did he decide to come to this particular track meet? I wondered.

Drawing my attention back to the race, I noticed that I had almost run out of my lane. The race was nearly over, and I would have plenty of time to mull over his motives after the race . . . but now was the time for running.

So, I put forth all of my strength into the remaining fifty meters. I crossed the finish line and went looking for my dad. Walking back to where I had seen him standing, I met my sister, Carly, and my mom, who were both eager to congratulate me on my success. My mom rambled on and on about how well I had done, saying stuff like, "You're fantastic." I kept trying and trying to tell her what

I had seen, but you know how moms are—she kept right on talking about how great I had done.

"MOM!" I finally yelled impatiently. She looked startled and hurt. "Sorry," I said in an undertone, but my voice then strengthened. "I saw Dad! He was watching me run!" My face was glowing. "I can't find him now, though. Can you *please* help me look?"

And so we searched. We looked around the track, the concessions, by the field events, we even looked in the parking lot—and then we searched them all over again. My heart sank as I realized that my dad was clearly gone.

The ride home was a long one. *Why did he leave?* I kept questioning myself. But, he *had* come. I had finally seen him after three long months of separation.

A few hours after we had reached our home, a soft knocking announced the arrival of an unexpected guest. Carly opened the door and welcomed the principal of our small-town high school. Mom greeted him, and he spoke to her in a very grave manner.

"We need to talk. . . ." He gave Carly and me a quick glance. "Privately. It's serious." Much to our dismay, Carly and I were sent down the street to play with the neighbor kids. When we returned, we fully expected our mom to have lost her teaching position at the high school, but what we stumbled upon was much more unsettling.

Sitting in the chair, my mom was sobbing into her hands. I was shocked at what I saw and sat down next to her on the couch. Carly took the loveseat. We waited for an explanation. After a moment's recuperation, my mom spoke.

"Girls . . ." she said gravely. There was a long pause. "Your dad has passed away." The words entered my head, racing from one side of my brain to the other as if trying to truly comprehend what they meant—but I knew.

"When?" I asked quietly, staring blankly at my folded hands.

"Last night, er . . . early this morning." Mom fought back her anguish. "The coroner said he . . . he. . . ." She choked back tears. "It happened around one or two this morning."

I sat in shock, unable to cry, unable to feel. How could he have died and left me when I hadn't spoken to him for three months? How could he have left me with nothing but a three-month-old good-bye? In fact, how could he even be *dead*? This was *not* a very funny joke. How could he have possibly been at my track meet if he had died before the track meet even started? A bit of hope helped lift my head enough to look at my mother's red, swollen eyes, which tore me back down. My mom couldn't act, and honestly, who would pull a joke this sick? Nobody. He was gone. Somehow, mysteriously, he had appeared to me at that race in a final gesture to me—as if it was his way of saying good-bye.

Now that I am nearly sixteen, I have finally learned to accept that he's really gone. I have been holding on to a false hope that he would return or that I would experience one last hug. But after more than six years of dreaming about memories I never had, I realized something very important that now lives in my thoughts every day: One cannot live while thinking on what might have been. Time holds misfortunes that are inevitable, but time still passes and never returns. We must be happy with what we *do* have right now, in this moment, and not let time get the better of us.

Kirsten Lee Strough, 15

Sarah's Story

Every child has a right to a good home.

Ettie Lee

I remember everything about Russia.

I was adopted from there when I was only four years old. It was a very sad life back then. People there didn't have enough money or enough food to eat, and it was hard to find warmth in such a cold place. For some people in Russia, it still is a very sad life, but I understand that the country is now building up and becoming a stronger community.

When I was just four years old, my mom contracted a disease called tuberculosis, which made it hard for her lungs to do their job. My mom also walked with a cane. Eventually, she couldn't take care of my sister, Anna, who was then fourteen, my eleven year-old brother, Michael, or me.

As amazing as it might seem, I don't remember ever seeing my father. I know he lived with us, but he left for work early in the morning before I woke up and came home late at night when I was already asleep. He worked hard so that he could earn money for our family, but he didn't make enough money to take care of all of us.

Although my mom was sick and my dad worked all the time, this is how my being adopted really started: There's this rule in Russia that says you can't walk after dark by yourself if you are a child. My sister, Anna, was fourteen then, and she was walking in a forest by our house. The police saw her and took her home.

When the police got to our house, they came in and looked around. They saw that we had no food, nowhere to sleep, no clothes and a mother who couldn't take care of us. They told our mother that they would have to take us each to a different agency and put us up for adoption. So the next morning, that's what they did. I felt so confused; I didn't know what was going on.

I lived in an orphanage for about six months after that. That's another rule—you have to be in an orphanage for six months before you get adopted.

The orphanage was just like a school. We had a teacher, a daycare person and a principal. We worked at our desks everyday with teachers and had lockers that we decorated. That was a lot of fun. After school, we went to the daycare center, where we played for a couple of hours. All of the children were friendly at the orphanage. We had a lot of toys to play with, like Russian dolls and pretend telephones. There was even a piano that the teacher played everyday. I also remember that the grown-ups were very nice.

All the children slept in a big room that had lots of beds and a blue ceiling with stars hanging from it. It felt warm and cozy. But there were still times when I felt lonely. I remember having lots of questions in my head. I wondered why I was there. I really missed my big sister. I wondered if I would see my family again.

One day, a woman named Grace came in, holding a little boy in her arms. She had just adopted this little boy and also wanted to adopt a little girl, so they introduced her to me. Grace didn't speak Russian, so she had an interpreter who helped us communicate. Grace came right up to me and began hugging me. She had brought a bag of gifts, and she gave me coloring books and a bow for my hair. My new mom put the bow in my hair, and I loved it.

Before we left the orphanage, we took a picture right in front of the orphanage with all of my teachers and my new family. I remember that my teachers were crying. As we left the orphanage, all of the children were waving from the windows and yelling good-bye. I felt so happy to have a mom again, but sad to be leaving the friends I had made at the orphanage.

We left the orphanage, stayed one night at the interpreter's house and then got on the plane the next day. It took more than twenty-four hours to get to my new home, where I was shown the room that I would share with my baby brother, Andrew. There was a dresser, a crib for my brother, a bed for me and a closet with some clothes in it. Then, my new mom's friend brought over a big box filled with shoes. My mouth was open, and my eyes were huge! I'd never seen so many shoes in my life. And they were all for me!

I had no idea what would happen next in my life. I just took it day by day. Every night I practiced my English, my ABCs and my numbers with my new mom. It took me about two months to learn to speak English. Sometimes people made fun of the way I talked, but when they found out I was just learning, they stopped making fun of me.

I felt comfortable in my new home in America. I loved my new family. I didn't think about my old family in Russia during the day, but I still dreamed about them sometimes at night. One night at my new house, just a few days after arriving, I had a nightmare. In my dream, a witch was chasing my sister and me through my old house in Russia. Anna and I hid behind a large chest. I woke up frightened and ran to my new mom's bedroom. I jumped in her bed and slept the rest of the night. I felt comfortable with her, even after only a few days.

As Andrew and I grew up, we became as close as any biological siblings. I remember times when I felt jealous of the attention he got as a baby, just like any older sibling would. There were lots of times when we would fight and argue, but now we are close. We share secrets, play together and get along really well.

I have been in the United States for almost eight years. I am eleven years old and in the sixth grade. My mom works a lot, but she makes sure to spend quality and fun times with Andrew and me. Sometimes on the weekends we go on bike rides, go to movies or play board games. I love my family. My mom is always trying to help Andrew and me as we go through rough situations. She is forgiving, loving and helpful. I can always trust my mom.

I have never heard from my biological mom or siblings. I hope someday I can know more about them or maybe even get to see them again. Sometimes I dream that my sister comes to find me and that we become close again. I would love to have a big sister to teach me things about growing up, to go shopping with and to be close friends with.

When I grow up, I want to be a cancer surgeon and a teacher. I am a good athlete, and I hope to be a college athlete and maybe a professional athlete, too. I also want to have a family someday. And if I can, I want to adopt two children—maybe even children from Russia.

Sarah Crunican, 11

Home

Call it a clan, call it a network, call it a tribe, call it a family: Whatever you call it, whoever you are, you need one.

Jane Howard

Has it really been fourteen years since I was placed into the invisible hands of the government? Fourteen years since Social Services first gained control of my life?

After all this time, I remember it so clearly, as if it were only yesterday. I was eight years old and sitting in a group home waiting patiently for Mom. Unfortunately, she did not return. Three months later, I found myself in a foster home. From that day on, my life became a case file; just a large manila folder held snugly under the arm of a complete stranger.

I learned to accept the foster home as I saw it; a place that I stayed. It was not a home to me but merely a house with four walls and a roof, just a building that Social Services deemed fit for my living requirements. It was a place that I slept and ate in, but it held nothing for me; no love, no family and no values.

I spent the first five years of foster care secretly envying my friends . . . secretly wishing for everything that they had. I wanted to know what it felt like to be so loved. I yearned to have a "real" home as they all had. I wanted so much to belong, to know what it was like to not feel like an intruder in somebody else's home. I ached deeply to not spend each day believing that I owed these people something for accepting me into their house.

At thirteen, right after I had just spent three months in the hospital for anorexia nervosa, I learned that I would be leaving the foster home that I had been in for the past five years, and I was going to be placed into a new foster home. I really didn't believe things could get much worse. It felt as though my world was crashing down upon me once more. I cried at the cold realization that my first foster family was not going to show me the meaning of "home."

The tears fell for days as my heart slowly began to understand. A home in my world was like a fairytale, a far-off place of magical beings and magical events where everything was fit perfectly to end in love and happiness. A world that would make me feel wonder and fascination, but deep in my heart, I felt like such a place could not truly exist. I never had known "home," and I suspected that this would always remain the same for me.

I was sent to what they call a relief home after I got out of the hospital. It felt comfortable, and the family was very loving. I felt at ease the first time I had stepped within the warm, cozy walls. But I knew I could not get too comfortable, because shortly, I would have to surrender to being sent to the second foster home. Then, when my two weeks in the relief home were nearly up and my anticipation and terror of being sent to a new home was in full force, the world I had come to know changed.

My "relief" family sat me down at the kitchen table one

evening just before bed, and as they all glanced in my direction, the mom spoke in gentle, soothing words.

"We know that you have gone through a lot after finding out that you were not returning to your first foster home." She went on with a quiet breath, "And we don't want to scare you off, or force you into any decision that you don't want to make—but we really want you to stay here with us and be a part of our family."

I stared at her in shock. I couldn't believe what I was hearing. The others smiled as I glanced their way.

"We want you to think about it. Take as much time as you need." I nodded and quietly rose from the table and went to the room where I had been staying while I was living there. I put my pajamas on, and I lay down in bed and silently cried many tears. They weren't just tears of sadness, but also tears of happiness and tears of relief. A part of my life was ending and now a greater part of my life was about to begin. If I would let it.

Later that night, as my tears finally began to dry, the youngest daughter popped her head into my room.

"Are you asleep?" she asked. I shook my head in reply. "Have you made a decision yet?"

This time I nodded, and she waited for my an swer. Without thinking anymore about it, I replied with a quiet "yes."

"She's going to stay!" she yelled as she ran out of the room.

I slowly got out of bed and prepared to be welcomed by my new family. I smiled as I walked out the door. For the first time in my life, I felt I belonged. For the first time in my life, I felt comfortable and cared for. For the first time in my life, I was a daughter and a sister. I was finally a normal girl.

For the first time in my life, I truly knew home.

Cynthia Charlton

5

SISTER SISTER

When you're all alone
And feeling down
You need someone
To change your frown.

She'll make you laugh
When you want to cry
You have to tell her the truth
Because she'll know if you lie.

You can count on her
And she can count on you
When she says, "I promise . . ."
You know that it's true.

She is there by your side
No matter what you do
Your sister's more than just family
She's a friend through and through.

Samantha Ott, 12

Ready or Not

One is not born a woman, one becomes one.

Simone de Beauvoir

I was wiped out. After two hours of grueling swim practice, the zipper on my bag felt like it had been cemented shut. I couldn't even lift the towel. I was starving, but how was I going to pick up a fork? I flopped down on the bench in the locker room, barely able to hold up my head. Breathing in and out took what little energy I had left. Maybe my skanky, bleach-smelling hair didn't need to be washed tonight? Couldn't I just dry off and shuffle home to dinner? I hauled my weary body to the mirror and tried to get away with "styling" my mop with the towel.

Oh, no! What is that under my arm? I wondered, quickly yanking my elbow down to my side before anyone else could see. Cautiously, with every attempt to appear calm, I slowly lifted my arm just high enough to peek underneath. *Yep! It was there! A hair! A black, plain-as-day-so-everybody-could-see hair!* I quickly scanned the locker room to figure out if any of the girls had noticed that my body had completely changed. *Whew.* No one seemed to have noticed.

Suddenly, I had energy. I couldn't wait to run home, so I threw on only the most necessary clothes, which wasn't easy, since I wasn't willing to separate my elbow from my hip. Taking no time to chat, or even complain about the workout, I whisked out of the locker room and sprinted home.

"Mom! I'm home! I'll eat later!" I shouted as I flew up to my room. I almost ripped my shirt off and stood about a millimeter away from the mirror, carefully examining this newfound evidence that I was becoming a woman. I was thrilled that I was actually, finally, growing up, but I was terrified that I was actually, finally, growing up. The thoughts starting streaming through my brain. . . .

Oh, I can't wait to swagger into the locker room and show the other girls the real bra I am surely going to need soon, now that I have armpit hair. It will be so wonderful to be allowed to shave my legs, which my mom will just have to permit, now that I have armpit hair. But how long will it be before I absolutely have to wear deodorant so I won't gag the kids next to me in class? Armpit hair is kind of cool, but the thought of hair . . . um . . . down there, still freaks me out. Will that show through my swimsuit? And then there is the whole period thing, which is particularly a pain for swimmers. What if I get my period when I have a swim meet? What if it's the state championships? What if my first period comes and I don't know it until I get up on the starting blocks in front of the whole team, all their parents, all the other teams, and people start pointing and whispering? As all these thoughts whizzed through my head, I slumped down on my bed. Why couldn't I get all the cool stuff that comes with growing up and just say, "No thanks," to all the stuff I wasn't ready for?

"Hey, Snotwad," my older sister, Elizabeth, said cheerily, as she walked into my room.

"Don't you ever knock?" I rolled over on my side to face

the wall.

"What's up with you?"

"Nothing."

"Yeah, I believe that," she laughed. "Seriously, what's up? You look stressed."

I turned toward her and whispered into the pillow, "I have hair."

"Yeah, and your point is?"

"No," I rolled my eyes, "not the hair on my head!"

"Oh, you got a pube? Congratulations!"

I groaned. "No, not a pubic hair, thank goodness—an armpit hair."

"Just one? That's no big deal."

I jerked up to a sitting position and glared at her. "Yes, it's just one, but it wasn't there one day and suddenly today it is, and it's long and black, and I've never had one before, and I don't want hair anywhere else, and what if I get my period, and. . . ."

"Hey, hey, slow down!"

My sister gently sat down on the bed next me and put her hand on mine. "It'll be okay. You got one hair under your arm, but it's not that big a deal. One hair doesn't mean you're suddenly going to have a triple-D chest and get all hairy everywhere. It all takes a whole lot more time than that."

"Yeah?" I looked at her.

"Yeah," she said softly. "It takes years for all that stuff to take place. Didn't you listen in health class?"

"Sort of. Mostly I was embarrassed, listening to Mr. Williams talk about breasts and stuff."

"Gross. At least I had a woman teacher, Mrs. Kilgore."

"Elizabeth, what was it like for you . . . you know, changing?"

"Don't you remember how I washed my face like ten times a day? My face was always a big grease bomb. At least no one can see your pit hair."

"That's true," I said. "When did you get hairs?"

She looked at the ceiling, trying to recall. "I don't really remember. I got sort of wigged out when it happened, like you are now, but I got over it."

"Do you think Mom will let me buy a real bra?"

"For what? You don't have anything to put in one!"

My face turned scarlet, and my eyes started stinging. Elizabeth leaned over. "Hey, I'm sorry. Don't worry—you'll get breasts. I didn't really need a bra for a long time, but it might be different for you. Just don't go crying to Mom about 'When am I ever going to get breasts?' When I did that, she made up this totally lame little poem, 'Hush little pancake, don't you cry; you'll have cupcakes by and by.'"

We both fell back on the bed from laughing so hard. When we caught our breath and sat up, I looked at her in a new way.

"Wow, am I ever glad you're the oldest!"

Elizabeth tried looking serious. "Are you done freaking out now?"

"Yeah, I guess. It's just that I don't know what to do!"

"Don't worry, I'm here for you, and I'll bet your friends will be, too," she reassured me. Then she suggested, "If you start going nutty about something, go online and find the info you need."

"Going online would be good. And I suppose I could ask Mom about some of it, too. I can't stop all this body stuff from happening anyway, huh?"

"Nope, but then, you don't want to be a little kid forever, do you?"

"No, I guess not."

Of course I didn't. I was just freaking out about it all being out of my control. My body was going to do things, and I didn't get to say a thing about it! Growing up would be a whole lot easier if you could order the changes you were ready for, when you were ready for them.

I did change over time, and I was okay. My big sister and I are closer than ever before, and I think it all started with that conversation. She really helped me by being kind and understanding when I was panicking. I only wish that I had a little sister. I'd like to help her know that the first armpit hair is no big deal.

Morri Spang

Jackie's Little Sister

The best and most beautiful things in the world cannot be seen or even touched—they must be felt with the heart.

Helen Keller

It was hard being the youngest of two sisters—I got all the hand-me-downs, I never got to do anything first and my teachers always said, "Oh, you're Jackie's little sister." It was so hard not to be like, "No, I am LAUREN!" I never liked being the youngest.

Don't get me wrong. Jackie and I got along—with a few fights here and there. We're two years apart, and I am one grade behind her. But sometimes it just really used to bug me to be called "Jackie's little sister" all the time.

Then a few years ago, Jackie and I were in a very bad car accident. She came out with a few bumps and bruises, but she was basically okay. I, on the other hand, had a broken arm and, worse, about 100 stitches in my face. Needless to say, I didn't feel like the belle of the ball when I looked into the mirror.

About a month after the accident, I returned to school.

The stitches were gone, but a very large scar remained. Jackie reassured me that I looked great and I shouldn't worry about the scar. (If you have a big sister, you know that this means a lot coming from her.) My friends did their best not to say anything and not to stare, but the scar was very noticeable.

One day, we were riding home from school on the bus. This guy named Jordan, who rode the bus with us, started teasing me about my scar. He is in the same grade as Jackie and older than me. She was sitting pretty far from where I was sitting and didn't hear him. When we got off the bus, I didn't say anything to her about what he had done. Almost every day, he would do it again, and I would get off the bus crying. This went on for about a month, until I finally broke down and told Jackie. She was furious.

The day after I told her what had been happening, when Jordan made fun of me the next time, Jackie stood up, walked to where he was sitting and said something into his ear. I don't know exactly what she said, but he never said one word to me again.

So, even though getting all of the hand-me-downs may not be the best, I am very grateful to have a big sister like Jackie looking out for me. I know that if I were ever in trouble, she would come running.

Ever since that day, when anyone asks, I tell them, "Yep, I'm 'Jackie's little sister.'" And I am proud of it.

Lauren Alyson Schara, 16

Big Sister

*You have to have confidence in your ability,
and then be tough enough to follow through.*

Rosalynn Carter

Susan wasn't just my big sister, she was my idol, the one person in the world I wanted to be like. I felt so little by comparison. I felt like I didn't quite have the self-confidence to try to follow a big sister act like Susan's.

Not that Susan was big by physical standards—she was much smaller in stature than I was. But bigness isn't always measured by size. In my mind she was my big sister; someone I looked up to—a person who could do anything and do it well. That is, until one night. . . .

We were at a school dance when Susan began acting silly, almost as if she were drunk. At first I couldn't believe it, then I started asking around. It didn't take me too long to find out that someone with a bottle had dared Susan to prove she could handle a drink. Susan was so sure of herself that she took the dare. It was her first taste of alcohol.

I was devastated. I had never faced that kind of situation where my big sister was concerned.

The next morning, Susan acted as if nothing had happened. *Maybe it hadn't,* I told myself. *Maybe I had only been suspicious. Maybe the kids had lied to me about Susan.*

But the following weekend it happened again at the school dance. I watched Susan when she thought I wasn't looking. She tried to play it cool by avoiding the bottle when it was passed around. But the kids kept pressing her until she had to either admit she was afraid of the liquor or take a drink. So she took a drink. Just one. It was enough to make her drunk.

After that, getting Susan drunk became a game her group of friends played. They competed with each other to get Susan to prove she could handle liquor. And Susan tried; she wasn't the kind of girl to take defeat easily. I was sick about Susan's losing battle with alcohol. Her friends were laughing at her—not with her. They liked seeing someone as sure of herself as Susan stumble and fall. It made their weaknesses seem less glaring if Susan— the ideal all-American girl—could be brought down to their level.

By then I was more than sick. I was angry. Big sister or not, Susan needed help. Who else but me could I depend on?

The next weekend, Susan went to the school dance ahead of me, leaving early with a group of her new friends. When I got to the dance hall, Susan had apparently already been drinking. I tried to find her, but everyone was vague about my big sister's whereabouts. *Susan must be hiding from me,* I thought. *Now what do I do?*

The more I thought, the angrier I got. I had to do something. Obviously, the first thing to do was to find Susan. Her drinking buddies must have warned her that I was looking for her. She was probably hiding somewhere, keeping out of sight while I was around.

I thought of checking the girls' lounge again. The room

was crowded, and I looked around slowly. All the girls hanging around seemed suddenly very busy—too busy. I noticed that I was being watched out of the corners of their eyes. I double-checked the toilet stalls. Susan wasn't there. Still, the feeling persisted that everyone was sort of waiting for "the little sister" to leave. Then I noticed a group of girls huddled around one of the vanities by a large waste paper basket. I moved closer. The huddle moved closer, too.

Then I saw a wisp of curly hair sticking up from behind the wastebasket. Susan! I pushed my way through the girls and looked down, right into the eyes of my big sister, who was tucked behind the paper-filled container. I didn't hesitate. "Come on, Susan, we're going home!" I ordered.

Susan rose slowly to her feet. For once, she didn't look big or sure of herself—she looked little, defenseless. "Don't talk to me that way! I'm your big sister!" she exclaimed.

I didn't argue. For once, my size was an advantage. I pushed the basket out of the way, threw Susan over my shoulder, and carried her out of the lounge and across the crowded dance floor.

"Put me down! I'm your big sister!" Susan cried, kicking and pounding my back with clenched fists.

I kept right on going.

The music stopped. Couples parted to let us get through. By the time I got to the other side, a round of applause cheered me on.

An older friend of mine offered to drive us home. Susan collapsed in a heap of tears in the back seat. I was on the verge of tears myself—I couldn't believe what I had just done.

That was the last time Susan got drunk. Maybe the humiliation of being carried home by her little sister in front of everyone had been too much for her. At any rate,

I didn't feel like a "little" sister any more. I felt just like a sister, an ordinary sister. That is a pretty big role to play. Bigness isn't always measured by size, you know.

Olga Cossi

If Only

There are two ways of meeting difficulties. You alter the difficulties or you alter yourself to meet them.

Phyllis Bottome

I stepped up into the school bus and looked for a back seat that was quiet and empty. My sister, Debbie, got onto the bus shortly after I did and looked for a seat close to the back too, chattering as she walked with her best friend, Shelli. They kept peeking over their shoulders, and I glanced behind them to see what could be so interesting.

Two boys cruised down the aisle just behind my sister. I sighed. All Debbie did was giggle at boys. I was a year older than she was, and usually I had no interest in guys at all.

But today was different. Jack was a boy Debbie had been chasing for some time already, and I had to admit that he was pretty cool.

Debbie and Shelli chose the seat directly in front of me and plopped their books down on the floor. The boys, Wes and Jack, sat in the seat across from me. I was sure I caught a glimmer of a smile from Jack. *No, it can't be,* I thought. Boys never paid any attention to me.

When the bus stopped at our white farmhouse, I hoped I could get away from the uncomfortable feelings I was beginning to have. I noticed Jack and his pal looking straight at me when I got out of my seat. Wes nudged Jack in the side, and they both laughed.

I walked down our long driveway as Debbie informed me of her latest plans. "Shelli wants me to go to her house tomorrow to spend the night," she said. "Jack will be coming over to do some work on cars or something with Wes. It'll be so fun!"

I shook my head. "Does he even know you exist?"

"You're just jealous because you don't have a boyfriend," Debbie said. Usually I ignored her teasing, but this time it bothered me.

I walked to the house and tried my best to ignore her. I opened the front door and went straight to my upstairs bedroom. "I'm going to get my homework done now," I told my mom when I passed her in the hallway. I climbed the steps two at a time and slammed my door loudly. Then I plopped my books and myself down onto my bed and sighed.

It couldn't have been more than a half hour before the phone rang. I knew it wouldn't be for me, so I continued to read my history book.

"Rita, you're wanted on the phone," my mom called. Maybe it was my best friend, Lyndie. I went downstairs and took the phone from my mom.

"Hello," I said.

"Hi," came a masculine voice from the other end.

"Uh, who is this?" I asked, although I recognized the voice as belonging to Jack.

"It's Jack, you know, from the bus."

"Oh."

"Would you like to go out with me?" he asked right out. I panicked. My heart began to thump wildly in my chest, and I felt sort of dizzy. He was the guy my *sister* was interested in. If I valued my life, I should have hung the phone up right then. But I thought I should get the situation straight.

"But my sister Debbie likes you!" I blurted into the receiver.

"Yeah, but *you're* the one *I* like," Jack answered.

"Is this a joke?" I asked.

"It's no joke, Rita."

I suddenly felt my mind go blank. I thought for a moment, and then I answered, "Okay."

I guess that's all he wanted to hear, because we quickly said good-bye and the whole thing was done. Just like that, I was going out with Jack. I couldn't believe it. I turned to tell my mom about the conversation without any thought to Debbie whatsoever. But Debbie had been standing nearby and heard every word of the phone conversation. She immediately stormed out of the room. Somehow, I didn't feel too bad for her. I figured that she had plenty more boys to choose from at school.

Later that night, I began to feel a little sorry about the whole thing. Debbie was hurt. I went to her room to try and talk to her. "Go away" was all she said in reply. So I did. I went to my room to study and think, but mainly to dream about my new boyfriend.

I was baffled the next day when I saw Jack and his pals in the school hallway. They walked right past me, and Jack never even said hi. The way he ignored me on the school bus later that day was worse. I didn't say anything because I was afraid to make a fool out of myself. Maybe it had been all a big joke after all.

After Jack ignored me for nearly a week, he called.

"Do you want me to sit with you on the bus and hold

your hand?" he asked. I couldn't believe he asked. I didn't understand boys at all.

"I don't care," was my response. As soon as the words came out of my mouth, I regretted them. But it was too late.

"You don't care?" Jack asked.

"Uh, yeah. You can if you want."

"I can what?"

"Hold my hand," I said. This weird relationship didn't seem to be working out too well.

It turned out that the relationship never did take off. Jack continued to ignore me when we saw each other, and he never did sit with me or hold my hand. Debbie told me later that Jack had a new girlfriend—her friend Hope. I hated the satisfied grin on my sister's face, but I knew that I deserved it. It was my sister that I would be in a relationship with forever. Selfishly, I had ignored her feelings just so I could say that I had a boyfriend, who turned out to not really be my boyfriend at all.

Rita M. Tubbs

The Wild Hair

It was evening and time for my little sister and me to take our showers and get ready for bed. As I passed the mirror in the bathroom, there it was—a wild hair right in the middle of my forehead, threatening to be the beginning of a third eyebrow. I went into the shower trying to think of a solution, and then I spotted the razor. I took it and started trying to shave off the savage hair.

Usually I would trust my mom's advice about what to do in this sort of situation, but this was just too complicated for her—or so I thought. Well, while I was shaving that hair off, the razor slipped, and I ended up shaving off half my eyebrow! Then I did what any girl would do in this situation—I tried to even them out. When I was finished, I looked in the mirror. It was a *disaster!* I tried to figure out if there was any way to fix this mess. Thankfully, I found a way to hide my mistake. I put my bangs over my eyebrows. It worked perfectly!

Just then my parents called me to come and say good night. Nobody noticed *my* eyebrows, but they did notice my little sister's eyebrows! It turns out that while I was fighting the stray hair, she had found another razor in the drawer and began copying me. Now *her* eyebrows were

COMPLETELY missing! My parents were very confused until they finally noticed that half my eyebrows were gone as well. After a lot of questioning, I broke down and confessed to what had happened.

I thought that my parents would be mad at me forever until my mom took me aside to tell me that when she was a preteen, she had done a similar thing. In her case, it was her underarms. While away at camp on a swimming day, she was extremely embarrassed because she had some long hairs in her armpits. My grandma, her mom, had told her she was too young to shave yet. But she went against her mom's wishes and borrowed her friend's razor and shaved her armpits. Then she wrote her mom a confession letter telling her that she had done a terrible thing and that she was very sorry. At the very end of this long two-page letter, she finally told her mom what she had done. As my grandma read through the letter, she was so worried about this terrible thing that her daughter had done that by the end of the letter she laughed, because she was just so relieved to find out about what had actually happened. My grandmother totally understood how my mom had felt, just like my mom now understood me.

This ended up bringing my mom and me even closer together. I still wouldn't ever recommend trying to shave your eyebrows. I suggest that you find a different way to get closer to your mom!

As for my little sister, it took a long time for her eyebrows to grow back in. From then on, I've learned to be a better example to her because she still copies EVERYTHING I do!

Ariel G. Subrahmanyam, 12

The Gift of Faith

The desire to be and have a sister is a primitive and profound one that may have everything and nothing to do with the family a woman is born to.

Elizabeth Fishel

It was the February when I was in the fourth grade. I had just come home from school when I saw my mother rushing in and out of my room putting new toys and stuffed bears on the bed. "Mom, what are you doing?" I asked.

"Two people from Social Services are bringing your new baby sister right now!" my mom said. I was so happy! We had been trying to adopt a little girl, and I was finally getting a sister! I had three brothers, and sometimes it got really boring and a little bit annoying having just boys for siblings. I had no idea that I was going to get a sister this soon.

My brother Nick and I looked out of the upstairs window waiting for her to arrive. We saw a white jeep pull up in front of the house and a woman get out of the car. She opened up the car door and pulled out a small, chubby, pale, very pretty little girl and carried her to the front door. I straightened myself up and came downstairs.

She was sitting on the floor with my little brother, Darius, playing with a toy. Her name was Faith. She had just turned three years old. She had big blue eyes and reddish brown hair. I sat down to talk to her, but she was very, very quiet. I am sure that she must have been scared. We talked to the social worker for a while and tried to learn more about Faith. We found out that this would be her eleventh home.

Once the social worker left, we went out to McDonald's. We had so much fun, and Faith enjoyed all of the attention. I thought she was the cutest little girl I had ever seen. She played with her toys that she got from her Happy Meal and started calling me "sister." I was very happy. She seemed happy too. We were sisters.

When we got home, Faith and I went to play in the room that we would now share. Then when my mom said it was time for everyone to go to bed, Faith had a fit! Because she had lived in ten other homes, I understood why she didn't listen too well. I couldn't imagine being in ten different homes by the age of three. She probably thought that she would have to move again in the morning. I realized how lucky I had been to have a secure home. When she was told to go to sleep, she burst out crying. I was so shocked at how long she could cry! After about fifteen minutes of crying, my mom brought her downstairs so that she could recover.

It wasn't as fun—or as easy—as I thought it would be at first. Faith had horrible asthma attacks, and she cried every night—all night long. She even cried when she just had to tell me that she had to go to the bathroom. Faith was always getting in trouble too. She was very sneaky and rarely told the truth. My new little sister would break my toys, color on my homework, and use all of my nail polish and perfume. She was always in someone else's conversation and doing things just to get people to notice her. She wanted attention, and it was not cute at all. She had a hard time getting used to the rules that she had to learn. I guess she thought that it just didn't matter, because she would be moved to a different home soon.

After a very long time, Faith finally learned how to stay out of trouble, and I learned how to share. I also learned how to put my things away so that she would not get into them. We both had to learn. She still forgets sometimes. So do I.

At first, Faith had a lot of trouble keeping up with us. She was a little chubby. At the rate she was going, she was going to weigh about 100 pounds by kindergarten. She ate huge amounts of food. My mom had her eat a little less and made her stop coming back and forth to the kitchen getting snacks and juice all of the time. We began to give her fruit to snack on and water to drink. We even bought a tricycle for her to ride and a stroller to push her dolls around in. It took just a few months for her to lose her baby fat. Soon, she was running up and down the street like everyone else.

Now she follows me everywhere I go—even when I don't want her to. At five years old, Faith is a very smart and talented little girl. After only two weeks of kindergarten, she was skipped to the first grade. While the new kindergarteners were learning to write their names, Faith was already spelling, reading and doing math. Now she has spelling tests and is learning more about addition and subtraction. I always try to help her with her homework and be a good example. Sometimes she gets a little lazy when it comes to reading and spelling, but once she gets the hang of it, I know that she will be okay.

We are also taking ballet and acting classes. It is so much

more fun to go with my sister. I always thought that she would be successful in acting because she is so full of drama. Faith repeats what she hears on television and pretends to do commercials in front of the mirror. She and our nine-year-old brother, Darius, even put on shows for us in the garage. Maybe one day she will be rich and famous.

It's funny. I can't even remember Faith not being here. When I wake up, the first thing I see is my sister, and when I go to sleep, the last thing I see is my sister. Faith is a nice little girl whose favorite color is purple and who loves to skate. She hates getting her hair combed, dressing up and having to help clean our room. Most of all, she hates brushing her teeth!

I'm glad I have Faith as a sister because she is fun and she makes me laugh. I don't think that the people who had Faith before us gave her a chance to get settled in with them. Besides, they could not have loved her as much as we do. One day, I bet that they will be sitting at home on their couch watching television and will see Faith when she is a star.

No matter what she does in the future, Faith will always be a star in my heart. How lucky I am to have the gift of Faith.

Nydja K. Minor, 12

Best Friend

Anger makes you smaller, while forgiveness forces you to grow beyond what you were.

Cherie Carter-Scott

During sixth grade, the world seemed to be far from my fingertips. I was under the rule of my "evil" parents—my mom and my stepdad. Somehow, I felt like they thought I could never do anything right. I struggled with my grades in history class, and kids at my school thought I was a little bit of a nerd. Overall, I was lonely, disgusted with myself and felt like life had dealt me the worst hand of cards! Then, as if God had heard my cry of despair, I was sent some company—however, it was not exactly what I had in mind.

At Christmas, my stepsister, Courtney, moved in—my new so-called best friend. My mom and her dad had gotten married after my parent's divorce. Although I had known her for five years, I had only seen her a few times— but even on those rare occasions, each time, there had always been tension between us, and we had never gotten along.

For the first month after she came to live with us, I ignored her as much as I could and almost completely avoided getting to know her. I had made up my mind that I hated her from the second that she had walked through the door. I did not know how to live with another person my age. Frankly, I wasn't up for the competition. I had been an only child for eleven years, and I wasn't about to let some prissy blond thirteen-year-old girl move in and take away all of my hard-earned attention! Oh no, not me.

Of course, my parents forced me to talk to her, which didn't change how I felt at all. Without a thought about how she might have felt about having to move in with us, I went about becoming the most mean-spirited sibling in the history of mankind. I plotted and schemed about how I could make her life miserable and drive her away. I stole her possessions, ate her "secret" stash of chocolate and even framed her, so that my older sister would end up having to do more chores than me. I became her worst nightmare.

One day after school, we started fighting as we walked home. We entered the house and began our homework while we still argued over a topic I can't even remember now. Then she did it! She called me a name that I will not mention. Anger rose up into my chest, and I looked around for something to throw at her. I found a pile of my school textbooks nearby. I picked them up and threw them at her, one at a time, with a force that amazed even me. After I ran out of textbooks, I was still in a rage, so I searched for something else to throw at her that could cause damage. I saw our new telephone out of the corner of my eye. I ran to it, ripped it out of the wall and chucked it at her without even a thought of what could come later.

My parents were horrified to find two extremely upset girls when they arrived home, not to mention the debris of their brand-new phone scattered on the floor along with my textbooks. That afternoon's occurrences were explained, and then Courtney and I were both sent to our rooms while they thought up a punishment.

Once I was able to calm down, I sat in my room and remembered all of the other times that I had lost control and injured Courtney physically and emotionally since she had come to live with us. I could not think of any legitimate excuse for me to treat her the way that I had, and I become conscious that I had acted out all of these heinous crimes for ridiculous, selfish reasons. I started to search my heart and recognized all of the wonderful qualities she possessed. With a shock, I realized that not only was I not lonely anymore, Courtney had actually brought a lot of fun into my life.

That night, my parents lectured me for hours. My sentence was that I had to pay for another phone, in addition to having lots of extra chores added to my normal duties. As I walked back to my room, I could hear Courtney crying in hers. For the first time in my life, I was sincerely sorry for the pain I had caused her. I stood in front of her door, trying to think of ways to apologize. Even though I was afraid I might be too late, I went in anyway. I found her in the dark, weeping on her bed. Because of her brokenhearted crying, she didn't hear me enter her room or my whispered apology. But when I lay down and wrapped my arms around her to comfort her, she knew how truly sorry I was.

After that night, she and I called a truce. Eventually, we began to get along better and even started hanging out together. Somewhere along the line, we discovered that we could get up on the roof of our apartment complex through a window in the laundry room. Having our own little private place to share secrets or just to talk, as we lay up on the roof looking at the stars or getting some sun, has been a special thing that we have shared for the past few years.

Over time, I have realized that it's really pretty nice having a sister and a friend to go through life with. Courtney and I have shared many triumphs and tragedies together, and she has been my rock through it all. Now, I can't imagine my life without her. She and I rarely argue anymore, and when we do, the disagreements are short-lived for we have learned that it is better to be happy and loved than it is to win the argument.

I can truly say that after all we've been through, my stepsister Courtney is my very best friend.

Bethany Gail Hicks, 16

6
TOUGH STUFF

Ever watched someone step on a butterfly's wing
Or have someone take one of your things
Thought you saw the truth in someone's eyes
Then you find out later it was all just a lie
Ever had someone change from friend to foe
As the world around you is stuck on "go"
You want to keep on dreaming a wonderful
   dream
To realize later it's not what it seems
You wanted to run, but found you can't hide
In a room where there's no one there by
   your side
I've been where you've been . . .
I've seen what you've seen
So my word of advice—for your life please
   take care
What you have now might not always be there.

                    Katelyn Krieger, 13

For Michelle

My doctrine is this, that if we see cruelty or wrong that we have the power to stop, and do nothing, we make ourselves sharers in the guilt.

Anna Sewell

Every day, five 12-year-old girls waited together for the school bus to take them home. I was one of them. Jessica was the bully. She picked on everyone. Emily and Clarissa were Jessica's sidekicks because they were afraid if they weren't on her side, they would become targets of her cruelty. Then there was Sarah, a nice girl who didn't like Jessica but was friends with Clarissa. I didn't like anyone except Sarah. Occasionally, a sixth girl named Brittany waited with us too. She despised Jessica but was liked by everyone else.

One day a new girl, Michelle, started waiting with us. She was shy and plain looking, but very nice to anyone who would talk to her. Although she was a year older, she was in a class with Brittany and me. Nobody else knew her. I sometimes sat with her on the bus and noticed she stuttered and had trouble saying a sentence clearly. She always spoke very highly of Brittany and considered her to be a good friend. She didn't have any friends besides Brittany and me. Most people didn't notice she was even there, but if they did, they made comments about her stuttering.

I was generally accepted in our little group, so when I brought Michelle with me, nobody objected. Things were okay until Jessica suddenly decided she didn't like Michelle and didn't want her to sit with us. Jessica started laughing at Michelle's stuttering. Then the "jokes" got more and more vicious. Emily and Clarissa would laugh along, but Sarah and I did not. We told them to stop. Then Jessica started to make fun of us too, so we backed down.

Meanwhile, I was privately becoming closer friends with Michelle, who confided in me how hurt she felt when everyone picked on her and how it had happened all her life. But whenever I got the nerve to stand up for her, I was always outnumbered, so I stopped trying.

One day Brittany overheard Jessica, Emily and Clarissa talking about wanting to ditch Michelle. Brittany took it upon herself to be the leader, and so the next day Brittany announced that we all didn't want Michelle to sit with us anymore because we thought she was a freak. Even though I didn't feel that way at all, I didn't say anything. I just sat there, stunned that Brittany had said what she said.

I'll never forget Michelle's expression. Despair, pain and anger were all mixed together on her face. Brittany, one of the girls she had trusted the most in her world, had told her she was a freak and didn't want to see her again. She silently picked up her backpack and moved to a nearby table with her back to us. I knew she was crying. One of my biggest regrets was that at that moment I didn't say out loud that I didn't want her to go. I should have called her back—but I was a coward.

So Sarah and I sat there without saying a word, while the others laughed at the thought of Michelle crying in front of us.

Though I was still friendly to Michelle in private, it wasn't the same. Michelle stopped showing the same eagerness to me when I spoke to her. She started taking the bus less and less frequently until she finally stopped altogether. Her mother drove her home. Then I lost touch with her, because the class we had had together finished, and she no longer rode the bus. She moved away later that semester.

One year later, Sarah ran up to me at school and blurted, "Michelle died . . . she committed suicide."

"What?" I asked, not believing what I just heard.

"Her mother put an obituary in the local paper," said Sarah, as shaken as me.

"But . . . didn't she move to the other side of the country?"

"Yeah, but it was in our newspaper for some reason. . . ."

I went home that day, still not thinking clearly. *Had I caused her to kill herself? If I had only stood up for her, would she still be alive today?* Those questions ran through my mind over and over. When I got home, I told my mother the whole story, from the very beginning when Michelle first entered my life—to the end, where she left.

Guilt-ridden and miserable, I stayed up that night crying uncontrollably, talking to my mother until 3:00 A.M. When I woke up the next day, my eyes were so swollen and puffy they would hardly open. I felt responsible for her death. I could still picture her face when Brittany told her not to sit with us anymore. It became obvious to me what had happened in her life. She had grown up always being picked on, without any friends to help her. When Brittany and I came into her life, she had clung to us, feeling that we were the only ones besides her family who cared about her. But we both let her down terribly. Moving is difficult for anyone, but for her, it must have been devastating. Not being able to handle it all, without any friends, only enemies, she must have decided she couldn't live with that kind of misery. Perhaps if I had only been kinder to her, she would still be alive.

"Oh, that's too bad," Emily and Clarissa both said, with fake sorrow in their voices, when they heard what had happened to Michelle. Jessica just snickered. Their reaction made me sick! How could they act so inhumanely about her, let alone laugh at her, even in death? After a minute, they forgot their would-be sorrow and went on to make fun of a sixth-grade boy with glasses sitting nearby. Sarah was just as shocked as I was at their cold reaction.

Now, two years after Michelle first entered my life, I'm not the same girl that I was. When I see someone— anyone—being picked on or harassed, I always try to help them, no matter what.

Michelle's memory still haunts me, but I will always think of her as a gift . . . a gift to me and to anyone else who has ever experienced bullying—a gift that reminds me to never make that mistake again.

Satya Pennington, 12

[EDITORS' NOTE: *If you, or someone you know, is thinking about suicide, call 1-800-suicide or log on to* www.kidshealth .org/teen/ *(keyword search: "suicide").*]

The Day My Life Ended

I had taken my father for granted. Now that I had lost him, I felt an emptiness that could never be filled.

Benazir Bhutto

"He only has a few weeks to live."

Try having someone tell you this about your own father.

Try having to watch your father die for two years.

Try having your father die in December, just before Christmas, just a month after your sister got married.

Try being me.

During sixth grade, I loved school. Not because it was fun, but because it was an escape from my home reality— a place where I could forget that back at my house my dad was dying. A place where I could forget that at any time, colon cancer would finally take my dad's life. Try getting good grades while you think about that 24/7.

I hated coming home every day after school and seeing my dad hooked up to an oxygen tank. I hated going to the hospital after school to visit him when he was really sick. I can still remember that horrible smell of death when I walked into his hospital room and seeing my dad not even able to lift his head because he was so weak. I hated knowing that my dad was going to die before Christmas day.

It was a chilly December day, and I woke up to the sound of birds chirping outside as the rays of sunlight poured through my bedroom window. I can still remember the sweet smell of pancakes being cooked, coming from the kitchen. I got up, took a shower, got dressed and went into the kitchen to get some food. As I walked past the front room where my dad was, I stopped and kissed him good morning. It looked like he was sleeping, but he wasn't. For the past two days, he had been hooked up to oxygen and hadn't been able to talk or open his eyes. It was Saturday, so I ate my breakfast slowly since there was no reason to rush. After I finished eating, my mom put my dad's favorite movie on, and I sat down next to him and watched it. After it was over, I decided I needed some fresh air, so I went on a really long walk. Actually, I didn't need fresh air, I just needed to get out of that house since the mood was very depressing and sad.

Later on that evening, my mom, sister, her husband, my aunts and uncles, and my cousins were sitting in the front room with my dad when I heard the phone ring. I picked it up, and it was my friend from down the street. She asked me if I wanted to spend the night with her. I was so happy when my mom said yes. I couldn't stand being in that sad environment. I packed my stuff, said good-bye to everyone and kissed my dad good-bye. My sister, brother-in-law and cousin walked me down to my friend's house.

I hadn't been there for more than twenty minutes when I heard my brother-in-law's voice coming from the front door. The minute I went into the hallway and saw his face, I knew. Before I could ask, he said, "He went." Those were the two words I had been dreading for two years since my father was diagnosed with cancer. At that moment, my life stopped. Nothing made sense anymore. How could my father die? I should have been there when he went. But I wasn't, and I regret it to this day.

That night I experienced two of the hardest moments of my life. One, my father died. Two, later on that evening, I kissed my dad good-bye, and as I did I whispered, "I love you," for I knew that it would be the last time I would see him. I went into my room because the people from the mortuary were there. When I came back out, he was gone and I had to accept the fact that my dad wasn't coming back.

I wish I had spent more time with my father. Now he won't ever teach me how to cook, drive a car, or walk me down the aisle on my wedding day. I wanted him to be there to see me graduate from high school and go to college. I just wish he could have seen me pass the sixth grade.

Every day I try my hardest at whatever I am doing, because I know up in heaven Dad is watching me. I try, because I want him to be proud of me. I'm sure that he is. I loved my dad very much. No matter what happens, I know that will be one fact that will never change.

Sammie Luther, 15

Cancer, the Only Word I Can't Say

Silence is no certain token that no secret grief is there; Sorrow which is never spoken is the heaviest load to bear.

Frances Ridley Havergal

I remember the day so vividly. It was early fall, and it wasn't too cold yet—the kind of weather when all you need is a spring jacket and you'll be fine. I was in the third grade. When I walked into the kitchen to look for my mom after school, I heard her talking on the phone.

"She's home, I have to go," she said.

She hung up the phone and gave me a tiny smile. "Do you want to go for a drive?" she asked me. "I need to tell you something."

I nodded my head, feeling that whatever she was going to share with me wouldn't be good, but I knew I had to hear it.

We drove around listening to music. When we reached my school, she drove into the parking lot, stopped the car and looked at me.

"Remember what Grandma had?" she asked.

"Cancer, right?" I replied.

"Yes. Well, when I was in the shower the other day, I noticed an unusual bump on my breast. I went to the doctor's, and he has diagnosed me with cancer," she said. Then she started to cry.

I wanted to cry too, but I didn't. I felt like I had to comfort her and reassure her that she'd be okay, so I needed to stay strong. As long as I kept telling her it would be all right, I felt like it was.

And she was okay—for a while. She had radiation and chemotherapy. It made her throw up everyday, and she lost her hair. But the cancer disappeared. The whole time I was in the fourth grade, she was completely fine.

Then I went into fifth grade. One day when I got home from school, my mom was sitting on her recliner, crying.

I *knew* it was back. "It's back . . . the cancer, isn't it?" I asked.

She nodded her head, and I began to cry. I ran over to her and gave her the biggest hug I have ever given anyone. She told me that it was still breast cancer, but the cells had moved to her liver.

Again, she lost her hair because of the chemotherapy and radiation. We also sent her to Chicago once a month to get a special treatment.

Then in March, my mom went into the hospital. She was only there for one and a half weeks, but during her stay she got a lot better. The doctors sent her home. She was doing great . . . until one day she couldn't move without hurting.

She was at the point where she had to be in bed all the time, and she couldn't even talk without it hurting like 100 stabbing knives. My family got ready to say good-bye because we all knew she wouldn't be around much longer.

One morning, my mom seemed to be in more pain than

usual. My brother Josh and I sat by her bed for over three hours, while I held her hand. Then she became quiet. Josh called the hospital and asked if someone could come over to check on her.

A short while later, a nurse arrived and checked her heartbeat. "She's gone. I'm sorry," he said quietly

I actually started to laugh because I couldn't believe it. I was eleven! Eleven-year-olds only lose their moms in movies—not in real life. Even though I knew that it was going to happen, it still didn't seem true.

Some days, I am great. Other days, I just can't believe she's gone. On those days, I want her back so badly that no words can do it justice. I'm sure that sometimes you probably think your parents are just out to ruin your life. Believe me; it's really hard to go on without them.

Cancer, the only word I can't say without crying or wanting to cry. I just hope my children, or other people I may love in the future, will never have to go through the same pain that I have had to. Many people survive cancer. I guess my mom just wasn't lucky enough.

Sammi Lupher, 11

[EDITORS' NOTE: *If you have a loved one with cancer or another life-threatening illness, or you have already lost a loved one to illness, go to* www.kidskonnected.org *or call 800-899-2866 for friendship, understanding, education and support.*]

It's Never Your Fault

Yesterday I dared to struggle, today I dare to win.

Bernadette Devlin

I sat there with my body trembling from head to toe, wondering what was happening to me and what would happen next. I knew that what was occurring was not right, but I didn't know how to stop it. I wanted with all my might to push his dark soul away from me, but being about three feet tall and only weighing around forty-five pounds, I didn't have the physical capability.

I was four, and my parents were busy with work and social lives, so they began looking for baby-sitters near our house who could watch my sister and me at night. They found two guys who lived down the street who were more than willing to be our baby-sitters. Although they looked a little scary when I first saw them, my parents assured me that everything would be okay and that I should be on my best behavior. I still had a feeling of insecurity running through my veins. I didn't know why, but I thought the men weren't good people.

After they were there for a couple of hours, I needed to go to the bathroom, so I went upstairs and shut the door. Shortly after, the door opened and in came the older of the two. I thought at first that maybe he just thought I needed some help since I was so young, but then he just stayed there and watched me. As I was getting up to leave, he started feeling me in places that aren't meant to be seen by other people. I didn't do anything to stop it. I was so small, and he was so big. Eventually he stopped, probably so my sister wouldn't become suspicious. He told me not to tell anyone what had happened and that it was to be kept a secret.

Having an older sister, I knew what secrets were and I knew that they were meant to be kept, so I never said a word to anyone. Each time he came over to baby-sit, the same pattern would occur, and I began to feel really uncomfortable and violated; but he was starting to get more threatening and I was beginning to fear losing my life if I told, so I remained quiet.

In elementary school, visitors from child abuse organizations would come and talk to us. That's when I learned that what was happening to me was called sexual molestation and that it's never the victim's fault. Up to that point, I had been blaming it on myself. They also said that it is very important to tell someone as soon as it happens to you and that telling is the most important thing to do. I really wanted to say something after hearing this, but I still didn't have the courage. I feared that he might come after me if the cops came after him.

The summer before sixth grade, I was walking back to my house after swim team practice. Normally, I walked back with my best friend, but she was staying at the pool all day, so I walked back on my own. As I headed up the long hill, a car started passing by very slowly, and the guys in the car were watching me. I could only make out one person—my former baby-sitter—and I started to run. I ran in between houses and went through backyards. I did everything possible to avoid getting into that car. After a half hour of that car chasing me, I made it into my house. I told my sister what had happened, and she called my mom at work, but she said that we should just lock the doors and watch for the car. I never saw that car ever again.

My junior year, I was on my high school's dance team. We had just finished performing our half-time routine and were in the process of heading back to the bleachers, where we had our bags, when someone who looked kind of familiar spit at me from over the fence and cursed at me. I wasn't sure at the time where I knew the face from, but I got extremely scared. A senior member on the team overheard what had happened and took me to the coaches. She explained to them what had happened, and my coach was about ready to jump over the fence and punch the guy's lights out, but I knew that wouldn't solve anything. That would only make me seem weak and would show that I let his hostility get to me. I wanted to be stronger than that and not give in, so I asked my coach if we could just forget about what happened and just enjoy the rest of the game.

Although I wanted to forget what had happened, I couldn't. I started having panic attacks and nightmares with flashbacks from that football game. I lost my appetite and became really depressed. After a couple months of not being able to eat much at all, my family and friends became very worried and wanted to help in any way that they could. However, I wasn't ready to admit the fact that I had a problem.

One night, after a dance practice, I got these intense pains in my side, and my mom rushed me to the hospital. I was given many tests, but they couldn't figure out what was wrong with me. I wasn't too sure myself. Finally, they took me back for a question-and-answer session, and a psychologist started asking me a ton of questions and had me respond to them. He asked me if I had ever had sexual contact. I wasn't quite sure how to answer that because I never had any willingly, but it did happen, so I told him the whole story. He was shocked to hear me say it so quickly and was glad that I did—and so was I. He asked why it had taken me so many years to tell, and I answered that I had been worried that I would be hunted down if I ever told. He found that quite understandable and contacted some social workers and legal offices to see if anything could be done about the sexual molester. Since I had waited so long and didn't have a witness, there really wasn't anything that could be done except that I should start seeing a psychologist regularly and that would help all the physical pain my body had been enduring.

I'm telling this story not to get sympathy, but because it was an important lesson that I learned. If something happens to you that you suspect isn't right, tell someone *right away*. It will only help. Your life will become more tranquil. I used to have nightmares any time my eyes would shut, but after telling someone, I can now sleep peacefully. My only regret is not having told earlier.

Hattie Frost, 18

[EDITORS' NOTE: *To get help with child abuse issues of any kind, call Childhelp USA at 800-4-A-CHILD.*]

BFF

Sorrow has its reward. It never leaves us where it found us.

Mary Baker Eddy

Whenever something bad would happen to me, I would think that nothing could be worse than when I had to move away from my home and leave my best friends behind. Flying away from my small home in Colchester, Connecticut, at the age of seven, I felt that it was the hardest thing I had ever done—or ever would do. But I was wrong. I was very, very wrong.

I was just about to go out the door, when I heard the phone ringing. "Hello?" I said into the receiver.

"Courtney? This is Mrs. Lynch."

"Oh! Hey, Mrs. Lynch! My. . . ."

Mrs. Lynch cut me right off. "Courtney, please let me talk to your mom."

"Sure, well . . . she's walking out the door to go to dinner group, but I'm sure she'd want to talk to you!" I went to get my mom. I caught her just as she was pulling out of the driveway with my dad.

"Mom! Mom!" I called, motioning for her to stop the car. "It's Mrs. Lynch, and it sounds really urgent!" I yelled, thrusting the phone at her. I started to walk away but then stopped because I heard the car door open and then slam shut.

I heard my mother say to Dad, "You go ahead and drop off this bread pudding. I have to stay here with Court and the girls." I was really confused. I had never heard Mrs. Lynch sound so . . . stressed out . . . or serious . . . or anything like the way she had been when I just talked to her.

"Courtney, come here, Honey. I have to tell you something."

"Why did Mrs. Lynch sound like that?" I asked, realizing that my mom looked very concerned and like she was choosing her words very carefully.

"Kelly and Jenn . . . ," she trailed off. Then she took a deep breath and started again. "Kelly and Jenn have been in a very serious sledding accident." Her words filtered into my head very slowly. Everything started to feel strange. Nothing was making any sense. I was confused. "What about Christiane? What happened? What do you mean?" All of a sudden, my mind sped up again and everything my mom was saying to me started to sink in and I had a very bad feeling in my stomach.

"We don't know very much except that they both have serious head injuries and they were flown from Colchester to Hartford by Life Star. Then Hartford Hospital transferred them to Boston Children's. They are both still in the air right now, on the way to Boston. Jenn was sent first because her injuries are more serious than Kelly's." Everything was spilling out of her like she was having a talking race with someone. There were tears in her eyes, and as I saw hers I felt a warm stream of tears running down my cheeks as well. I was too overwhelmed to do anything but hug my mom.

My mother told me to call Christiane because she didn't want to talk to anyone but me right now. I didn't want
to talk to anyone either. The only thing I could think
about was Kelly and Jenn. The three of them were my best
friends in the whole world. Christiane and I were like sisters. We had done everything together since . . . well, forever. Kelly, Christiane, Jenn and me. That's it. We were all
best friends—BFF—best friends forever. Now two of them
were almost gone?

I ran to the parlor and cried. I didn't stop. Everything
seemed to be blocked out of me. I wanted to run. I wanted
to be with Christiane. I had to be with her. We needed each
other right now, and we were a thousand miles apart.

As the night wore on, I heard the phone ring. My mom
answered and murmured something into the receiver.
Then I heard footsteps coming down the hall . . . my
mom's footsteps. Not wanting to talk, I rolled over and
pretended to be asleep. My mom came over to my bed
and handed me the phone. I pushed it back. I didn't want
to talk to anyone. I couldn't. "Courtney, it's Chris. She
won't talk to anyone but you. She needs you right now.
You need each other," she said quietly but firmly. She
pushed the phone back toward me, and this time she didn't allow me to push it back. There I was, trying to think
of what to say to my best friend.

"Hi, Christiane," I said very quietly.

"Hi, Court," Chris said back.

"I don't really know what to say. I am so confused.
None of this is sinking in right now."

"Ya. It hasn't sunk in for me either, and the scary part is
that I could have been on that sled with them."

"Oh please, Chris! Don't even go there! Please! Please!"

There was a long moment of silence between us. Then I
said I had to go, even though I really didn't. I just didn't
know what else to say. So we just hung up.

A few hours later, I woke up not realizing where I was or what was happening. I looked at my alarm clock and saw that it was very early in the morning. I had no idea why I was awake. Then I remembered. Tears came into my eyes, and I wiped them away. I climbed out of bed and went downstairs. I saw my mom, just sitting at the table, looking out the window. I knew something was terribly wrong.

She hugged me hard as she gave me the worst news of my life. "Oh, Court," she said softly. "Jenni died this morning."

And that was it. I screamed and ran. Then there was nothing. I wanted to be with Jenn—to laugh with her, do stuff like we used to—just to see her. I never would again.

Now I'm on the plane again. We are going back to Colchester for Jenni's funeral. I haven't sorted through my feelings enough to understand how to deal with what has happened. I know I will get there eventually, but I'm not there yet. All I can think about is Kelly and Chris and what I will say when I see them. And poor Jenni. I look out the window, and the tears run down my face. I had always thought that plane rides were supposed to be for fun, for an adventure . . . but never again will I think that.

Courtney VanDyne, 12

[EDITORS' NOTE: *For more information about how to deal with death and grief, log on to* www.kidshealth.org/teen/ *(keyword search: "death and grief").*]

Hero

Who ran to help me when I fell
And would some pretty story tell
Or kiss the place to make it well?
My mother.

Jane Taylor

Have you ever had someone in your life who made you think you could conquer anything? Someone who could make you smile even when you felt like all you could do was cry? My mom was that for me.

My mom took the bad things in life and turned them into miracles. If I was upset and crying, she was there with a bright smile that made all the troubles in the world seem minuscule compared to her brightly lit face. Sometimes I think she could have eclipsed the sun with that smile. I still see that smile sometimes—like when I wake up to a loud alarm clock beeping in my ear telling me it's time to start another day, or when I'm sitting in class and I just can't conjugate that Spanish sentence. I'm about to give up, and then there it is, that beautiful smile.

As a child, your worst fear is death. You don't really

know what it is. You know it's sad. You know that it's something you don't want to happen to the two people in your life that you love the most . . . your parents. As scary moments go, that's one of the worst. As you get older, you come to the realization that nothing lasts forever and that you aren't going to last forever either.

But we never think that it is going to happen to us immediately. When people usually talk about death, we speak as if it's something that's going to happen so far into the future that we needn't worry about it. Sometimes we may wonder how it's going to happen—if it will be painful. We wonder if we will get to tell those friends and family members just how much they meant to us.

When I thought about my parents dying, I always thought of them as being old when it happened, and it stopped there. I never got past the old part. I never made it to what actually happened.

Thoughts like that were running through my mind the day my mom died. So many things were running through my mind—unanswered questions and unspoken words are what I remember pounding in my head. I can remember every second of the day my mom died, every single tear that streamed down my face.

I was thirteen, on the brink of leaving my preteen years behind me. I woke up that morning refreshed. It was Sunday. Mom was still asleep on the couch, so I figured I would just pull out some food and turn on the TV and keep the volume low. At around two o'clock, my mom started snoring really loudly. I turned around and looked at her; she looked really peaceful, but she sounded like a train. Later I would find out why.

I just smiled and went back to my program. A few minutes later, I decided that I needed to take a shower and get packed to go to my dad's house. I showered, and then I picked out my outfit and played with my mom's makeup.

I looked in the mirror and I just knew that Mom was going to tell me how pretty I looked. I was excited. I loved hearing her say things like that. I needed that—I needed it to keep me going. Being a teenager can be tough—but with her there, I knew I could make it.

A few years ago, Mom and I got into this letter thing. We would write letters and little notes and strategically place them around the house. Things like, "Smile, God loves you," or "I'm proud of my beautiful daughter/mother." So, with that in mind, I grabbed some paper, a pen and some tape. I placed a note on her mirror and looked at it satisfyingly. *Now, I'll wake her up and she can find it. Then she'll tell me she feels the same way and that I'm pretty, and then we can go,* I thought.

When I walked into the living room to wake her up, I didn't do it immediately, even though I wanted to. I always felt a little bit scared in the dark room when there were no lights on. My mom had covered the windows with heavy drapes to keep the sunlight out when she slept in the living room. I sat down on the chair beside the couch and looked at the clock, which read "3:26." I sat there in the dark, staring at the couch. I couldn't see my mom, but I knew she was there. Finally, after a few minutes, I got up and knelt beside her. I knew that she usually jerked awake when someone tried to wake her up, so I didn't want to give her too much of a shock.

I reached over and shook her shoulder. I did it again. Again. Again. Nothing. I felt my heart stop. The thought that she was gone didn't even enter my mind yet. It was just irking me that she wasn't waking up. I reached up and turned on the lamp. When that light hit and I looked down, I knew. My head knew, but my heart didn't. I shook her again. No. No! "Mom, come on," I pleaded. But when she didn't respond, it really hit me. My mom was gone.

At that point, the tears came. I sat there thinking, *My*

mom is dead, I'm in a brand-new apartment, I'm all alone and I don't even know the address. Our phone wasn't even hooked up yet. I ran to the door and ran outside. It was like a scene from a horror movie.

Tears were running down my cheeks, and I was screaming, "Somebody help me! My mom!" I ran back in for a second and looked at her. I'm not really sure why. Maybe I wanted to see if I had been mistaken. Maybe she was just in a deep sleep and she was sitting up and was about to ask me why I was screaming. I ran back outside and a man and woman were getting out of their car. They asked me what was going on. The man went in to check on my mom while the lady helped me call the police and my grandparents. The man came back out and announced that she was gone. I wanted to scream at him, "What do you know? Shut up! Shut up!" I didn't though. And then they came with an ambulance and took my mom to the hospital.

My mom used to tell me when she was little there were times that her mother, my Mawmaw, would have these attacks where she couldn't breathe. I had never seen one. But that afternoon, while I was in the hospital waiting room with Mawmaw, I saw it. She tried to bend over, but she just couldn't get her breath. I get these attacks now. I started getting them that very day. When the doctor came into the waiting room, he told us that there was a lot of fluid in my mom's lungs and that was why she had died. We found later that it was caused by a mix of prescriptions.

Her death was marked accidental. *Accidental? This wasn't an accident. Someone did this.* That's what I was thinking at the time, but I don't think that way anymore. Sometimes life throws us things that are unfair, but we are never thrown anything we can't handle.

The most important thing that my mom taught me was that your life experiences are what make you who you are. It's the little moments that make up the big ones. As important as those little moments are, it's what you do after something huge happens that really counts. That's what really matters.

That day, I had one of those experiences my mom was always talking about. But, when my big moment came, all I could think was, *What happens now? What if I don't make it?*

I look back on that day and I think about how I've handled life afterward. I think I've done fairly well. I was back at school by Thursday. On Friday, we went to clean out her apartment. Walking in there was probably one of the hardest things I have ever done in my life.

I looked around Mom's apartment. My chicken from lunch the day she died was still on the table. I walked into the bathroom and looked in the mirror. On the mirror, on a little piece of yellow paper, were written the words, "I love you." My mom had never seen that note. I tore it down.

I remembered one day when I was at my mom's, I was sitting on the couch, watching *Buffy the Vampire Slayer* while my mom read a book. I noticed that every few minutes she would look over at me. She would give me that beautiful smile of hers and then go back to her book. She finished the book, and I kept watching the show.

"You really like this Buffy girl, don't you?" she asked me. I looked over at her.

"Yeah, I do," I smiled.

She paused before she asked her next question.

"So, I guess she's your hero then, huh?"

I had never thought of it that way. I just went back to watching my show. Now when I think about that little moment, I realize that as close as we were, there were still things that she didn't know about me.

Buffy wasn't my hero . . . she was.

Brittany Shope, 14

Behind the Bathroom Door

The willingness to accept responsibility for one's own life is the source from which self-respect springs.

Joan Didion

I stepped onto the cold tile and silently closed the bathroom door. There I was again, staring into that deep hole. I jolted forward, releasing all my sadness and anger that had somehow turned into food. I flushed the toilet, washed my mouth, wiped my eyes and walked back into reality. I forced a smile on my face and sat down with my family. They didn't know what really happened when their perfect daughter closed the bathroom door.

Dreams of being perfect had filled my head since elementary school. By the seventh grade, my dreams of being beautiful had taken me to unhealthy extremes.

It began like any other diet. I felt the need to be skinny because I was a gymnast and cheerleader and all of my best friends were always skinnier than me. I weighed eighty-eight pounds in seventh grade, when counting calories and reducing food intake became the main

priority in my life. I stopped eating. Once the first pound
was lost, there was no turning back. Every tip of the scale
managed to put a smile on my face.

The thought of being "fat" soon became my biggest fear.
I grew afraid of eating in public. I always thought the person next to me was thinking, "Gosh what a pig! No wonder she's fat!" I wouldn't eat anything at all for days,
craving food the whole time. I would finally give in to my
cravings and find myself with a half-eaten bag of chips and
an empty tub of ice cream in my hands. Then I would stop
eating again. This went on for about five months until I
decided that there was only one thing left to do. I taught
myself to throw up. I would starve myself until I couldn't
stand it anymore and then eat everything I could get my
hands on. After every food binge, I would walk up the
stairs, step onto the cold tile and close the bathroom door.

Ironically, my eating disorder pulled me further and
further away from the perfection and acceptance that I
worked so hard toward. Convinced that I was incapable
of being loved, I isolated myself from the world.
Everyday, I walked through the hallway at school with
my head down. I didn't enjoy talking to anyone. Not even
my family. When the day would end, I would lock myself
in my room and cry. I sometimes even pressed a sharp
blade upon my skin in a strange attempt to feel something besides hunger and unhappiness. I never slept. I
stayed awake every night praying for a change in my life.

I continued to hold this dreadful secret through my
freshman year. I would stop eating for days, then binge
and purge. This lasted my entire ninth-grade year. Then,
in my sophomore year, I quit starving myself and just
binged and purged.

Fortunately, after years of starving, throwing up and
crying endless tears, I realized that I needed to rid myself
of this demon that ate away all my happiness. I had

always thought that I was alone and nobody loved me enough to care. Strangely enough, through the years, I managed to overlook my family and friends reaching out to help me for so long.

December 9th of my sophomore year began just like any other day. However, it was the day my life would change. As I sat in the hall during activity period, someone brought me a message from the guidance counselor. I made my way to her office, and as I opened the door, I found my best friend sitting in the middle of two chairs. The counselor sat to the left of her. The chair on the right was for me. As they looked at me, they didn't need to say a thing—I knew what was going to happen. There was no more running away. I sat down, stared at the floor and began to cry. For the first time in four years, I revealed my secret. I finally began the long journey I would have to take to get well.

Recovery drove me down a dark difficult road. It was a journey consisting of lessons and life-altering decisions. At first, I continued to lie to myself, as well as to my family, and denied every medication and doctor I came close to. My family never gave up on me. They continued to give their support and love to make me better. Luckily, I began to see the truth behind this deadly illness that I had. My family's support gave me the courage that I needed to open my eyes to a life without anorexia or bulimia.

Through the tough times, I learned a lot about myself, self-control and self-acceptance. I finally understood that for other people to accept me into their lives, I had to accept myself. I came to know that my striving for perfection would never end. However, taking it out on myself would never offer me comfort. I began accepting compliments, refrained from comparing myself to others and eventually began to smile again. Rather than letting my eating disorder control me, I finally learned to control myself and the terrible thoughts that previously had owned my mind.

As I walked onto my high school's football field at the beginning of my senior year, cheers erupted from the crowd as the former Homecoming Queen carried a brand-new tiara in her hands. As I waited in anticipation, I closed my eyes as memories of my five-year battle with the horrible demon ran through my mind. I remembered all the self-hatred, lack of control, and then all the lessons that I learned about myself and my disorder on my road to recovery.

When I opened my eyes, I found the beautiful tiara being placed upon my head. My heart began to race as the announcer shouted my name as the Homecoming Queen. Cheers erupted from the crowd as all my friends ran toward me. Tears ran down my cheeks as I realized that I had finally won my battle with the demon because I had found the strength inside of me to overcome it.

Katy Van Hoy, 18

Sleep-Away Camp

Sometimes if you want to be a winner, you have to be willing to bear the scars from the fight.

Petra Salvaje

"I'll have a single scoop of the butter pecan in a cone," I say to the guy behind the counter at the ice cream shop. I look over, and sitting in a booth behind me is a kid in my grade at school. It's Cory, one of the boys who made fun of me all year long after finding out that I had been hospitalized for depression. He used to pass me in the school hallways, look down at the scars on my arms where I cut myself, make karate chop gestures and say things like, "Why don't you go kill yourself?"

The thing was, I never wanted to die. I just cut myself to escape the emotional pain I felt. Some days, I would lie in bed for hours—not sleeping, not reading—just lying there. I would sit in my room, cry, loathe myself and wallow in self-pity while I wrote morbid poetry about how great life would be once I was dead. Then one muggy summer morning, my mom found me lying in bed, blood staining my clothing and sheets. I looked and felt like a zombie. That's how I ended up in the hospital.

It all started when my parents got divorced.

I had always been a daddy's girl, and when my father moved 3,000 miles away, I grew numb and angry. To this day, I still don't remember much of what happened during that time, even though I was ten years old. All I remember is that I began to get angry easier, especially at my mom. After the divorce was final, my mom sold the house and that made me mad. Then we moved to a place where I felt like I didn't fit in. I cried all the time because I was different from everybody else. Being multiracial in a predominantly white town set me apart, but I was also different in how I was. I was a tomboy. I was the kind of girl who spoke up for what I believed in, no matter what the cost. Most of the time, eleven- and twelve-year-olds don't want to hear one of their peers telling them to stop acting out.

Some people write when they feel sad, or they go running to get the pain out. They have constructive ways to cope—but I didn't. My method for dealing with depression was a razor blade and a locked bedroom door. But the deepest scars that I carry are the memories of feeling that nobody else understood me and a sense of feeling abandoned and helpless.

That morning when Mom found me lying in my bloody bed, I was admitted to the hospital where I spent almost an entire month.

At first, I hated the hospital. I thought they were making me worse. Looking back, I think I didn't really want to get better. Being depressed was easy, because not caring meant I was numb; I didn't have to feel the pain inside. I soon began to attend group therapy. We'd talk about our issues, and even though I heard every other kid in the group talk about being sad and lonely and wanting to die or trying to die, I still felt like nobody in the world understood me or cared. My only pain was the blood I released through my arms.

I continued to cut myself with whatever I could find at the hospital, although it wasn't easy since they locked up anything potentially dangerous. I took pen caps and used them to cut my arms. I took plastic knifes out of the cafeteria and cut myself with them. I hated the therapists and didn't open up to them. I blamed everybody and anybody but myself for all of my problems. And I was embarrassed to be in a mental facility. Was I crazy? Maybe. But looking around me I realized that I was surrounded by completely normal kids.

Nicole, a dancer, was funny and smart; she had stopped eating and wasted away to seventy-two pounds at five foot six. Even Tina, a beautiful soccer player, cut, binged and had attempted suicide. On the surface, the kids at the hospital looked normal, yet there was nothing normal about Tina needing a straitjacket after having an anxiety attack and trying to kill herself. Kids who would normally be playing softball were sitting on couches, looking like zombies because their medication had just been changed.

When one of us was finally released to go home, everybody signed her discharge journal. These were like yearbooks, with inscriptions and signatures in it, promising things like, "Keep in touch" and "Never forget you." Almost like a real summer sleep-away camp, only this one was for the emotionally challenged.

Mental illness doesn't get knocked out like an infection after you take an antibiotic. It's a multistep process, so it's not easy to describe how I got better. Through weeks of intensive therapy, painful sessions in which I let down my guard and let myself cry, and group sessions in which I actually contributed, I began to recover. I was placed on medicines that helped ease my depression. I personally made an effort and slowly it began to show. With the combination of these things and support from family and friends, I learned to laugh again. I stopped hurting myself.

Now I am past my preteen years, and I'm a teenager. I have recovered from my depression. I'm alive. I am enjoying life, and I cannot believe that I was so depressed that I cut myself so viciously. I try to grasp onto whatever pieces of my childhood I lost in that month in the hospital and the months leading up to it.

Depression is a disease, not an excuse to treat others poorly. People have called me crazy, but I know that I wasn't crazy. I was sick and now I have recovered. I notice other people around me who cut themselves, who write the same dark poetry that I wrote. In science class one day, a girl was being picked on because somebody noticed cuts on her arms. I immediately came to her defense and even caused a disturbance in the class because I felt so strongly that this was not something to harass somebody about.

So today, at the ice cream shop, I get my ice cream and I look back—right at Cory. I realize that I may still have my scars, but I don't have my depression anymore. He can harass me all he wants, but his words can't drive me to drag a blade across my skin like they would have a year ago. I won. I'm a winner, and like Petra Salvaje said, I have the scars to prove it.

Butter pecan ice cream has never tasted sweeter.

Kellyrose Andrews, 15

[EDITORS' NOTE: *For more information about cutting, log on to* www.kidshealth.org/teen/ *(keyword search: "cutting").*]

7

THE
PRESSURE'S
ON

Weighing down upon me heavily,
I feel it surrounding me daily.
I try not to give in,
But it seems so hard to win.
If I can't be perfect, I think I'm a nobody.
And must follow them to be somebody.
Then when I feel like I've finally succeeded
To do, and have, everything needed,
Once again the pressure surrounds me
But this time it won't win and I will be free.

Lindsay Oberst, 14

So Which Will It Be? Us—or Her?

The only way not to break a friendship is not to drop it.

Julie Holz

Jodie was the most popular girl in seventh grade. She was petite and blond and wore black eyeliner and mascara. It seemed like Jodie had an endless clothing budget—she set the style for the rest of our junior high school with clothes that looked like they came straight from a magazine.

Jodie and her friends laughed easily with boys, openly flirted in and out of class, and passed notes back and forth detailing their current crush. All year I had hoped to be included in Jodie's group—the popular crowd. When Jodie invited me to her birthday party, she let me know I should feel honored.

"We'll see how you fit in," she told me. "You're nice, but do you fit?" I desperately hoped I could find a place in the group. After my mother dropped me off at Jodie's party, I discovered that her parents weren't even going to be home for the slumber party I had mistakenly assumed was for girls only. As the music blared, Jodie turned the lights down low, and couples began to dance close together and kiss.

I sat by myself on a couch. All I could think was, *We're only in seventh grade. Do we have to do all this now?*

When a game of Truth or Dare got out of hand, I panicked and called my mom to pick me up early. I wasn't ready to discuss things I'd only read about in books, yet Jodie and her friends already seemed to know about sex and drugs and alcohol. I was relieved to get home and spend the rest of the evening with my puppy. Yet part of me wanted to be like Jodie and her friends—cool and confident with boys, secure in their popular status, superior to the rest of the seventh-grade class.

I might have hung around more with Jodie and her group had she not given me an ultimatum. She asked me to dump someone who had been one of my best friends since fifth grade.

Marleigh and I had been friends from the day when she marched up to me on the playground and said, "You can call me M."

Marleigh and I lived in the same neighborhood, both loved to read and were good students. We were soon in and out of each other's houses on a daily basis. I didn't care that she wore glasses and had kinky-curly short hair instead of long, straight hair like the popular girls. Marleigh and I understood each other, and she was a loyal friend.

Jodie's ultimatum caught me off guard.

"Even though you left my party early, we voted to ask you to join our group," she said, tossing her perky head. "There's just one thing, though."

My stomach flip-flopped up when I saw several of Jodie's friends pass a knowing look between them. Jodie pointed to the edge of the playground where Marleigh stood.

"She's a problem," Tiffany, Jodie's number-two-in-command, said.

"We don't like her," Jodie said. "She's too weird. If you want to hang out with us, you need to dump her."

I stood surrounded by the most popular girls in seventh grade. I looked at their perfect clothes and confident smiles. I wanted to be like them.

"So which will it be? Us? Or her?" Jodie put her hands on her tiny waist and cocked her head to the side. "We need to know if we can count on you."

"What difference does it make who else I'm friends with?" I asked timidly.

"We look bad if you hang around with us *and* her. She's a geek," Jodie said.

I couldn't tell if Marleigh was watching us, but I did see that she was standing there all alone. I wanted to be part of Jodie's group so badly I could taste it. I looked at Marleigh—at Jodie—at Marleigh—at Jodie.

"Then I guess I'm a geek, too," I said finally, "because Marleigh's my friend."

Jodie gasped as I turned away from her and "the group." I felt their eyes on my back as I walked up to Marleigh, who seemed to have been expecting me. Her eyes shone from behind her thick glasses and her face became animated as she started telling me about a movie she'd seen on TV the night before. We stood and talked until the bell rang to tell us lunchtime was over.

In the hallway during passing period, I saw Jodie leaning against her locker, chatting with an eighth-grade boy. I was surprised when she smiled at me, just as I was surprised that the other girls in her group were friendlier to me than they had been before. I was nice to them in return, but the burning desire to be part of the "in group" was gone. A few years later, Jodie and her friends were also gone—they had dropped out of school or moved to other cities. Marleigh remained a good and faithful friend through high school, college and into adulthood. And me? I realized that popularity wasn't worth changing who I was or giving up a friend.

Anne Broyles

Danny's Courage

*Patterning your life around other's opinions is
nothing more than slavery.*

Lawana Blackwell

I was in seventh grade when Danny transferred to my
school and became my first real crush. He had the darkest
of brown eyes and light blond hair with a dark complex-
ion. I fell for Danny the first day he arrived, and many of
the girls in my class felt the same way. That, however,
soon changed.

Danny had been going to our school for about a week
when his parents picked him up in an old beat-up car that
spewed exhaust and made loud banging sounds. The girls
who had previously adored him looked disgusted. It was
obvious that Danny was poor and that was that. He was
no longer boyfriend material.

I had a poor family as well; I just hid it from everyone. I
was so ashamed of how we lived that I never had kids
come over to my house. Even though I couldn't do a thing
about it, I felt like the kids in my class would judge me if
they knew the truth. It was a lot of work keeping my

secret, but I figured it was easier than it would be to not have any friends.

One day, our teacher, Mr. Sims, announced that the seventh-grade field trip would be to an amusement park. The classroom buzzed with excitement as the girls discussed what they would wear and what they should bring with them. I sat back and listened, knowing that my parents did not have the money to send me. It made me angry to feel so left out. But not Danny. He simply told everyone that he wouldn't be going. When Mr. Sims asked him why, Danny stood up and stated, "It's too much money right now. My dad hurt his back and has been out of work for a while. I'm not asking my parents for money."

Sitting back down in his seat, Danny held his head up proudly, even though whispering had begun. I could only shrink in my seat, knowing those whispers could be about me when they found out I would not be going either.

"Dan, I'm very proud of you for understanding the situation that your parents are in. Not every student your age has that capability," he replied.

Glaring at the students whispering in the back, Mr. Sims spoke again, only louder.

"This year, we're going to do things differently. The trip is not until the end of the month, so we have plenty of time for fund-raising. Each student will be responsible for bringing in at least one idea for a fund-raising drive. Bring them in tomorrow. If a student does not want to contribute to the drive, then he or she will be spending the field trip day here at the school. Any questions?"

Of course, Shelly, the most popular girl in the class, spoke up.

"Well, Mr. Sims, my parents can afford it. Do I still have to help?"

"Shelly, this is not a matter of being able to afford it. Money is not just something that is handed to you when you get older. This will be a great learning experience for everyone, whether you have the money or not."

While walking home from school that day, I noticed three of the boys from our class talking with Danny. I worried that they were giving him a hard time, but as I got closer, I realized they weren't harassing him. They were all just debating about the best ideas for a fund-raiser.

Although not everyone accepted Danny after that day, he won over the respect of many of us. I was especially awed by how he didn't cave under peer pressure. For so long, I could never admit to my friends that I could not afford to go somewhere. Instead, in order to continue to fit in, I lied about why I couldn't do things and came up with excuse after excuse.

By standing up and admitting he was poor, Danny changed my life. His self-confidence made it easier for all of us to understand that what his parents had or didn't have did not determine who he was. After that, I no longer felt I had to lie about my family's situation. And the funny thing was, those who were truly my friends stuck by me when I finally let them get closer.

And Danny, more because of his courage and honesty than his great looks, is someone I will never forget.

Penny S. Harmon

You Are Never Too Young to Take a Stand

"There's nothing wrong with it!" he exclaims to me, his tone convincing. "C'mon, take it!" In the very back of my mind I hear a small, persistent voice. And I listen to it. I listen because I know better. I listen and I shove the cigarette back. "You are not in my cool group!" he shouts in my face. It is then that I realize that I'm a loner . . . and proud of it.

Jennifer Lynn Clay, 12

When I was eleven, I looked older than I was; in fact, I looked like I was about fifteen or sixteen. I felt older than most of my classmates, and I just never fit in. I had always been tall for my age too, and that really didn't help. Most of the kids I hung out with were at least two years ahead of me in school. One day I reached a turning point when I realized that it isn't your age that makes you mature, it is a personal thing.

One of my best friends, Linda, asked me to go to the high school football game with her. Of course I went, not only because I loved hanging out with her but because I also had the biggest crush on her older brother. When we got to the game, I didn't see too many people I knew from school, but Linda had a lot of friends there. I thought how it was so awesome to have as many friends as she did, and I wished I was more like her. She was fun, and she had a great personality.

The game was winding down, and our team was losing big time. A lot of people had already left the game because it was so obvious that we weren't going to win. A large group of girls came by and saw Linda and asked her to come over and talk to them. She told me she would be right back and went and sat with them.

After a few minutes passed, she turned and yelled for me to come down and sit with them too. I did, never thinking it to be a big deal. After a while, they all started smoking, and they offered Linda a cigarette. These were girls from her neighborhood, and I guess she wanted them to think of her as being tough, so she accepted.

She asked, "What about my friend?" and they said, "Sure, would you like a cigarette?" At that moment, I felt so shocked, so embarrassed and so young. *These girls are only thirteen,* I thought, with a shock. *Does two years make such a huge difference in our ages?* Only two years but they were far beyond me, or so I thought to myself.

I was humiliated. I knew my parents trusted me to make right choices, or else they would have never let me go to the game. Of course, they trusted Linda too—she was older and supposedly looking out for me.

It seemed like hours passed in that short minute, with all the thoughts going through my head. *Should I take a cigarette? Will they laugh at me and make fun of me if I don't? Will they want to beat me up because they'll think that I think I am too good to take what they have offered me?* Finally, with all those thoughts racing through my brain, I just said, "No . . .

thank you, but I don't smoke." Then I got up and went back to the seat where we were originally sitting and just sat there in the stands all by myself.

Linda finished her cigarette and came up to where I was sitting and sat down by me. After the game, we went on as if nothing had happened. That was fine with me—I just wanted to go home and cry. It may sound silly now, but that is how I felt.

Several months passed and things went on as usual. Then one Sunday at our church youth group, we had a special service, and a lot of people were giving testimonies—it was just such an inspirational service. After the service was over, Linda came over to where I was standing and cornered me. She told me that she needed to tell me something.

"I just wanted to tell you what an inspiration you were to me when you were offered a cigarette, and everyone around you was smoking—including me—and you said no . . . and you stood by what you knew was right for you. It meant a lot to me, and I will never forget it."

I was so stunned. I never realized that when I had taken my stand and said no, the decision I had made would influence someone else—even someone older than I was.

Later in life, I realized that saying no to something as simple as a cigarette made me stronger and more able to stand up and say no to other things as time went by. I was offered so much more as I got older while hanging out with my peers.

At eleven, I learned that when you think you are all alone, sitting by yourself, others are watching what you are doing. Your actions may help other people take a stand for what they believe in when they are not strong enough to do it alone.

Maudie Conrad

Trying to Handle It

*The weak are the most treacherous of us all.
They come to the strong and drain them.*

Bette Davis

"Becca ran away," my instant message screen said, "and my sharp knives are missing." It was my friend Becca's screen name, but the message said, "This is Becca's mom. Is she with you?"

Everything inside me lurched. "No," I typed. "When did she leave?" The computer clock showed 10 A.M.; early for a Saturday.

"Early this morning," the message said. "It's all my fault. We had a fight."

Becca and I had been best friends for about six months. She was the funniest person I knew. She was always smiling, and she made me smile, too. For instance, when she had to go to the bathroom, she danced around with her knees together and even if I was upset with her, I'd have to bust out laughing.

People who knew Becca warned me that she was bad news, but I thought they were being too hard on her. She was failing school, but her parents didn't seem to care and neither did she. She'd laugh at herself and joke, "I'm going to Clowntown University."

Pretty soon, it seemed like every time we got together, trouble followed. Becca was also wearing me out by wanting to be with me or talk to me every single minute. Every time I tried to get a little "me" space or spend time with someone else, Becca seemed to have another crisis. And I was there for her.

One day she came to school with a Band-Aid over one eye and bruises all over her arms. She said she'd pierced her own eyebrow, but when her mom saw it, she "flipped" and ripped it right out and beat Becca up. Sometimes, she talked about cutting herself or wanting to kill herself—especially when I'd get mad at her or want time to myself.

This situation, though, was the worst ever. I called for my mom, and she came running.

At first, Mom seemed as upset as I was, but when she looked at the messages, a new one popped up. "What should I do?"

"Why would she be asking you?" Mom wondered. It made me stop shaking and think for a moment.

"Oh my gosh! She's outside right now," the screen flashed. "Should I go out and talk to her?"

Even *I* knew it was crazy for a mom to be sitting talking on the computer while her runaway daughter was out on the driveway. Her daughter was supposedly running away and trying to kill herself, and she was asking a middle school kid what to do?

Then I noticed all the misspellings. Funny how much they looked like Becca's D-minus workmanship. "Come on, Becca," I typed. "I know it's you."

She quickly went off-line, which made me suspect even more that it was her all along. Man, had she used me. I felt like such a fool! I was mad, but as Mom and I talked, I

realized Becca really did have problems. She needed serious help—not just my holding her hand all the time. I
wasn't qualified to give her the kind of help she really
needed. And trying to be her everything put way too
much pressure on me.

We were already in the middle of another big "Becca
mess" at the time, which Becca had dragged me into. My
dad had just received a call from the manager at the local
7-Eleven. As soon as he hung up, he said, "You're not
allowed in the store anymore. She said she had proof from
the security camera of Becca and you taking things." But
that couldn't be true because I never stole anything!

I remembered those times at the mall, when store man-
agers had kicked us out. At the time, it had made me mad.
I thought they were just prejudiced against kids. But I
began thinking about how many new things Becca
always had, which she always said were on sale, and the
expensive Christmas gift she gave her mother, which she
had stuffed in her purse, because she said she "threw
away the bag." I realized that all those gifts Becca had
given me, which I'd thought were so nice of her, were
probably stolen, too.

I was so scared, I thought I was going to throw up. I
called Becca to see if she had heard from the manager. She
had taken the call and said that her mom wasn't home.
She warned me that if her mom found out, she'd beat her.
That turned out to be Becca's way of keeping us from
telling her anything.

My mom demanded that Becca and I go back to the
store and try to make things right. She tried to reach
Becca's mom on the phone for about a week, but she
never seemed to be home—nor did she return any calls,
probably because Becca screened all the messages first.

So Mom and I finally went over to her house. Becca met
us at the door, and she didn't look glad to see us. "Mom's

getting ready for work," she said. "She's in the shower."

We kept after her, though, and finally the moms had that talk. At first, Becca's mom didn't want to believe what we were telling her, but a week later, she ended up thanking us and said Becca was in counseling, and they were working through their problems. But she didn't make Becca go back to the 7-Eleven and apologize like my mom did. Facing the manager was one of the hardest things I've ever had to do, even though I knew I was innocent. The manager said she'd been trying and trying to reach Becca's mom but could never get through.

"I didn't take anything—really," I told her. "And if Becca did, I didn't know it."

"But you were with her," she said. "That makes you responsible, too. I believe you, though," she said. "If you need to come into the store for something, it's all right. But that other girl's never coming back in here."

After that, Becca and I never hung out again, but we still say hi. I don't want to think of how I would have felt if Becca really did kill herself. And I'm glad that my mom and I made her mom more aware of what was going on with Becca. I really cared for her, but for six months of our friendship Becca manipulated me and put way too much pressure on me as her only friend. I now know it was because she was so messed up, and I wasn't doing either of us any favor by trying to handle it all alone. Her issues were way beyond my ability to fix. She needed help long before she met me, and I was too young and unable to give it to her. I'm just glad to know she's still alive, maybe partly because of me.

Marcela Dario Fuentes, 17

The Party That Lasted a Lifetime

*I think that somehow, we learn who we really
are and then live with that decision.*

Eleanor Roosevelt

"It's just a party," Alicia said. "Come on, it'll be fun."

I was both panicked and excited by my cousin's words.
My parents had gone to Europe on vacation for two
weeks that summer, and I was thrilled at the opportunity
to stay with my Aunt Sarah and my favorite cousin, Alicia.
I absolutely idolized Alicia, who was everything I wanted
to be—seventeen years old, athletic, a popular cheerleader
and beautiful.

"Sure, I'm cool with that," I said. I was honored that she
wanted me to go with her, even though I knew my parents wouldn't approve of me going, since I had only just
turned fourteen.

"What do we tell your mom?" I asked, hoping I sounded
like I really didn't care.

"We'll just tell her we are going to the movies with some
of my friends." Alicia started talking about the party and
who was going to be there, as she stood in her closet and

began throwing out some of her clothes for me to try on.

"Okay, we need two outfits, one for Mom to see us leaving in—and the other to change into for the party. Pick out what you want to borrow, and I'll help you get ready. We can do your makeup in the car," Alicia said while we tried on a dozen different outfits. My emotions seesawed between not believing my good luck and being nervous. I wondered what a high school party would actually be like. I had been to boy/girl parties before, and I had even made out with Joey Razzone in the back of the skating rink, but that was all junior high stuff. This was a *high school* party. The thing I was most worried about was that everyone would think I was just a stupid little kid.

"Alicia, everyone's going to know I'm barely fourteen," I whined, while trying my favorite outfit on again. It was a lime green tank top (not very well filled out) and a blue jean miniskirt Alicia had decided against wearing, with a pair of white sandals.

"No, they won't . . . here . . . ," Alicia responded as she tossed me one of her strapless bras and a box of Kleenex.

"Oh my gosh, Alicia, I can't do that!" I said.

"Why not?" she answered as she shoved a few tissues in her own bra. Then she crammed our party clothes, makeup, hair spray and a brush into her bag. "All right, little cousin, it's time to go!"

I felt a small pang of panic. I was going to my first high school party, and Alicia wouldn't dare take me with her if she thought I would embarrass her—right?

We parked Alicia's Honda down the street from the house where the party was. Real butterflies had started in the pit of my stomach. *Don't you dare throw up,* I scolded myself. *Ugh,* I thought, *how did I get into this?*

"Let's go!" Alicia said excitedly, after we had changed our outfits and completed our makeup. I followed her out of the car. *Don't forget to smile,* I kept repeating to myself. I don't really know why I felt that was so important—maybe I didn't want anyone to notice how scared I was, but more likely it was because Alicia's smile seemed to be cemented on her face.

As we walked up the sidewalk toward the house, I noticed small groups of people on the front lawn. They were all laughing and talking, and most had a beer in their hand. I heard music coming from inside the house, and I looked over at Alicia, who didn't appear to be nervous at all.

"Cory! Hey, how's it going?" she yelled across the lawn to a group of guys in football jerseys.

"Hey, Alicia!" the boy shouted, as my cousin bounced across the yard.

"Leigh! Over here!" Alicia called. I walked over to where my cousin was standing with the group of older-looking boys—men almost. I couldn't believe this is what the boys at my school were going to grow into. Alicia introduced me to Cory and the others, and although they really didn't include me in their conversation, thankfully, they didn't laugh at me either. *Maybe this won't be so bad,* I thought.

After a while in the front yard, we made our way into the house. It was packed with people. The sound system was on full volume. There were groups of teenagers everywhere—most drinking, some kissing and quite a few doing both. I was amazed. This was not like any boy/girl party I had been to before.

Everywhere I went, I was offered a beer that I didn't want, and when I refused it, whoever I was talking to would just shrug, turn around and walk off. No matter how hard I tried to fit in, I kept finding myself alone, and after a few hours, I was very ready to go home. Finally, I walked up to Alicia, who was talking to a boy, and said quietly, "Alicia, I'm ready to go." I didn't really want to be a pain in the you-know-what, but I was tired and not enjoying myself at all.

"Who's this?" Cory asked, nodding his head in my general direction.

"It's my cousin, Leigh. You met her earlier," Alicia answered, never taking her eyes off Cory.

"Well, make her go away," he snapped, as he started kissing Alicia right in front of me.

Devastated, I didn't even wait for Alicia's response. I just turned and quickly walked away. I felt tears welling up in my eyes and didn't want anyone at the party to see me cry—especially Alicia. I felt so alone and stupid. I was embarrassed about coming to the party in the first place, much less letting those idiots get to me. I walked as fast as I could to the bathroom, then closed and locked the door.

The first thing I did was look in the mirror. I was so disgusted with myself for the way I looked. As my tears fell, the mascara Alicia had caked on my eyelashes was now thick, black streaks on my face. My hair was a huge blob of hairspray, and—thanks to the tissues—my breasts were two times larger than they should have been. I didn't look like a seventeen-year-old—I just looked like a clown. I stood there, staring at my awful reflection and cried for what seemed a really long time. Then I started scrubbing. I washed all the makeup off my face and found a brush in the medicine cabinet to brush out my hair. I took the wads of tissues out of my bra, threw them in the toilet and triumphantly flushed. I regretted the tank top and miniskirt now too, and I wanted to go get my other clothes in the car, but I didn't want to have to interrupt Alicia again to ask for the keys.

When I finally felt presentable—and more like me—I left the bathroom. My face was a little puffy from the tears, but that was okay. I knew I couldn't look any worse than I had looked all night long. I found a comfy spot on the couch and sat down to wait. Alicia had disappeared somewhere with Cory, and I didn't know where she was. I sat there for a long time, hoping I was really as invisible as I felt.

"Hey, are you okay?" came out of nowhere. I looked up, and there was a boy standing in front of me. His blue eyes seemed to plead with me to ask him to sit down.

"Yeah, fine, . . . you?" I managed nervously. I was shocked that someone was actually talking to me, and truthfully I was slightly disappointed that my invisibility had worn off.

"Can I please sit down?" he asked, while fidgeting with his hands in his pockets. *He looks harmless,* I thought.

"Sure." This was really not going well. Conversation seemed so easy for Alicia, why couldn't I squeak out more than one word at a time?

"So, what's your name and how do you know Brian?" The boy was staring straight into my eyes now. *Does he know I've been crying? Is this some sort of pity chat?*

"Who's Brian?" I asked, trying to sound as cool as I could.

"The guy who lives in this house, dummy!" he began to chuckle. "What's your name, anyway?"

"I'm here with my cousin, Alicia, who has left me alone for the millionth time tonight. I don't know anyone here, and for your information, I'm not a dummy," I said defiantly, now somewhat angry at him for laughing at me.

"I didn't mean that! I'm sorry if I hurt your feelings. I was just trying to lighten you up, girl. My name is Anthony; it's nice to meet you," he said, and as he sat down, he flashed a brilliant smile and stuck his hand out toward mine. *Wow, he's kind of cute,* I thought.

I reluctantly put my hand into his. When I could, I finally spoke, "My name is Leigh . . . nice to meet you, too." My face was blazing red now, and my heart was pounding so loud I was afraid he could hear it.

"Leigh, that's a really pretty name," he said as he gently squeezed my hand before letting it go.

Anthony and I sat and talked on the couch for a while. I was starting to feel a little more comfortable. I was happy to be talking to Anthony. He was fifteen, a freshman at my cousin's school and played drums in the high school band. His older brother was Brian, so this was his house, too. He hardly knew anyone either—these were all Brian's friends—and he was pretty upset that his brother was having this party while their parents were out of town.

"I'm going to the kitchen. Want a beer?" Anthony asked.

"No, thanks, I don't drink," I mumbled, praying this wouldn't be the wrong answer.

"That's cool . . . me neither! How about a Coke?" he asked, as he got up from the couch. Miraculously, he was back in just a few minutes with two cans of soda pop. I had truly expected him to take advantage of this perfect escape.

"Where's your cousin, anyway?" he asked as he took a big gulp of his soda. I just stared at him—he really was cute.

I suddenly realized I didn't care at all where Alicia was. I was finally having a good time in my own element and, most important, acting my own age—not hers. I had spent so much time trying hard to walk in her footsteps (and fill her bra) that it had been hard for me to even think about walking in my own. In that one night, my wise and gentle friend Anthony taught me a lesson that some people need a lifetime to learn: Just being yourself is the best you can ever hope to be.

Leigh Hughes

Suffocating

I am suffocating
And I just need to breathe
I'm smothered under pressure
I must be relieved.

Nothing I do is right,
Nothing they say is fair
I cry and scream and throw a fit,
But no one seems to care.

Nobody will listen,
To what I have to say.
My life is not important,
Yet I'm living every day.

I can't do what I want
I cannot stay out late
Here I sit and write this poem
To release my pain and hate.

I'm confused and I'm alone
I'm lost inside my mind.
No one will search beyond my looks
To see what they might find.

So many thoughts confuse me,
Feelings I can't perceive,
In this time of adolescence
And I just need to leave.

None of it makes sense
None of this seems real.
And noone understands
The emotions that I feel.

I'm still suffocating
And I still need to breathe.
I'm smothered under feelings
Let me be relieved.

Marion Distante, 13

To Have a Boyfriend—or Not?

The best protection any woman can have . . . is courage.

Elizabeth Cady Stanton

All of a sudden it seemed like all my friends were starting to have boyfriends. Last year in eighth grade, when we talked on the phone, we had talked about all kinds of stuff; like horses, our 'rents, homework and boys, but it wasn't *all* about boys. Now every conversation was all, "My boyfriend this, my boyfriend that," and I had nothing to contribute. The last straw was when one of my best friends told me about her upcoming birthday party.

"Since my birthday is so close to Valentine's Day, my mom said I can have a couples-only party, Patty. Isn't that cool?"

Huh? Cool? Definitely NOT, I thought. *I am the only one without a member of the opposite sex in my life, and I sure won't have one by next weekend.* "Yeah, that's cool, Heather," I managed to stammer out, and I hung up the phone. *Great. Just great.*

The very next day that all changed when I ran into

Tyrone Raymond—literally. I was late to one of my classes (as usual), and as I was barreling around the corner of the building, I ran right into Ty, scattering my books and homework everywhere. He bent down to help me pick up my papers, and as he stacked up what he could reach, he looked up at me and grinned. *Not bad,* I realized with a shock. *Not too bad at all. In fact, kinda cute.*

Ty Raymond was in our class, but he was a year younger than the rest of us because he had skipped a year of school somewhere along the way to ninth grade. We all figured he must be really smart to have done that. I had heard that his parents had gotten a divorce over the summer and that it had been really hard on Ty and his three little brothers. Other than that, I didn't know much about him; except that now, looking at him, I realized that he was much better looking than I had remembered. His deep brown eyes were dark and sparkling under long eyelashes as he gazed up at me, and his black hair wasn't just a careless buzz cut anymore—it had actually grown into kind of a neat style.

"Patty . . ."

I snapped back into reality as I realized he was trying to hand me my papers.

"Huh?"

"I've got to get to class. Here's your stuff. . . ."

"Oh . . . thanks. Ummm . . . hey, Ty, would you like to go to a party with me on Friday?" *Ohmigod. I can't believe I just said that.*

"Ahhhh . . . sure," he answered.

What?????? I was astounded.

He continued, "Give me your number, and I'll call you after school. Sounds like fun." I scribbled my phone number on one of the pieces of paper and gave it to him. Then he turned and walked away, leaving me with my jaw hanging open. That was the beginning.

Ty did call me that night. And every night after that. And he called me in the morning before school every morning to tell me where we would meet so that we could walk to school together. As we walked together, Ty would do one of three things to show the rest of the world that I was HIS—he would have his arm around my back with his hand in the back pocket of my jeans, or wrap his arm around my waist, or grab the back of my neck with his hand as we tried to maneuver though the busy school halls like some cojoined weird set of Siamese twins.

That first couple of days, I was in heaven. Ty obviously liked me a lot. No boy had ever shown me this kind of attention before, and I felt proud of his possessive attitude and that he was always by my side.

On Friday night, my dad drove me over to Ty's house to pick him up for the party. His mom seemed like a nice person but kind of frazzled. It looked like she depended on Ty to help her take care of his three wild little brothers, and she asked us more than once what time the party would be over and when he would be coming back home. Before we left, she asked if I could come over for a family dinner on Sunday, and when I looked to my dad for the answer, he nodded yes, so I accepted. More than ever, I was convinced that this was my first real relationship.

When we got to Heather's house, I was excited. Her family room was dimly lit, and love songs were coming from the sound system. It was the first time I had gone to a party with a guy, and it felt *so* romantic . . . at first.

After about two hours of slow dancing with our faces stuck together from nervous sweat and Ty's hands roaming around my back as he held me tightly against him, I was ready to go home. I realized, too late, that I hated kissing Ty. He mashed his mouth so hard against mine that it HURT. I turned my face away so that he couldn't kiss me anymore and managed to mumble something about my braces hurting my lips, so he stopped for a while—but then he started right up again. When I went to the bathroom, he followed me and waited outside of the door until I was done. If I wanted food or something to drink, we visited the table together. I started to feel dizzy and sick from the sweating, the groping, the music, the lack of air in the room and Ty trying to kiss me. I felt trapped and suffocated.

Finally, FINALLY . . . my dad came to get us. As we dropped Ty off at his house, Ty turned to me, smiled and said, "I'll see you on Sunday, Patty."

"Uhhh . . . okay . . . see ya." When he closed the door of the car and went into his house, I heaved a sigh of relief. I couldn't wait to get home and hide beneath the covers of my bed. My bed in my room. Away from him.

All day Saturday, I thought about Ty and how I was feeling. Every time the phone rang, I let my mom or dad answer it. When he did call, I was conveniently too busy to answer. *If this is how a relationship is supposed to be*, I thought, *I don't want any part of it.* I felt like I couldn't breathe. I didn't know how to tell him that I just couldn't do this anymore, so I did the logical thing—I chickened out. On Sunday, I pleaded with my mom to call Ty's mom to let her know I wasn't feeling well enough to go to dinner at their house. It actually was the truth—just the thought of seeing Ty right then made my stomach turn.

As I expected, Ty called me the first thing on Monday morning.

"What happened to you yesterday, Patty? My mom was looking forward to having you for dinner, and she missed seeing you. And what about all day Saturday? I called and called but I never got you."

My mind was spinning like an animal in a cage. *What am I going to say to get out of this?*

"Never mind," Ty said. "You can tell me all about it on the way to school. I'll meet you at the usual corner."

"Uh, Ty, I'm not going to walk to school with you," I blurted.

"WHAT!!?" He shouted.

"I don't want to date you anymore. I want to break up," I ventured timidly.

"What are you talking about? Is there someone else? That's it—you have been seeing someone else behind my back. Who is it? I'm going to beat the snot out of him! I'm going to. . . ."

"Ty!" I interrupted. "I'm not seeing anyone at all. It isn't that! I think I'm just not ready for a boyfriend. I don't want to date anyone yet." I was barely able to breathe from the pressure of trying to understand my own feelings and to explain myself. "I don't want to *belong* to someone. I . . . I just don't want to . . . ."

"All right, you baby. Whatever!" And he slammed the phone down.

I barely made it to school at all that day. My mom had to give me a tardy excuse because it took me so long to stop crying and to do something about my red swollen eyes. But the reality is I *did* make it to school. And I made it the next day and the next—and I walked down the halls alone or with my girlfriends. I didn't need Ty to be glued to my side to be okay. He moved shortly after that, and luckily I didn't have to worry about running into him in the halls anymore.

It took me a while to realize that Ty's possessive behavior wasn't normal and that wasn't how a healthy relationship should be. You should never feel pressured into doing something you are not ready to do, like you are trapped or owned, or be made to feel guilty if you want to hang out with your friends or like you can't do anything on your own without making your boyfriend mad at you. It's just way better to be a boyfriend have-not!

Patty Hansen

NO RODEO®

NO RODEO. ©Robert Berardi. Used by permission.

Easy as 1, 2, . . . 3

People tell you what to do, what to wear, who to like, how to behave. People put demands on you when all you really want to do is be loved and accepted for who you are.

Malinda Fillingim

We had gone to a movie, and he was walking me to the door. Just as I was about to go inside, something stopped me and I turned around. He was smiling a little, and the stars in the background twinkled as if to say, "Go for it!" We both leaned in carefully and our lips met. My stomach was doing cartwheels of joy—it was the perfect first kiss.

Wait a minute! That wasn't my first kiss—the last time I've seen anything that flawless was in the movies.

No, my first kiss was not touched by the twinkle of the stars or perfect movie timing, though I had dreamed about it long enough to hope that it would be. In my dreams, my lips met a boy's in perfect sync, our eyes closed and our hearts pulsed together at hyperspeed. Plenty of other girls my age had already started kissing, and they all made it sound so easy. Even though I had imagined all the details of that moment in my mind, I hadn't considered the possibility that I wasn't really ready for the real deal. Instead of imagining it as a personal thing that I would have to grow into, I treasured kissing as a step toward growing up, one that all girls must do at the same age.

I didn't realize how wrong I was until I finally had my first kiss.

My first boyfriend and I were watching a movie. It seemed like the classic setup for a kiss—watching a movie alone with a boy I thought I really liked. So why was I so shocked when he suddenly moved toward me, apparently hoping for more than just a hug? Why did I feel so uncomfortable and unprepared? When my lips met his, it felt like they were fumbling around in the dark, clueless and confused—and I didn't like it.

In my cloud of confusion, I tried to make sense of my feelings. My friends all knew how to kiss and *they* liked it—at least they made it sound that way. After feeling so unsure about my first kiss, I became scared of trying it again.

Hoping to buy some time over the kissing confusion, I talked to my boyfriend about it. "Maybe we could just take it a little slower," I suggested. I told him I just didn't feel ready to kiss, but it wasn't because I didn't like him. I simply wasn't comfortable with all that lip-locking. He didn't get it—he said he didn't really understand why kissing, of all things, was an issue.

I was shocked. So he was just like the rest, who believed that kissing was something that everyone our age did with no problem. He couldn't believe that I would somehow be uncomfortable with it. I had thought that he was a boy I could trust and be respected by, and I didn't want to change myself or force myself to kiss him just so I could have a boyfriend.

Obviously he didn't want a girl who was honest with

him like I was, and so we broke up—which hurt a lot at the time. It made no sense that a boy could like me one minute and then ditch me the next, just because I wasn't ready for kissing. I trusted my feelings though, and I believed that when the time was right, the kissing would be, too.

A few years later, the time was finally right. I had been seeing a new guy who had a different attitude and personality from my first boyfriend. I started to think that maybe not only was the time right for the kiss, but the boy was right, too. After hearing about my kissing phobia, he had not run in the other direction laughing. One night under the stars, while saying good night to him, I noticed that my stomach was no longer telling me *No!* As I gazed into his eyes, wondering if after we kissed I would feel comfortable about it, he sweetly offered to meet me halfway.

"Emily," he said, holding my hand, "how about this? I'll count to three. I'll just count to three, and we'll kiss."

I smiled and felt relief push me closer toward him. "Okay," I replied.

And then, in the most understanding voice, he counted: "One, two, . . . three." We leaned forward, eyes closed, and we kissed. Instead of looking at him in shock afterward, I wrapped my arms around him. It was the only way I knew to thank him for such a wonderful moment. To know that someone could care about me and respect me enough to go at my pace made me happier than if I had been kissing boy after boy for many years.

The wait for the right kiss had seemed so long, but now I can trust that it was worth it. The kiss we counted out that night was better than the movies and the kisses my friends had been having, because at the heart of it was deep caring and respect.

Finally, when everything seemed right, kissing was as easy as one, two, . . . three.

Emily A. Malloy

Intimidation

Whatever you fear most has no power—it is your fear that has the power.

Oprah Winfrey

I was terrified to answer the phone. I loved being out of the house where I would never have to hear it ring, where I did not have to pray that someone was going to shout "Carrie Joy, telephone!" I was thirteen years old and I thought my life was over. In short, I was being bullied.

The first phone call came on a Sunday in November. I remember answering the phone and being surprised to hear giggling. "Shhhhh!" said one of them, then, "Carrie?"

"Yeah?"

"This is Natasha. How are you?" More giggles.

"I'm fine," I mumbled as I tried to figure out what was going on. Natasha had never called me before. She was extremely popular and we barely talked at school.

"Did you kiss Alex?" she asked sweetly.

"What?" I asked, trying to stall for time. I could feel my heart starting to pound. Alex was Natasha's ex-boyfriend.

"Did you kiss my boyfriend?"

What? Her BOYFRIEND? "No . . . I mean yes, but I didn't know that he was still your boyfriend. I thought you guys were broken up. . . . I'm sorry, I didn't know that you still liked him . . . ," I trailed off.

"We were *sort of* broken up, but you really should know better, Carrie. Don't you think she should have known better?" she said to someone in the background.

"Of course she should have."

"Maybe she's just too stupid."

"She *is* stupid, and you know what else you are, Carrie? You are *so* ugly. I don't even know why Alex would want to kiss you. Don't you think she is ugly, girls?" They laughed as I silently started to cry.

"Carrie, you really look like a dog with your poodle hair," Natasha continued on. "So why don't you bark for us?"

BARK *for them? Was she kidding?* I stayed quiet.

"C'mon, Carrie! *Bark* you stupid poodle!"

"I am not going to bark for you, Natasha." My voice quavered as I said it. Too humiliated to think clearly, I hung up the phone. It rang again, and I listened as the answering machine picked it up. It was Natasha, and this time there was no giggling or fake sweetness.

"You are going to be *so* sorry, Carrie. I am going to make your life hell. Get ready to eat dog food tomorrow." *Click.* I burst into tears.

Monday came and went—with no dog food. I saw Natasha briefly in class, but there was nothing she could say in front of the teacher. I ate my lunch in my classroom. When I got home from school, there was a message waiting for me. Amid laughter, I could hear Natasha and her friends reading a list titled, "Ten Reasons Why Carrie Is an Ugly Dog."

On Tuesday, Natasha marched into my third-period class with her friend, Diana, and told the teacher I was wanted in the counseling office. As the teacher excused me, I started to shake. We walked in silence and arrived at the counseling office to find it empty. "I need to talk with you in private," Natasha said with a smirk. I stared at her.

Our "counseling session" was Natasha telling me that I was ugly and stupid and had no respect for people and their boyfriends. She told me that I had really hurt her and that she was not trying to hurt me, but this is what I deserved. She swore that if I told anyone about our situation she was going to beat me up. It was pure intimidation.

While we were in the room, Diana, her friend, found a picture of a horse in an old stack of magazines. Natasha held it up next to my face and said I looked just like it. "Don't you think that you look like a horse?"

"I guess," I mumbled back.

"And why are you so pale? Are you an albino or something?" I shrugged. I did not think she wanted to hear that it was because of my German and Irish blood. "You should wear more makeup." She pulled a compact out of her backpack and started to smear concealer on my face. I wanted to tell her to stop, but I was frozen. This girl had taken over my life.

The next few months went on like this. Natasha and her friends screamed obscenities at me in the hallways and called my house to threaten me every night. The bathroom stalls were covered with obscene words claiming that I was easy with the boys. I got used to people whispering about me. I cried in almost every class. The best part of my day was when I first woke up in the morning and, for a few seconds, forgot that anything was wrong. Then my stomach would twist into a knot, and the constant feeling of dread would wash over me again.

I started to feel like there was no way out, that there was no one who could fix this problem and make my life go back to normal.

In early February, I was eating lunch with a few friends

in my fifth-period classroom, where I had hung out during lunch period ever since the first phone call. One of my friends came in to tell me that Natasha was looking for me. There was a closet in the room that could be locked from the outside and I told them to lock me in the closet.

Knowing that I was trapped but safe, I listened as Natasha came to the door of the classroom. The girls told her they had not seen me, and Natasha left angrily. When they unlocked the door, I was shaking and crying. I could barely form a sentence as my friends marched me to the counseling office and I told Ms. Mulligan the whole story.

It was difficult to remember all the hurtful things Natasha had said, but Ms. Mulligan needed facts and so out they all came. As I watched her fill up pages and pages with the horrible events of the past three months, I started to feel a sense of relief. *This was all going to end.*

I cannot say that Natasha was a changed person after that. She never apologized. In fact, she ignored me completely as if she had forgotten that I existed. I, on the other hand, remember her well. I will remember her for the rest of my life. She changed me forever. As I stood in the dark closet that day, I realized that I had lost all respect for myself. I had allowed someone to take away my happiness, and I had given up control over my own life. Never again will I let that happen.

No one can tell me what to think or how to act. I know now that I do not have to listen to hurtful words. I am always free to hang up the phone. And more important, I am now always happy to answer it.

Carrie Joy Carson

[EDITORS' NOTE: *For information about dealing with bullying, log on to* www.kidshealth.org/teen/ *(keyword search: "bullying").*]

8

CRUSHIN' HARD

As you enter the classroom
Laughing and joking with your friends,
I see you break away from the group.
You are headed my way!

You stop to talk to me.
It only lasts a few moments,
But I feel as if I rule the world
And I have accomplished a lifelong dream.

Jennifer Lynn Clay, 12

My Story

A kiss can be a comma, a question mark or an exclamation point. That's the basic spelling that every woman ought to know.

Mistinguette

It was weird how it happened. Actually, it was weird that it happened at all.

I was down in my friend Kyle's basement with him. We were jamming on our guitars. Totally normal. Just hanging and playing. I was working on a song, concentrating really hard, trying to get the solo down. And that's when it happened.

Kyle kissed me. I was shocked. Stupefied. Anyway, I didn't handle it well. I mean, I sort of screamed. Well, not screamed, exactly—it was more like a yelp. He had taken me by surprise. I had been concentrating on the song, not preparing for a kiss. *The* kiss. My first kiss. And it came out of nowhere. Kyle and I were friends. Buds. Totally tight, but not in a boy-girl kind of way.

"Uhh . . . sorry," Kyle stammered after my yelp.

"Sure. No. I mean, that's okay," I mumbled incoherently,

grabbing my stuff. "I should probably go." Kyle didn't even slightly try to stop me. He just backed out of my way as I zoomed out of the door.

I cried that night. Really hard. I kept thinking about Kyle's kiss. *Why did I yelp? Why did I do that? Lame, lame, LAME!!!* It wasn't as if I hadn't imagined him kissing me a thousand times. I had. I just never thought he would. We'd been friends since the fourth grade. It had pretty much seemed as though he didn't even realize I was a girl. I was happy just to be his friend. But then he kissed me. And it was so weird, because I knew the kind of girl Kyle liked. He'd been crushing on Courtney Davis all last year. She was blond. Popular. A Barbie. And I wasn't. Anyway, I was sure I had blown it with Kyle. Now I was sure he thought I was the world's biggest dork.

I didn't talk to Kyle for the rest of the summer. My aunt in California had just had twins, and I went to help her. I was sort of like their nanny for the summer. It was a good job, and my aunt paid me big bucks—and she had a pool. But I kept thinking about Kyle, his kiss and wondering if we were still friends. Over the entire summer, confused thoughts ran through my head. *Why had he kissed me? Why was I such a moron?*

On our first day back to school, I was nervous. My palms were sweaty, and I felt sort of excited and nauseous. Kyle didn't show up to walk to school with Megan and me like he usually did. Things were not looking good.

"I can't believe Kyle ditched us," Megan said for the hundredth time as we walked Kyle-less to school. "What's up with him?"

The thing is, I never told her about Kyle's kiss. I don't know why exactly, I usually tell her everything. But I didn't tell her this. And now, walking to school, I still couldn't bring myself to say anything. I mean, what could I say? "I'm a dork"? I was literally unable to choke the words out. It hurt too much. The thought was just too brutal. Instead I tried to concentrate on the new school year. New classes. New friends. New opportunities. I tried to think, *You never know, things can turn out great.*

When we got to school, we found Kyle at his locker, talking with Courtney. Seeing them together was like a punch in the stomach. Extreme pain. Before I could stop her, Megan marched over to Kyle.

"We waited for you this morning. What happened?"

"He walked with me," Courtney informed us with a smile, looking smug.

The bell rang, and I headed for homeroom feeling like the world's biggest jerk. I'd thought about Kyle all summer long. Thought about his kiss. But obviously, Kyle didn't waste his time thinking about me, because over the summer he got what he wanted. COURTNEY. Trauma, trauma, trauma.

I crept into fourth period just as the tardy bell rang. It was the class I'd been dreading all day because it was band, and I knew I'd have to face Kyle. I avoided his gaze as I slipped into the seat. Actually, I avoided his gaze all during class. But I was unable to avoid him once class was over. He was beside me before I had a chance to dart away.

"Look, let's talk a minute, okay?"

"No. Not now. I'm late." I tried to rush off, before I cried or something. But he grabbed my arm, making me stay.

"Just for a minute," he said calmly. I glared up at him, trying to keep my tears back. "I'm sorry I didn't show this morning. Courtney came by, and . . . I don't know, I've been afraid things might be weird between us—between you and me."

I looked away from him, muttering, "You should have called."

"Yeah. I know. I'm sorry."

"Whatever." I wiggled free of his hold and headed for the door. "See ya."

At lunch, I told Megan what Kyle had said. She was more understanding than I had been.

"Well, Courtney went to his house—not the other way around," she reasoned. "I guess that's not his fault. Besides, he's had a crush on her forever. Give him a break."

"Well, he should have called," I sulked, still feeling a knife in my back.

"Face it," Megan said, "guys are spazzes when they like a girl."

Moments later, Kyle walked by with Courtney and a group of her friends. I slunk down in my seat, my heart sinking at the sight of them. I hated this new school year. I wished everything could go back to the way things were last year, when Kyle just drooled over Courtney from a distance. Those were the good old days. Feeling gloomy, I was surprised to see Kyle leave Courtney and her followers to come sit across from Megan and me.

"Are you still mad?" he asked.

I looked down at the table, not wanting to answer. How could I possibly answer?

"I'm not mad at you, Kyle," Megan piped in. "I'm not. I totally understand. So, don't think I'm storming away." We watched Megan skip off in silence. Then Kyle turned to me.

"I'm sorry I didn't show up today. Seriously. I was afraid to face you. But I thought about you all summer."

"Right," I scoffed. "While you were getting together with Courtney." He shook his head in disbelief.

"We're not together. Seriously. All summer long, all I could think about was you. About all the fun we used to have—at least until I kissed you. I really blew it, huh?" I dropped my jaw.

"*You* didn't blow it."

"But the way you acted. . . ."

"I didn't know how to act. I was surprised."

He grinned. "You screamed!"

My face reddened. "I *didn't* scream! I yelped!"

Then I looked at Kyle's grinning face, and I knew it was all okay.

And so that's my story. My first kiss—my first day back to school. MY FIRST BOYFRIEND!!! Good story, huh?

Melanie Marks

A "Bite" of All Right!

Life's under no obligation to give us what we expect.

Margaret Mitchell

At eleven years old, I had already had boyfriends. I had even held hands with a couple of them and kissed one on the lips. It all seemed very exciting. Then . . . I met Ben.

No one else saw Ben the way I did. To others, he was arrogant and mischievous—even if that was true, he made my tummy wobble every time I saw him.

He was in my class, which meant I got to sit and gaze at him during lessons, although this got me into trouble on a couple of occasions for not concentrating; I was concentrating, but on Ben—not the lesson.

All my friends thought I was crazy, but I didn't care. I wanted Ben to be my boyfriend. So, I got my friends to find out if he liked me, and in turn, his friends were doing the same—to see if I liked him. There were messages going in all directions. It was like torture, not knowing for sure if he liked me or not, and I was too shy to just ask him.

As I walked down the hallway one morning before class, Ben suddenly stopped dead right in front of me. My heart was racing; I didn't know whether to smile, speak or giggle. "Will you go out with me?" he said with no warning. I wasn't sure if he was just joking, but he looked serious.

"Yes," I mumbled, embarrassed.

"Good," he replied, and that was that. We were the newest couple in school.

We had a "normal" relationship for a couple of weeks. Every few days I would dump him, or he would dump me, then our friends would pass messages, and we would get back together again.

Then one day he said we should kiss. *But we have kissed,* I thought. *On the lips!* But he meant a "real" kiss, a "mouth-open kiss" he told me. Not wanting to seem immature, I agreed—but I was terrified. I didn't really know what he meant.

We met that evening, and with a group of friends, we went up the road from our house. There was a house there that was empty, and Ben had said we could go round to the back of the house. The others waited at the front of the house.

When we got to the back of the house, my heart was pounding. I just didn't want to mess it up. I would have to follow his lead. "Don't worry," he said quietly, "just close your eyes and open your mouth a little." How difficult could that be? I could feel his breath on my face as we got closer, and then his open mouth gently touched against my lips. Then without a warning, he slipped his tongue into my mouth—it was slimy and disgusting, and without a second thought, I clamped my mouth shut!

"Ouch!" he yelled. "You bit me!"

The other kids laughed a lot, and for a few days it was the gossip around the school. Even the teachers looked like they were grinning at me. But they soon forgot about it and moved on to laugh at someone else who had done something embarrassing.

For me, however, I will never forget my first "real" kiss.

Paula Goldsmith

Never Should Have

Never regret. If it's good, it's wonderful. If it's bad, it's experience.

Victoria Holt

On June 13th, my friend C. J. had an end-of-the-school-year party. Naturally, I went with my friends Kalah and Ashley. We were having the time of our lives! Then I noticed *him* as he was walking through the door. I knew who he was—his name was Greg and he had been in my health class. I had sat by him a few times, and we had talked a little, but I never thought he would be the guy I would end up crushing on.

I told Ashley and Kalah, "Let's go sit on the trampoline with Greg." They were wondering why, but they sat with him anyways. There were tons of girls on the trampoline, and Greg was basically in the middle. I was next to him on his left. I knew in that instant that I liked him. We both laughed. We didn't talk much more except that he said that I was the only hot girl on the trampoline. I smiled and blushed. We all went back inside C. J.'s house and waited while everyone's parents came to pick them up. Greg,

Kalah, Ashley and I were the last to leave, so we got to hang out for awhile longer.

Ashley had asked Kalah and me if we wanted to stay overnight with her, and the three of us sat up all night talking about how much fun the party was! Then I finally 'fessed up to them about liking Greg. Kalah ran into the kitchen to get the phone book. We looked and looked for his number and finally found it! I was overjoyed, and we agreed to call him the next day. Kalah's mom picked her up in the morning, but I got to stay at Ashley's longer.

Ashley and I went to this little concert at the park. We walked down the sidewalk for a bit until we found a bench by the docks. It was time. I get nervous asking guys out, so Ashley called Greg for me.

"Do you like Kristen?" she demanded. He replied, "Yes . . . yes, I do. She is really nice." He fidgeted and said, "Uhh . . . does she . . . umm . . . like me, too?" Ashley told him to hold on, and she asked me.

I said, "DUH! I told you last night!" Greg was happy to hear that I liked him, and Ashley asked him out for me. He said yes!! I felt like the happiest girl on earth. We talked for about thirty minutes on my cell phone and found out loads of things about each other. We were really a good couple.

A few days later, I asked my mom if I could go see a movie with Greg, and she said it was fine. I called Greg and asked him. He said he really wanted to see me but he couldn't go. I said it was okay, and I would just talk to him later on the computer. It ended up being like that a lot. It was like he couldn't see me that much because he was either grounded, riding his dirt bike or going to church. I wanted to see him so bad, and I would be going away to camp for a week.

Right before I went away to camp, I got onto the computer and told Greg that I would miss him and asked him to write to me. He sent me one letter, and I wrote him back a letter. I told him bye when I had to leave, and he said bye, too, and promised to write to me. I cried when I left home, although I told my mom it was just because I would miss her and my sister and my dogs.

After I had been at camp for a couple of days, I wrote Greg a letter. I told him about the hiking, dances, lunch/dinner/breakfast food, I told him everything—even about the dance. At my camp, when someone asks you to dance, you HAVE to do it. At the first dance we had, this boy named Trevor asked me to dance a lot! I didn't mind too much because he was a nice guy. From then on, I noticed that every activity I did, he did as well. I asked him about it, and he confessed that he liked me. I told him I already had a boyfriend, but he said he didn't care about my boyfriend. For a while, it annoyed me and bugged me that he was always around, but then at the last dance, I danced with him again. When the song came on, he SANG IT to me! I was so touched. That's when I realized that I kind of liked him. I told him that I was tired, and he offered to carry me to my cabin. I laughed and said, "It's okay, you don't need to."

The next day it was time to go home. I realized that I was going to miss being at camp. I really did, and I still do. When I got home, I explained all the fun I had had at camp to my mom, my sitter and her boyfriend. They were glad I was back, and so was I in a way. I was looking forward to being able to see Greg and talk to him and stuff like that. But somehow I was missing Trevor. I was so confused. I finally came to the worst decision of my life—I was going to break up with Greg.

When I took my overnight bag into my bedroom, I looked on my bed and there was an envelope. I recognized the address—it was from Greg. I jumped on my bed and ripped it open. It said: "Dear Kristen, I have missed you so much and I am glad to hear you've been having fun. That whole dance thing—it doesn't bug me because I know you are true to me. I have been really bored because I haven't been talking to you! I cannot wait to see your screen name on my buddy list again or your phone number on my caller ID. I miss you a lot. Hurry home. Love, Greg."

I just couldn't believe it! I started crying, but I decided that I still wanted to go through with breaking up with him. I went to my computer and signed on. I wasn't surprised to see that he was online. He instant messaged me and said, "WELCOME BACK! I MISSED YOU A LOT!" I said, "Thanks, I missed you, too." Then he told me that he wanted to tell me something very important that he had wanted to say for a while. I thought he wanted to break up, but that wasn't it. Then he said it—the three words that mean the most—*I love you*. I told him to not say that because of what I was about to do to him. He didn't say anything back, so I asked him if he was there. Then he answered me, "I think I know what you are going to say."

I said, "What am I about to say?"

"WHY is all I want to know!"

I didn't have to say a word, and he already knew. When I told him about Trevor, he was, like, "Oh. . . . We are still friends though, right?"

"Yes, of course," I replied.

He said okay and left. I signed off and ran to my room and lay on my bed, stuffing my face into my pillow. I thought about it over and over again, and then I came to this conclusion—I shouldn't have dumped him for a guy who lives over two hours away from me. It was such a stupid idea and a stupid thing to do. But I couldn't ask Greg out again because I figured after I had hurt him he wouldn't want me back.

Trevor and I won't see each other for another year, and I do not even know if he is going back to camp again. It was a terrible mistake to break up with Greg. I should have stayed true to him and not allowed myself to feel anything except for friendship toward Trevor. That way I wouldn't have hurt Greg.

These days, Greg and I still talk with each other on the computer. He has a girlfriend now, and she is a nice person. Even though I am friends with her, sometimes it still hurts me. I think he knows how I still feel about him. He doesn't forgive me for what I did, and I do not blame him. But he still talks to me. At least I have that.

Kristen Weil, 13

My First Kiss

For it was not into my ear you whispered, but into my heart. It was not my lips you kissed, but my soul.

Judy Garland

Sunsets and sunrises,
This moment locked in time
My breath stops, our eyes lock
Your heart beats next to mine
The ground shakes, my body shivers
It feels like total bliss
I have allover tingles
This is my first kiss.

Khristine J. Quibilan

NO RODEO®

Secret Crush

A crush is the path to a secret heartache.

Gina Romanello

Jason. He was the boy of my dreams. He started coming to my school when I was in the second grade, but he was in a different class than me, so I barely caught a glimpse of him. In the third grade he wasn't in my class either, but then came fourth grade. That was the first year we had the same teacher, and the first time I really got to see him, hear him, watch him, . . . I fell madly in love with him.

His blond hair was always cut just so, and his bangs hung straight down on his forehead. His blue eyes were the bluest of blues, and when he smiled . . . oh, that smile. His entire face lit up. He had the straightest, whitest teeth I'd ever seen. He was a dream. I was obsessed with him, and it was the beginning of a secret crush that I'd hold onto for years.

In fifth and sixth grade, Jason and I ended up having different teachers so I didn't see him as much, but he was on my mind and in my heart just the same. During lunch or recess, I'd steal glimpses of him. I couldn't erase his blue eyes out of my heart.

When sixth grade came to an end, we were off to junior high school. I knew I'd be meeting new boys, and Jason would be meeting new girls. I was excited and nervous. For three years, I secretly loved him, dreamed about him and never shared that with anyone.

Finally the first day of junior high school came. I hardly slept at all that night, I was so scared and nervous and anxious all at the same time.

When the bus arrived at our new school, I went to my first class and then my second—and there was no Jason. I went to my third class, then finally my fourth. I walked in the classroom and there he was, sitting alone at a desk. He gave me a huge grin as if he was so relieved to see a familiar face—mine! I sat right next to him, and we talked. We talked and talked and talked. It was different this time, we were in junior high, and we didn't know anyone else in the class except each other. We talked until the class started and then we talked at the end of class, and we walked out together! Except, I wasn't walking at all—I was floating!

That's how it was every day in fourth period during those first few weeks. Jason and I sat next to each other and talked. We became fast friends, more than we'd ever been before. Then one day, my heart almost exploded.

"I have an idea of what you can do today when you get home," Jason said to me as we walked out of the classroom.

"What?" I asked, curious.

"You can call me," he answered, and I was speechless. "Call me around three o'clock."

"Okay," I said, my lips and heart quivering.

With trembling hands, I picked up the phone. It was three o'clock, just like he said. I heard the phone ring, then another.

"Hello?" Jason answered.

"Hi," I said, hoping that he'd know it was me. He did. After the first few minutes, I began to relax, and he did too. We talked on the phone for more than an hour! I was dreaming, I was flying, my head was in the clouds! And to top it off, the first dance of the year was coming up that Friday, and I began to hope that Jason might ask *me* to the dance with him! Was my dream on the verge of coming true?

The next day I wanted to run to fourth-period class, but I didn't. I walked slowly, fighting the butterflies that were flying around my stomach.

I went and sat in my usual spot next to Jason. He looked at me and smiled. Right away, the teacher started talking, and try as I might, I couldn't pay attention. My heart was pounding in my chest as I sat next to the boy of my dreams, the boy I'd talked to on the phone for more than an *hour* the day before!

To my total surprise, he slipped a note on my desk. With trembling hands, I took the folded slip of paper. My face became hot, and I hoped it didn't look as red as it felt. *What could this be?* I thought. *Is he telling me that he likes me? Is he going to ask me to the dance? Is my dream coming true?* I carefully and quietly opened the piece of paper and saw one sentence written there. I looked closely and read the words, "Will you ask Shelly if she likes me? Thanks, Jason."

Fighting tears, I quickly folded it back up and put it in my book. I looked over at Jason and quickly nodded "yes" to him. The teacher rambled on, but I was in a broken-hearted world of my own.

I did Jason's asking for him, and I found out that Shelly didn't like him, but it didn't matter. For the first time ever, I'd experienced a broken heart, and I'd had enough. I decided right then and there that I wasn't going to spend another second of my life hanging onto a dream that was never going to come true. After much crying, I gave up on Jason.

Jason and I never got together, but I watched him with this girlfriend or that one. And he watched me, as I found new boyfriends who captured my heart.

He never knew that a blond-haired girl with green eyes and freckles loved him from afar. In fact, no one ever knew. He was my secret love for many years—until now.

Karin A. Lovold

The Truth

You can't be brave if you've only had wonderful things happen to you.

Mary Tyler Moore

Guys. Not a subject I have much experience with since I've only had one real boyfriend.

Seth—he was the popular one, while I was not popular. I had a crush on him, big time, and I finally had a chance to go out with him. I was on cloud nine! Two days later, I got a phone call from him saying he didn't want to go out anymore. I found out later from mutual friends that it had just been a dare. It hurt a lot, but I slowly got over it.

It took me four years to get a boyfriend because all I thought about when I met a new guy was, *Is this just another dare?*

Then David came along, and I knew that I wanted to go out with him. The first time I met him, I could actually talk to him. Around David I felt like I could be myself; say what I wanted or be silly—and I never felt ashamed. He would call me just to say hi, and we would talk for hours about nothing in particular.

And then things changed. It went from talking all the time, to five-minute phone calls—or none at all. Then I found out from one of my friends that David had told her that he couldn't be with me anymore. I told her that he needed to tell me himself, because he needed to deal with his problems on his own.

He called that night, and he acted really confused on the phone. I asked him if he needed to tell me anything, and he said no. That totally sucked. Here it was, two days before the prom, the most important night of my junior year, and he wasn't even going to bother to tell me that he wasn't going to go with me. I asked him straight up if he wanted to be with me or not. All I *really* wanted at that point was the truth. I was brave enough to deal with that.

"I dunno, . . . " was all he could say after a long pause. And then the famous line came: "I think we should just be friends."

"There you go," I said. "That's all you had to say. If you just want to be friends, then we'll just be friends."

I didn't cry. I didn't yell. I just got straight to the point. Oh, I cried later on, but I also smiled because I knew that I had been through this sort of thing before and I had survived. If I could live without him before, then I could live without him again.

I hear things now, rumors about him denying that he knows me, and that's fine. I see him with his new girl-friend, and I say hi. There's no, "Eww . . . she's ugly," or "He's such a loser," just a genuine hello and a smile.

Through all of this I have realized that relationships don't always last a lifetime, but the memories and the lessons that we learn from them can last forever.

Anna Bittner, 16

Learning How to Move On

I wanted a perfect ending. Now I've learned, the hard way, that some poems don't rhyme, and some stories don't have a clear beginning, middle and end. Life is about not knowing, having to change, taking the moment and making the best of it without knowing what's going to happen next.

Gilda Radner

I've never had much luck with guys. Oh, it's not because I'm not pretty or that I'm really mean or anything like that—it's just that things never really seem to work out. I don't have much confidence, and I've always admired those special girls who can turn the head of any guy and charm them all with just a smile.

When I was fourteen, I met this older guy who I really liked, and I got my hopes up only to get dumped after three or four days. Looking back now, it seems pretty insignificant, but at the time it was a big deal. I decided to just give up dating. I couldn't see the point in hurting myself like that again until I was ready for something serious. It worked quite well . . . for a while.

A few months later, I was at church one Wednesday night when my youth group announced that they were going caroling. A couple of my friends decided to stay at church, and I chose to stay with them. A little while later, this guy I'd seen once or twice at church events showed up. I didn't know his name or anything about him, but as soon as we started talking, I was immediately interested. He told me his name was Andy, and we proceeded to play our own warped version of dodge ball with my friend Melissa. We had a blast that night, and when it was time to go, I walked outside with him and told him he should come back soon. He gave me a hug when he left.

The next day, while I was hanging out around the house, my phone started ringing. I picked it up, and guess who it was? Andy. It turns out that he had gotten my number from one of my friends. Now, I have to admit, I'm a total sucker for a guy who makes the first move because I'm too terrified to do it myself. I thought it was an incredibly sweet thing to do, and we ended up staying on the phone for hours. For the next two weeks, he pursued me relentlessly, but I kept telling him no when he'd ask me out because I didn't want to get into another relationship that meant nothing and wouldn't last a month. In the end, though, he wore me down and I finally said yes.

We became inseparable. We saw each other every day, and I was always at his house or doing something with his family. He became my best friend, and I confided to him things that I'd never shared with anyone before. Not only could I tell him anything, but he shared things with me in return. I was the one he came running to when he got his first speeding ticket, and he was my shoulder to cry on when I found out my mom was dying. I thought nothing could come between us and that we would be together forever.

For Andy and me, forever was five months and one day. I called him one night because I felt as if he had been avoiding me, and I needed to know what was going on. He finally told me that he just wanted to be friends and that he didn't love me the same way that he used to— somewhere along the road it had changed. I cried during the entire conversation ... and for about two months after.

It was incredibly hard for me to face life without him because I had made my life revolve around him. All of a sudden I was alone. There was no one for me to talk to for hours on the phone, and since I had always been doing something with him and his family, I hadn't just lost him—I felt as if my second home had been taken away too.

It's been a long road since our breakup, and I've had a lot of heartache since then. But even though I thought I'd never be able to get over him, I've slowly begun to heal. I know I'm going to be okay without him. Yes, I still miss being with him and having someone to joke around with; someone who will just hold me when I need him to and who turns to me when he's feeling down. But I know that eventually the right guy will come along, and I'll be happier than I could have ever imagined.

I will always be grateful to Andy for what he gave me— my first real kiss, my first serious relationship and a wonderful experience. Even if things didn't work out between us, I still learned so many things, like how to open yourself up to someone and, most important, how to move on after it is over. These are lessons and memories that I will carry with me for the rest of my life, and for that, Andy, I thank you.

Elizabeth White, 15

Nineteen

Love makes your soul crawl out from its hiding place.

Zora Neale Hurston

There he was, standing out in the crowd at the mixer that the student council puts on every year at the beginning of school. He had grown well over six feet, gotten contacts, developed a tanned and chiseled face, and let his dark brown hair grow enough to curl adorably. It was the first time in two years that I'd seen him—Michael, my ex-boyfriend from back in middle school. He was the first boy I'd ever gone out with.

To get a better look at him, I gathered up the courage to ask him to dance, and he didn't run away screaming. We slow danced.

After the mixer, I couldn't stop thinking about him. I realized that the old crush I had had on him was reviving itself, and I wanted to see him again. Considering our history, I should have beaten my head with a board until I fell unconscious. Two years before, we had dated for a month and then he told me that he loved me. I dumped him because of it. A week later, when I told him what happened, we got back together. His friends took it upon themselves to disapprove. They kept telling me that I wasn't good enough for him, that I was going to break his heart. They told him the same thing. I guess they got the best of him, because he dumped me a few weeks later over the phone.

None of that mattered to me anymore. I wanted to get to know this ex-boyfriend again—this intriguing stranger.

I decided to take a walk and "just happened to pass by" Michael's house, which was a mile down the road from mine. I walked by it . . . passed it . . . turned around to pass it again . . . and again. I wanted so badly to go up and knock on the door, but I was scared. What if he thought I was a freak or a stalker?

I gathered some courage, headed up the walkway and banged on the door. I could hear his dogs going crazy inside the house, and soon Michael was standing at the front door, staring at me like I was some sort of mutant.

"Hey," his deep voice boomed.

"Hey," I managed to squeak. "I was just taking a walk and . . . ummm . . . I know this is weird . . . but do you want to . . . ummm . . . come for a walk with me?" I was so artic-ulate and intelligent sounding—NOT!

"Uh . . . sure." To my amazement, he went to get his shoes, and before I realized that the sky hadn't fallen, we were on our way, in the direction of my house.

We walked along and talked about what had happened in our lives while we were apart. Michael used to be unbearably shy, but he didn't seem afraid to talk to me anymore. We chatted on about ice hockey, school, my year at private school and everything else that we could manage. We wound up in a park near my house. I stopped and turned to face him when I reached the jungle gym. I curled one hand over the cool metal, leaning on it.

"You know, I still have all the notes you used to write me in eighth grade," I said, teasing him.

"Really?" He smiled as his entire face lit up at the thought. "I have all of yours, too."

"Are you serious?" I couldn't believe that he'd actually cared enough to keep them. I had thought myself sentimental, maybe even a little weird for doing the exact same thing.

That's when I felt his hand close over mine. I lowered my gaze to stare at it. His other hand wound around my waist. I glanced up into his eyes for a brief second, totally bewildered, and then, he kissed me.

Now, I've been kissed before, but I can still feel his gentle lips pressing down upon mine. It had to be the most impulsive thing that he'd ever done. We just stood there kissing, until I realized what was going on.

As I pulled away, I whispered, "Nineteen more."

While we were together in junior high, Michael had given me a little certificate that was good for twenty kisses. We never used it. I think maybe he was afraid of me or of kissing. Or both.

Michael didn't need me to explain it. He just smiled and leaned forward to kiss me again.

Kathleen Benefiel, 16

9

CHANGES, CHANGES AND MORE CHANGES

Not long ago, I was so self-assured
But recently, a lot has occurred
And I'm no longer a little girl
But I'm not a teen, that's for sure
Now life is strange and all I know
Is that I don't want my insecurity to show
From braces to bras, from zits to shaving
It's crazy how much my life is changing
But if I embrace both the laughter and tears
I think I'll survive my preteen years.

Irene Dunlap

Late Bloomer

*You have to have confidence in your ability, and
then be tough enough to follow through.*

Rosalynn Carter

Much to my dismay, as a young girl I carried with me an
unshakeable stigma. I was a "late bloomer." Everyone
knows that's just a nice way of saying that I had a flat
chest for much longer than most of the girls my age. I was
one of the youngest and smallest kids in my class, so while
all of the other girls were beginning to need training bras,
I could put on a baseball hat and a pair of jeans and pass
for a boy any day of the week. Needless to say, I tried not
to. By eighth grade, I actually *wanted* to wear eye shadow
and nail polish—to explore my newly acquired femininity
or, at the very least, my hope for it.

But it didn't seem to matter what I did. As long as I was
flat-as-a-board, I felt that I would never grow up. My great-
est fear was that I would turn into a scientific enigma: the
only thirty-year-old who never hit puberty. All sorts of
doctors would be called in to examine the freak who never
developed in all the right places. I would be infamous. I

would be a social outcast. My future children would starve if I tried to breastfeed them. I would make my living as a circus sideshow; "Step right up and see the woman who *still* has no need to wear a bra!"

All of the popular girls needed bras. Heck, all of the unpopular girls needed bras. *Everyone* needed a bra it seemed, except for me. While most of the girls in gym class would try to shower and dress quickly so that no one would see what they had to cover up, I tried to cover up the fact that I had nothing to cover up. I longed to be part of the over-the-shoulder-boulder-holder club, if only I had boulders to hold! Or small stones. Even pebbles would have been acceptable.

I was smart. I was a cheerleader. I had friends. But junior high can be vicious. And eighth-grade girls can be ferocious. Case in point: some girls from the locker room leaked to some of the boys that I didn't wear a bra. Short of "stuffing" (which I considered but couldn't figure out how to pull off the slow, natural growth rate), I couldn't hide my pancake look. But there still seemed to be some social expectation that I should wear a bra anyway. An eighth-grade code. Unwritten rule.

So some of the boys knew. But the worst was, Scott knew. Now it might seem that this was devastating because I liked Scott, but it's not true. Honestly. I'm openly sharing about the development of my mammary glands, so would I lie about liking a boy all this time after the fact? I promise, I *didn't* like him. Scott was the boy who, on a field trip, mooned a car from the back seat of the bus. He was the boy who was always getting in trouble for being loud, getting in fights and making a general nuisance of himself. He was a little bit of a class bully, or maybe more of a class clown, but he was friends with all of the popular guys—like Joey Jackson. And *he* was the boy I liked.

Ahh, Joey Jackson, a.k.a. Mr. Hottie. He was the cutest boy in the entire school. And I had the distinct privilege of sitting behind him in homeroom. When he would turn around to talk to the boy who sat behind me, there I was in the middle. One day when his friend behind me was sick, Joey talked to me. I think it was when I cracked a joke and he actually laughed that I knew I was in love.

It's easy to imagine how devastated I was to think that Sarah-told-Jenna-who-told-Brody-who-told-Scott-who-would-probably-tell-Joey that I wasn't exactly in need of a Victoria's Secret charge card. As if Joey couldn't have figured it out on his own. Nevertheless, I was horrified.

One of the cruel things boys did was to sneak up behind an unsuspecting girl to snap her bra—if, in fact, she wore a bra. Now, what could be more humiliating than a bra-snapping incident? Yep, that's right—*not* having a bra to snap!

One day I got tipped off that Scott intended to snap my bra, knowing that I wouldn't be wearing one, so he could announce to everyone (including Joey) that I was missing the ever-popular undergarment, thus leaving my self-esteem in the toilet.

I didn't know what to do. Should I go to the nurse's office and fake sick? Should I go to the locker room to see if someone accidentally left a bra lying around that I could borrow? I considered an emergency run to the nearest store, but my school was conveniently located nowhere near a mall. My options weren't great.

After math class, I shuffled out into the hallway with all of the other kids, glancing to my left and right to find Scott. I figured if I knew his whereabouts, I might just have a chance at hiding from him. When I spotted him coming out of Mrs. Walsh's class, I ducked, but it was too late. He had seen me too and was making a beeline toward me. If I turned to walk away, he'd have an easy target. If I broke into a full sprint, I would get in trouble for running. So I just stood there, back against the wall, holding my books in front of my less-than-voluptuous chest. He sauntered up, his eyes mocking me, saying nothing.

I don't know exactly what he expected me to do, but I think what he did not expect me to do was face him head on. As the class bully, he was pretty much used to getting his way. So I just stared him down with my powder blue-shadowed eyes.

Finally with my voice shaking, I warned, "Scott, don't touch me. Not now. Not ever." Then I ducked past, turned my back to him and walked away.

At that point, Scott could have gone through with his plan. My back was in a position of easy access for the "Braless Bra-Snap Caper." With one motion, he could have attempted to make my life miserable. But he didn't.

As I headed toward my next class, I didn't look back. Heart racing, breathing heavily, I feared what would happen next. But nothing did. I waited through my classes, through lunch, through the end of the day to hear something. I anticipated my worst fear coming true when Joey Jackson would walk up to me and say, "So when are you going to wear a bra like everyone else?" But he didn't. No one did.

By the next day, all of the kids in my class had moved on to some other topic of conversation, like Larissa's new too-tight pants. By the next week, I started wearing a bra. And by the next year (or two), I had begun to develop my much-anticipated front side. All was right with the world.

Julie Workman

NO RODEO®

NO RODEO. ©Robert Berardi. Used by permission.

ARB

What you can't get out of, get into wholeheartedly.
Mignon McLaughlin

"My mom says I have to get a bra," I told my best friend, Wendi, as we ran around the school field, training for the cross-country team.

"I won't hate you when you get it," she said.

"Thanks." I was afraid I was going to be the only girl in fifth grade with a bra. The boys would snap it, and the popular girls would make snide comments. Everyone would notice.

"I don't need a bra," I protested to my mom the next day as we walked into the lingerie section of the department store. The closest I'd ever come to this section was in the summer, when the bathing suits were hung beside the nightgowns. I scanned the aisles for a sign of my classmates. Mortified wouldn't even begin to express how I'd feel if one of them showed up.

"You'll survive, Alison," my mom said. She guided me toward the rows of creamy pink boxes. "The girls in your class will catch up to you soon."

"No, they won't."

A saleswoman approached us. I tried to hide behind my mom. This was the worst shopping trip I'd ever been on. My mom's voice sounded like it belonged on another planet as she said, "We're looking for the training bras." The sales woman looked down at me.

"For her?"

"Yes."

"Oh, she doesn't need a training bra." The saleswoman bit her lip as she studied me. I was elated. *Mom was wrong!* The saleswoman continued, "She'll need at least a B cup." My heart dropped as the saleswoman wrapped a measuring tape around my chest. "Yep, just as I thought, 32 inches. Follow me." I looked furtively around as we followed the woman to another section. The saleswoman told us to give her a wave when we'd found some to try on.

"The letter is the cup size," my mom explained, "and the number is the width around your chest." She pulled a bra off the hanger and held it out to me. "What do you think?" It was a white cotton bra with a little bow in between the cups.

"It's alright." God, I hoped none of my friends were out shopping today. "We should get you a bunch to try on. Is there any particular one you like?"

"No." They all looked the same. "Those look fine." I could rip off the bows.

"There's this style, too." I found myself holding four white bras (two with bows and two without) as I walked into the fitting rooms.

"Let me know if you want me to come in, dear," the saleswoman called. I slid the slotted door shut. I knew what I was doing. And if I didn't, I definitely did not want any help.

There wasn't much difference between the bras as I

tried each of them on. They all felt horrible. I couldn't imagine running cross-country with them on, especially the ones with the bows. The straps dug into my shoulders, and the tags itched. But somewhere below all my discontent with the foreign apparatus, I felt tingles. The more I looked at myself in the mirror, the more I liked what I saw. I didn't look like an awkward, loud ten-year-old who wore the wrong shoes, got her ears pierced at the wrong place and cared more about sports than boys. The shape that my chest rounded into with the bra on made me feel like a movie star. I thought that I looked more like a tall, sophisticated almost-teenager.

"Are you okay, dear?" The saleswoman knocked at the door. "I just want to make sure your straps are adjusted properly." I snapped back to reality.

"They're fine." I'd play around with the straps later. I unfastened the bra and threw my T-shirt back on. My chest felt looser without the bra on as I walked out of the dressing room. Glancing around the surrounding aisles first, I shoved the two white cotton bras with the white bows in the center into my mom's hands. "I'll take these."

"Are you sure?" she asked. "This is an important decision. Do they fit well?"

"Yes."

"And you really want the ones with the bows?"

"Yes!"

"Okay, you're the one who has to wear them." She carried the bras up to the cash register. "We've settled on these two," she told the saleswoman.

"I'll be over here, Mom," I called, wandering as far away from the transaction as I could.

Monday morning I walked into class wearing the darkest colored shirt I could find over my new bra. I kept my back arched, hoping to hide the strap lines. Thanks to Wendi, word got out fast that I was wearing a bra. During recess, boys dared each other to snap it. By Friday, the novelty had worn off. I'd made it through cross-country and soccer practice without incident. And I'd even worn a white T-shirt to gym class, showing the bra straps proudly. After all, I was the only girl in the fifth grade who owned one.

Alison Gunn

Headgear

The way I see it, if you want the rainbow, you gotta put up with the rain.

Dolly Parton

The moment he spoke those dreaded words, I knew my life was over.

"You need headgear!" Dr. Newman said, pointing to the horrible-looking device on the table in front of me.

I'm pretty sure the tears sprouted almost immediately. I knew I had crooked teeth. I was reminded everyday by one of my classmates calling me "Bugs." I could handle braces or a retainer, but I hoped and prayed since my mom brought me to the orthodontist that straightening my teeth would not include having to wear an ugly head strap attached to a metal wire. There was already a girl in my class with neck gear. She got teased constantly, and she only had the part that went around her neck and was easily covered by her hair.

But my hair would not easily cover the thing sitting on the table in front of me. In fact, it would be covering my hair, meaning an extreme amount of bad hair days in my future.

"Is this something she has to wear all day or just while she sleeps?" my mom asked.

This question caused the tears to stop for a brief moment as I hoped that he would say it was just something I could sleep in. That way, no one would ever have to see it.

"She should wear it for sixteen hours a day." Desperately, I began calculating the hours in a day and the hours spent at school. I was so distracted, I could barely focus on his explanation of how I would be fitted for the device and when I would get it. I figured out that if I wore it from the minute I got home until I left for school each morning, I could get by without wearing it to school.

"So, I don't have to wear this to school?" I interrupted.

Dr. Newman nodded. "Not as long as you wear it the full sixteen hours. But you also must take into consideration that you can't eat with it or wear it while playing sports."

I added in the hours at soccer practice, and I figured I could eat really fast. No matter what, I was going to avoid wearing it to school at all costs. Bugs Bunny was a much better nickname than what I imagined them calling me if they saw my headgear.

"You get your choice of two colors, tan or blue. You can have one to match either your hair or your eyes." He pointed to the two different versions of the same ugly headpiece.

"The one that matches my hair," I reluctantly answered. Only it didn't really match my hair. The light brown color did not blend in with my blond hair. On top of that, it would be impossible to wear my hair any way other than straight. The only style that wasn't in the way of the head straps was two ponytails sticking out the two sides like horns. There was no way I'd wear my hair like that.

I looked at him like he was insane. He must not have noticed my complete meltdown. My only consolation was that I was able to not wear it out in public. I kept to my plan, wearing it the minute I got home from school to the minute I left in the morning, minus soccer practice and meals. I hated the thing so much I began to limit any activities that might involve seeing anyone outside of my family when I had it on.

My mom finally got sick of me refusing to go anywhere. One day after school, she forced me to go grocery shopping with her. The worst part is she made me wear the headgear inside the store.

"You've only worn it for an hour today, and you have to wear it the full sixteen hours," she insisted as we drove to the store.

I didn't understand how wearing it for fifteen hours only one day would harm my teeth. But she wouldn't budge.

"You have to get used to wearing it out in public. I promise no one will stare at you. I bet you won't even see anyone you know!"

We didn't see anyone I knew for the first few aisles we went down. But as we turned down the soup aisle, I spotted Jeff. Jeff was one of the most popular—and meanest— boys in my class. Whenever my friend Trisha and I would walk by him, he'd call out, "Look, it's the nerd herd!"

I quickly ran to the next aisle and hid behind a display of cereal to avoid being spotted by him. My mom followed me.

"Thanks a lot! *Jeff* is here. If he sees me, I'll never hear the end of it. I'll be scarred for life," I told her.

She rolled her eyes, "I think you are being overly dramatic." She peeked down the aisle. "Is he the boy with the brown hair?" she asked.

I nodded and pulled her back. "Don't let him see us!"

My mom grinned. "Who cares if he sees us? I promise he won't make fun of you. Plus, I need soup."

I tried to protest, but she grabbed my hand and pulled me down the aisle. Of course, Jeff and his mom were standing right in front of the soup my mom wanted. I would have given anything to be invisible at that moment. I prayed that he wouldn't notice me. Once we got closer, I realized that he was trying to hide behind his mom. That's when I saw it. *He had headgear, too!* Not only that, he had neck gear. He had two white straps on his head and one white strap on his neck. Both were connected to a metal wire like mine on his teeth. Neither one of us said a word to each other.

My mom was right for once. The next day at school, Jeff acted like nothing had happened. When my friends and I walked by him, he ignored us.

"Jeff is quiet today," Trisha commented. "He usually loves to pick on us. Not that I'm complaining. I wonder what's up with him?"

I shrugged, "No clue."

Stephanie Dodson

Did She Say "Ovary"?

*You don't have to be afraid of change. You don't
have to worry about what's being taken away.
Just look to see what's been added.*

Jackie Greer

"And so you see, the OVARY is really the mother of all
human life!"

Silence filled the school library. Mrs. Bancroft's lecture
seemed inspiring to just her and her alone. All of us sixth-
grade girls were disgusted. Not just by the huge projec-
tion on the wall of a woman's parts, which strangely
resembled a cow's skull, but by the joy that Mrs. Bancroft
seemed to take in grossing us out.

My best friend, Erin, was ticking off tally marks on her
paper every time the woman said "ovary." It seemed to be
the word of the day. Luckily, we were saved by the bell.

After "life processes" class was over, Erin and I went to
our lockers. Her long black hair sashayed beautifully over
her back as she walked. She turned to me and whispered,
"Tasha, my ovaries may be the mother of all human life,
but my mom told me they are also the root of all evil. In

fact, if and when I ever start my period, my mom told me sharks will actually hunt me down and kill me if I even think about going swimming in a bikini at the beach."

Erin's mom always told her funny things that I thought sounded a bit wrong. But I couldn't help wondering who was right. Was it Mrs. Bancroft, with her excitement over the amazing science of it all? Or was it Erin's mom, who felt that women's functions were shameful and should be kept private? Or what about my mom's crazy-hippie, free-love ideas?

My mom grew up in the era of openness and feminism in the 1960s. The minute I turned twelve, she felt compelled to tell me every detail about why I should be totally excited to be a woman. Mom informed me about the "magic" of menstruation and how special I was because only women could create life.

The day after that lecture at school—and I cannot believe this—my mom actually started talking to Erin and me about all this stuff, loudly, in a shoe store!

"Tasha, you need to think about the kind of shoes you wear because you want them to reflect well on your body. The body is sacred. You will be a woman soon and . . ."

"Mother!" I gasped, mortified. She knew when I called her "mother" that she had crossed the line. My face felt hot with little pin prickles all over it. Those were the times when I wished we were a repressed mother-daughter duo that never talked about anything. But Erin was actually very interested in what my mom was saying.

Mom continued, this time in whisper-tones: "Honey, it's nothing to be ashamed of! The changes in your body will be the beginning of you becoming powerful. It's the start of a wonderful journey that only other women can understand."

"Okay, okay, I get it!" I said, my eyes darting down the sandal aisle, hoping no one had heard. My heart was thumping in my ears as I grabbed my purse and ran to a bench outside the store. I knew my mom was trying to share something with me in her weirdo way. I knew she loved me and wanted me to welcome the changes that, unfortunately, were coming any day now. But I did not want to talk about it, and I certainly didn't want to share anything about the power of my ovaries with Erin and the shoe salesman.

When we were driving home from the mall, Erin asked my mom to tell us more about what kind of power she was talking about.

"Please, Mom, don't!" I snorted, through gritted teeth. I was suddenly embarrassed by her tie-dye tank top. I wanted to disappear. I felt suffocated by the odor of her patchouli perfume that filled the car.

"Oh, come on, I'm curious, and you know *my* mom will say it has something to do with attracting all manner of insects and rabid dogs," Erin pleaded.

"Well," Mom began, looking over the top of her purple sparkly sunglasses. "Some cultures send girls into menstruation huts, in order to protect the other villagers from their power. That is, until the girl is given the knowledge she needs to wield that power responsibly." I thought, *What kind of power could a teenager in Glendale, California, have?* I couldn't even ride the city bus by myself yet. This seemed a little too wacky. I sat there in silence, while my mom rattled on . . . blah, blah, blah. . . .

After that day, my mom actually listened to me and did not talk about this kind of stuff in front of my friends. Erin and I endured the remaining week of "life processes" class with Mrs. Bancroft, and we passed the female biological systems test. But Mom continued to bring things up when she and I were alone together, every now and then, just to make sure I understood. She told me about breasts and how they make the perfectly nutritious food for babies that no scientist can imitate in the lab. No matter how I squirmed and hid my face, she told me every gory detail of the blood that would be coming out of me and about my ovaries releasing eggs. These eggs, she said, were the root of creation.

She quoted a verse by the Indian poet Mirabai, "Understand the body is like the ocean, rich with hidden treasures." The hidden treasures I saw were tiny bumps I hid behind a padded bra and zits that I covered up with concealer. Then she followed it up with, "Tasha, when you start your period, when your body changes, this will be just the beginning of your ability to realize that you can be a positive womanly force connected to everyone you meet. It's a physical reminder of all that is sacred about women. You can create life with a husband who values all that you are." I thought she was probably delusional.

One day that summer, when I went to the bathroom and saw a small red splotch on my underwear, I stared at it for about five minutes straight. It didn't seem all that important. Was it a life-changing event? Or was it just shark bait? I was pretty confused about what was going to happen to me now that I was a "woman." I would never be a real kid again. I was some sort of mutant—half kid, half woman.

Mom took me out to a special dinner that night to cele-brate. She said, "Your new name is woman. And at this time in history, more than any other, we have the oppor-tunity to affect our world by being educated, loving, strong, nurturing, creative and powerful women." No matter how corny that sounded and how hard I tried to feel like ordinary old me, the pride and wonder I felt about the whole world swelled up inside of me, and I actually cried over my raspberry cheesecake.

Now that I've made it through the changes we heard so much about, I try to remember through all the menstrual cramps, breakouts and chocolate cravings that they're all physical markings of womanhood.

And at last, I don't cringe every time I hear the word "ovary."

Tasha R. Howe

NO RODEO®

NO RODEO. ©Robert Berardi. Used by permission.

Hair Horror

The key to realizing a dream is to focus not on success, but significance—and then, even the small steps and little victories along your path will take on greater meaning.

Oprah Winfrey

There were times when I totally, completely disliked Julie Chartrand, and this was definitely one of them. She had a knack for stealing boys right out from under my nose. Not really stealing them (I was not exactly overflowing with opportunities to date), but completely destroying my chances of ever having a boyfriend. She would always say the worst thing about me at the worst possible time, scaring away any potential interest.

And now, in the middle of science lab, Julie decided to strike again. My lab partner was the cutest boy in school—Tim Anderson. I had developed a massive crush on him and had successfully managed to get past the giddy, weak-kneed, tongue-tied stage to the point where I thought I was actually flirting intelligently. Even more amazingly, Tim seemed to be returning the interest! I never dreamed in my wildest dreams that I could actually be excited about science class, but Tim made all the difference.

As I held out a test tube for Tim to put over the Bunsen burner, I flashed him a smile, and he grinned back; a cute, boyish grin that made me melt. Unfortunately, Julie saw it too, and eyes narrowed, she chose that exact moment to make a shocking announcement.

"Michelle, is that hair on your upper lip? Do you have a mustache? You DO!!"

I stopped in complete horror. I had noticed a few days before that soft, downy hair was beginning to grow on my upper lip and was thoroughly distressed by this turn of events. No one else I knew had hair on their upper lip—not even the boys! Was I some sort of freak of nature? I had no idea how to get rid of it, as tweezing really hurt and I was scared shaving would make it grow back even thicker. I hoped and prayed that no one would notice. However, I had forgotten to factor in the Wicked Witch of the West.

"She does? Let's see!" Tim suddenly morphed from my idol into an annoying, embarrassing, typical eighth-grade guy as he dropped the test tube to crowd in for a look. I ducked my head and stumbled for words.

"No—I don't! Julie's a dork. Why would I have a mustache?" I dropped into my seat and feigned great interest in my science textbook, praying that an earthquake would hit and swallow me up—or better yet, swallow up Julie. My heart sank as I gave up all hopes of ever having Tim as my first boyfriend.

After school was over, I raced to the drugstore. Scouring the hair removal aisle, I finally settled on a hair removal cream. I took my purchase home and hid it in my dresser drawer until it was close to bedtime, savoring the knowledge that soon my problem would be solved.

After brushing my teeth, I got a washcloth ready to

wipe the cream from my silky smooth lip when I was done. I was sure it would be a lip so soft, so clear—so kissable fresh. I opened the tube and spread a liberal amount onto my lip. It BURNED. My eyes started to water as the sensitive skin on my upper lip seared with pain. My lip smarted and tears poured down my face as I scraped the cream off with the washcloth. I splashed my face with cold water until all the cream was gone, but the damage was done. My upper lip was free from hair, but the problem was now much, much worse than I ever could have imagined. The skin between my nose and my mouth was an angry red, swollen and blistering on one side. I pressed another washcloth soaked in cold water against my lip, but it did little to abate the throbbing pain. Sneaking back down to my room, I picked up the box and read:

"If you have sensitive skin, be sure to do a test on a small patch of skin to check for allergic reaction." Having ignored the instructions, I ended up calling more attention to my upper lip than my wispy mustache ever had. *How in the world would I ever explain this to my parents? Even worse, how would I face everyone at school the next day?* I got into bed with a wounded soul, tears pouring down my face from the pain of my burning skin and the sure loss of my crush. *Why, oh why, had God placed Julie in my world?*

When I woke the next morning, I was relieved to find that the pain, swelling and redness were gone, along with the hair. A nasty scab had formed over the blisters on one side, but it didn't look too bad considering what my face had been through the night before.

Predictably, Julie was there to greet me in science lab that day. "What did you do to your face?" she asked loudly, glancing to see if Tim had heard.

"Oh, my curling iron slipped this morning, and I accidentally knocked myself in the face with it. Stupid, huh?" I tossed out casually, flipping my hair over my shoulder.

"Must've hurt," Tim said, sliding into the seat next to me. "Did you get those questions that were assigned for today? I couldn't figure out number seven."

"Sure," I said, flashing him a smile, and then, looking past him, I smiled sweetly to Julie who returned my smile with a scowl. Somehow, the memory of my swollen, burned lip dimmed in the moment of victory.

Michelle Peters

Strapped for Cash

A wise parent humors the desire for indepen-
dent action, so as to become the friend and
advisor when his absolute rule shall cease.

Elizabeth Gaskell

The stereo was blaring when Deb entered my room. She stood beside my bed, hands on hips, piercing blue eyes focused on me intensely.

"What?" I asked nervously. Deb didn't usually come into my room, or even have that much to do with me.

"I need to talk to you." Deb was my sister, actually my half-sister, and older by ten years. She took it upon herself to look after us younger kids, and I suppose that is why she was the one to come to my room instead of my mother.

"What?" I asked again, fidgeting with my pillow.

"I've been noticing that you've been changing," she said.

"Changing?" I asked innocently, but I knew what she meant. I had reached puberty and wasn't too happy about it, even going so far as to wear oversized T-shirts to hide it. I was a tomboy and proud of it. I didn't want boobs like some girly-girl.

"Robin Lynn, it's time you got a bra."

I rolled my eyes in embarrassment.

"I was thinking we could stop by Dad's office today and get some money. Then we could go to the mall and see what we can find for you."

"I don't want to ask Dad for money," I whined. "He'll know what it's for."

"No, he won't. He never has before," she said, looking toward the ceiling in thought. "Besides, if he does, you can just tell him you need it for something. He won't ask. Now get going."

"Is this really necessary?" I asked, wishing the whole situation would just disappear.

"You are not a boy, and it's time you started looking and acting like a girl," she advised. "I'm not going to argue about it. Get ready!"

As Deb shut the door, I flung myself backward, hitting the mattress hard and bouncing slightly. I closed my eyes and continued listening to my music until a sappy love song came on. That's when I grabbed my tennis shoes and headed downstairs.

Our fifteen-minute drive to town was unusually quiet. I was too embarrassed to talk about it, but nothing else was on my mind. *A bra. What would be next? A dress or pantyhose!?* Womanhood was not something I was looking forward to.

"I'll wait in the car," Deb said. "Hurry."

"Yeah, yeah," I answered unenthusiastically.

Dad's office was on the second floor of a huge building downtown. The building was old, and the dark stairwell gave me the creeps. I always took the stairs three at a time to hurry to the landing at the top, but each step still left an eerie echo.

Once at the top, I went into Dad's office. Dad's secretary was sitting at her desk. "Your dad is with a client. Let me buzz him," she offered.

She announced, "Robin's here."

"Send her in" was Dad's happy reply. He always told us we were more important than anyone else and could always come right in, but I was glad she checked first.

Dad sat behind his huge desk, which took up at least half of the room in the office. One side held pictures of us kids. Yellow legal pads were scattered in front of him, and a sign that read "J. R. Sokol, Attorney at Law" clasped the edge of the desk for all incoming clients to read. The faint smell of leather from all the law books filled the room.

His client sat in front of the desk in one of the four green leather office chairs. He was a round man in a blue three-piece suit. His thick black hair was slicked to his head as if he had used glue.

"Hello there, Robs. Where's your mother?" Dad asked casually.

"At home. Deb brought me to town."

"What do you need?" he asked, removing his black-framed glasses and rubbing the corner of his eyes. He had a permanently tired look about him; trying to raise seven kids would do that to a person.

"I need some money."

"For what?"

I thought, *Oh, no, now what?* I looked at Dad's client, who seemed to be interested in what I needed the money for, too. I looked back at Dad. "I just need some money, that's all." I felt my face start to heat up like a hot coal.

Dad's voice rose slightly, "What do you need the money for?"

I couldn't take it anymore, "Never mind," I yelled and turned to leave. I could feel the tears swell up in my eyes but tried to fight them and not be a sissy.

"Young lady, you come back here this minute and tell me what you need the money for!" From the firm tone of his voice, I knew I had to tell him.

I walked back to the corner of the desk, tears now running down my face, and yelled at the top of my lungs, arms waving, "I need a bra!"

Dad's eyes widened in surprise, "Oh, I see." The corners of his mouth curled upright, and he started to laugh. So did his client. They both roared with laughter, which only made me madder.

"It's not funny!" I yelled.

"Young lady, you settle down." Dad said firmly, trying to tone down the situation. He reached into his suit pocket and pulled out his wallet. He flipped it open and handed me a couple of twenty-dollar bills. "Here Robs," he said, still chuckling.

I grabbed the twenties firmly, spun on my heels, ran out of the office and bounced down the stairs.

I stopped on the landing at the bottom, cried a little more and then wiped the tears away. I was not going to let Deb know what happened.

At the supper table that night, I waited for Dad to say something about the day's events. I knew once the rest of the family knew, they would tease me relentlessly. But he never said a word about it.

Later that evening, there was a knock on my door.

"Yeah?" I asked.

"It's me. Can I come in a minute?" Dad asked quietly.

"Yeah."

He opened the door and stood inside, glancing around my room like he had never seen it before. I sat on the edge of my bed thinking I was in trouble for acting up today.

"Honey, I have an idea."

"Yeah," I answered, trying not to look him in the face.

"From now on, if you need money for something personal, why don't you just say it's for 'girls' stuff.' Then I'll know."

I felt my face get flushed again. "Okay."

"It's a deal then," he answered, lowering his eyes, as embarrassed as I was.

"A deal. Good night," I answered trying to end the conversation.

"Night. Don't let the bed bugs bite."

We both smiled as he shut the door.

I took the two new bras out of my drawer and laid them on my bed. One had two bears, dressed in jeans, kissing. The other had a moon and a sun imprinted on the front.

I put one on and pulled a baggy T-shirt on over it, looked in the mirror and smiled. Deb thought getting me a bra would turn me into a girl, but with a baggy shirt on no one would ever even be able to tell. *This won't be so bad,* I thought to myself.

Not so bad, that is, until my brothers found out I had been bra shopping.

The teasing lasted for weeks.

Robin Sokol

I Learned the Truth at Thirteen

You never find yourself until you face the truth.
                                                    Pearl Bailey

Big things were happening in my life the summer after I turned thirteen. I had just graduated from junior high, and I'd finally had a chance to dance with John, the boy I'd had a crush on all year. In the fall, I would begin high school. It was all very exciting, but a little scary, too. At least I knew I could always return to the safety of my family if things got rough.

Then, in the middle of summer, my parents shook my entire world and turned it upside down when they told me they were getting a divorce. When my mother said, "We think it's for the best," the words rang hollow in my ears. *For the best? How could that be?* I was shocked. I couldn't believe that our family was going to break up. Of course, at some level, I always knew my parents weren't very happy. They were rarely affectionate with one another, and they often fought. But I still didn't want anything to change. I wanted my family to stay the same—it was all I had ever known.

My life changed quite radically after the divorce. My mother and I moved into a small apartment across town, while my father and brother stayed in our house. I now became a visitor whenever I went to see my dad and brother on the weekends. I was at an age when I might be expected to start dating, but it was my mother who began going out for dinner and to parties with men she'd met at work or through friends. Then she did the unthinkable— she became engaged! I was immediately suspicious of my soon-to-be stepfather, Dan. I resisted all his attempts to get to know me. I was, in fact, pretty rude to him. Things were definitely bleak.

At the time, divorce was an uncommon occurrence. Since all of my friends' parents were still together, they couldn't relate to my situation and wondered why I was now quiet all the time. I still got together with them to go out to football games or dances, but I found I wasn't enjoying life the way I used to. I was clearly depressed, especially after Dan and my mother married and I realized that there was no way that things could change back to the way they were.

My salvation came from the last person on earth that I would have expected—Dan, my new stepfather. Even though I wasn't very nice to him, he never gave up on me. Gradually, I began to trust him. I realized that we actually had some things in common, especially when it came to movies and TV shows. We spent a lot of time together hanging out watching TV. That gave us a chance to talk and get to know each other. Then Dan invited me to go running, and I connected with it.

Better still, Dan showed an interest in me that I had never experienced from my own father. Dan was always around when I needed advice on school, friends or boys. I also learned a lot by watching Dan and my mom together.

They were often playful and affectionate with each other, so I saw firsthand what a good marriage looks like. Once I began to warm up to Dan, the three of us began spending a lot of time together. We often went out to eat, took short trips, and Dan and I even entered races and ran together. Eventually, I discovered that I finally had the happy family that I had always wanted.

I now realize my parents were right about getting the divorce. Their breakup was the best thing to happen for all of us. My father also found happiness—he remarried and had another child, my half-sister, Michelle.

At thirteen, I learned an important truth—change is not always the worst thing that can happen. Sometimes, it is just what we need the most.

Carol Ayer

10

FREE TO BE ME

C is for the Courage to not be embarrassed
O is for my Outstanding body and mind
N is Never saying never
F is for Finding out who I am
I is for Individuality
D is for celebrating Differences
E is for an Everlasting smile
N is for Nobody else quite like me
C is Congeniality
E is for Earning the strength that I have

I go to sleep happy because I am me!

Elizabeth Kay Kidd, 11

The Shy Girl

*From a shy, timid girl I had become a woman
of resolute character, who could no longer be
frightened by the struggle with troubles.*

Anna Dostoevsky

To say that I was shy when I was ten is an understate-
ment—I was basically afraid of people. Kids, adults, pretty
much everyone made me nervous. I was also what most
teachers and parents would call a "good kid." I followed
the rules, got good grades in school and rarely questioned
authority. But then one day, one single ride on a school
bus changed all that.

The school bus that day was crowded, hot, humid and
smelly. The windows were all rolled up—bus driver's
orders—it was simply raining too hard to have them
down. Only a few of my classmates were looking through
the windows at the torrents of water filling the street,
overflowing the curbs and drains; most of the other kids
were engaged in animated conversations, arguments and
games. I sat alone as usual, speaking to no one.

I thought that the road outside looked like a flooded

stream. I could make out tree limbs, bags, even an umbrella washing down the boulevard. People raced here and there, gripping umbrellas or covering their heads with bunched-up jackets and papers. Over and over, I carefully wiped a small circle through the cloud on my window so that I could see the rushing water outside.

The bus stopped, waiting for an accident to clear. The driver was particularly tense that day and had snapped at several kids who had been messing around, standing up in their seats, yelling, making faces at drivers in passing cars and even one kid who had been licking the window.

As I sat quietly, waiting and watching, I saw a kitty across the street on the other side of the road. *Poor cat,* I thought. He was all wet and didn't seem to know where to go to get out of the rain. I wanted to go get the kitty, but I knew that the bus driver, Mrs. Foster, would never allow me off the bus. It was against the rules to even stand up, so I knew that I would get in big trouble for trying to rescue a cat across a busy, rainy street. I also thought that if I pointed out the miserable cat, the other kids would probably think that I was weird, even weirder than they already thought I was. I was sure that some of the kids would laugh at the soaked, dripping animal; they would see his misery as their entertainment. I couldn't bear that; I didn't want things to get any worse than they already were.

My window was hazy again, and when I wiped the window clear, I could see that the kitty was now struggling in what seemed to be a surging, grimy river. He was up to his neck in cold water, grasping at the slippery metal bars covering the storm drain in the street. Twigs and other debris rushed past him and down into the black hole. His body had already been sucked into the dark opening of the storm drain, but his little front paws were clinging to the bars. I could see him shaking. He swallowed water and gasped for air as he fought the current

with all of his strength. His movements revealed a level of
fear that I had never witnessed before. I saw absolute terror in his dark, round eyes.

My heart was racing. Tears were rolling down my
cheeks. I felt like I was drowning along with the little
kitty. I wanted to rush off the bus without asking permission, and pull the stray cat from the drain, and wrap it up
in my warm jacket, safe in my arms. But I also pictured
getting into trouble before the cat could be saved, the
other kids staring and laughing, and my parents' disappointment in my behavior.

I sat motionless, unable to act. Helpless. The bus began
to move forward, the accident traffic finally in motion.

The cat's eyes locked on to mine. He was begging for
help. Although the bus was noisy with the clamor of active
children, I was sure that I heard his terrified meow. I could
see that he was panicking and needed help right away. I
glanced around, but no one else seemed to have noticed.

When Mrs. Foster yelled for me to sit down, I was
startled. I hadn't even realized that I was standing up. I
immediately sat back down. I did not break rules. I cried
as the bus lumbered into motion. I prayed that someone
else would notice and rescue my courageous friend. As
our bus slowly turned the corner away from the flailing
cat, I saw a car drive by the storm drain causing a wave to
rise up and over the kitty's head. He appeared again
coughing and sneezing but this time with some blood
trickling from his mouth and nose. One ear was completely folded back, like it was flipped inside out. The
weight of hopelessness blanketed down around me. None
of the people on the street seemed to notice the tiny
orange feline.

Somehow I managed to stand up again, directly dis-
obeying the bus driver.

"Mrs. Foster!" I cried.

Every single person on the bus stopped talking and looked at me. Waiting.

"A cat. There's a cat in the drain," I stammered. "If we don't help him, he'll drown." I held out a shaking hand and pointed.

The bus driver, to my amazement, did not yell at me. Nor did the other kids laugh at me. Instead, Mrs. Foster pulled the bus to the side of the busy road.

"Children," she said sternly. "No one is to leave this bus."

Then the woman rushed out into the traffic and rain. She sloshed across the street to the drain as we all watched in silence. Even the boys looked concerned. No one was laughing. I noticed that I wasn't the only one crying.

With one quick movement, Mrs. Foster grabbed the cat and pulled him into the safety of her arms. She cradled the terrified, clawing creature, removed her own coat to wrap him in it, and then she raced back to the bus. We all cheered until she motioned for us to be quiet.

"We'll have to look for his owners to see if he has a family already," Mrs. Foster said, as she handed me the sopping bundle.

"I know," I stammered.

"I'll help you," the girl sitting in the front seat whispered to me.

"Me too," came another voice, then another and another.

The other kids did help; we put flyers up all over town, one girl's dad put an advertisement in the paper, and we contacted the local animal shelters, veterinarians and pet stores. That means I was forced to talk to a lot of people, both kids and adults. There was no room for shyness and fear. To my surprise, I slowly gained more confidence in myself and made friends with some of the kids who had helped me. We never did find anyone to claim that cat, so he became a cherished member of my family.

Sure, I was still a pretty good kid after that day, but I learned to speak up, to overcome my shyness. I also learned to say a little prayer and then go for it when something really matters.

Laura Andrade

NO RODEO®

NO RODEO. ©Robert Berardi. Used by permission.

Never Cool Enough

I was always looking outside myself for strength and confidence, but it comes from within. It is there all the time.

Anna Freud

Why was it so easy for my blond-haired, blue-eyed twin sister, Allie, to make friends? She didn't even try, but they gravitated to her. It was so hard for me to be noticed when she was around. I didn't know why I wasn't like that. Her charming outgoing personality was too much for me to compete with.

I was the shy girl who sat in the corner. Why didn't people stop to think that maybe the person who doesn't talk the most might have the most to say? Why didn't any of the kids think that maybe I was just like them, but too intimidated to say anything? I was just as fun to be around as Allie was . . . if you got to know me. Yet I struggled all through elementary school trying to find friendships. I spent years lacking one of the most meaningful relationships a child can have.

Growing up is hard for everyone. For some it's harder

than for others. Especially the scramble we go through to find the right best friend—or just to find a friend at all.

By the time I reached eighth grade, I was lost. I had tried everything to become "cool" to fit in. I changed how I dressed, talked and presented myself. I copied other people's style, thinking that if I did, I would fit in with them and their friends. I tried the sporty look, then the preppy look—then came any other look you could think of. For a while, all my shirts were black and my jeans hung on my hips three sizes too big. You name it, I tried it.

I even changed the way I talked. I'd speak in a well-thought-out manner, very articulate. When people didn't notice that, I would speak like I had trouble putting a sentence together. I would change the tone of my voice. High pitched, different accents or just silly tones: Nothing could get me noticed. I just knew that if someone paid attention to me, I could win them over.

If that wasn't bad enough, there was the dreaded lunchroom where you can become very vulnerable to what others think and say about you. If you didn't sit with anyone, you were automatically a loser. Once one person thought you were a loser then everyone thought you were a loser. No one gave me a chance. There was also the constant fear of getting things thrown at you or in your general direction. I was struck many times with flying food. It was not an enjoyable experience. I ate lunch with my sister in elementary school because she felt sorry for me, but once we got to middle school, I wasn't cool enough to sit with her and her friends. I was forced to face what I thought was my destiny, sitting all alone at lunch over a tray of uneaten pizza.

So I felt horrible about myself. I continued to reinvent myself constantly in hopes I would be liked by at least one person. Surely *someone* wanted to hang with me. Allie blended in perfectly with the popular kids. She projected confidence, and people really responded to that.

Going through something like what I was going through was very difficult without Allie. Like perfect strangers, we didn't talk at school. We talked at home though, which was awkward. It became a hassle to try to make it seem like we were fine when both of us knew we weren't. We were twins. We have the same sense of humor. We talk the same, and most of the time, we think the same. We don't dress or act alike, but that isn't what matters. We went through everything together. I remember when I broke my arm, she went out of her way to make sure I had everything taken care of. I wouldn't even have to ask her to do something because it was already done. And when we moved, she stuck by me when I was having a hard time. Through thick and thin, it had always been the two of us. Having our relationship on the rocks made going through eighth grade anything but easy.

The only way I could cope with the ever-apparent reality of my situation was to act as though it didn't bother me. I pretended I didn't want to be popular. I acted like I hated everyone. I even became disruptive in class. I constantly made fun of the stupid things the popular kids did or said. I was all over it, mocking them in every way. Oddly enough, acting so rudely toward the popular kids attracted the attention of the self-declared rebels. Apparently being incredibly rude is a quality some people like. I decided it was easy to be rude, and it was finally going to be easy to make friends with these kids. All I had to say was that I hated "preps," and I was in. Way in.

I became a big part of that little group before I realized it was happening. The more mean and belligerent I became, the more these kids wanted to be around me. Inside, I was torn. I didn't want to be mean, but I wanted friends. I decided to do what at the time I thought was right. I had to start rolling with that crowd. Looking back,

I realize it was a big mistake.

I bought into their whole punk thing. I started dressing in a way that sent a message that didn't portray me, but portrayed *what* I had to be, to be in this group. Band T-shirts, leather wrist bands, studded belts—the whole nine. I took notes from my friends; I changed my way of thinking. Anything having to do with my family was no longer cool. The government was all wrong. Nothing was right.

I was becoming a completely different person, all for these people who I thought would never like me for me. When my friends started getting into drugs and other illegal activities, I felt really alone. I had no idea I was going to have to deal with these things at the tender age of fourteen. I had no idea how these people, my friends, could do this. Over the course of about six months, my friends started drinking and smoking. At first, they'd drink or smoke once a month. Gradually, it escalated into a weekly, then a daily, occurrence. They were constantly coming to school under the influence. I was dumbstruck by this, especially because the teachers didn't seem to notice or care. I prayed for the day when they would get caught. I thought then maybe they would shape up, and I would have my friends back. That day never came.

So I stood by, while my friends got trashed in their basements while their parents were upstairs. I stood by while they ditched class to go outside and smoke. But I was firm in my belief that participating in those activities was simply unacceptable. Finally, these friends began to distance themselves from me. Apparently, I wasn't cool enough for them because I didn't want to get high or wasted. At least that's what I thought. Maybe they just resented me for my values and couldn't stand the fact that they were weak enough to fall into that—and I wasn't.

I realized those kids weren't my real friends. It was hard to deal with that. I thought I had found a group that

I could stay friends with for a long time, but I wasn't about to throw my morals out the window for a few people. It was extremely difficult to face the fact that I had to choose between my morals and going back to being called names and always being alone. No one to eat with. No one to talk to.

At the beginning of ninth grade, I was flying solo again. Then something strange happened that year. I simply put my true self out there, which is what I should have done to begin with, but I had been too afraid. Finally, I was just being myself. I hadn't ever done that before.

Soon, I made friends with all kinds of kids—"preps," "punks," "nerds" and "losers." I looked at them individually instead of as being part of a group, and they began to respect me for that. I also started to get to know people instead of saying I couldn't be friends with them because they didn't think the exact same things as me. It didn't matter to me if they didn't dress like I did.

I became known as someone you could have fun with without doing anything illegal. I wasn't out every Friday night, but it had nothing to do with my popularity and everything to do with my values.

Finally, things at lunch are all good. I have yet to have a day this year when I have gotten pelted in the head with a grape or have nowhere to sit. People come and find me at lunch because they want to sit with me. They *want* to sit with me. I never thought that would be my reality. I was even voted Lady for the freshman class in the Homecoming Court!

I would have never guessed in eighth grade that I would be living the life I'm living today. I never knew it, but not once did I need to change a single thing about me.

I became cool by being myself.

Natalie Ver Woert, 16

Parting Ways

You can stand tall without standing on someone. You can be a victor without having victims.

Harriet Woods

When I was in first grade, my parents decided we needed to move to a bigger house. So that summer, we packed up our things and moved across town. And you know what that means—changing schools.

Lindsey's first words to me were, "Did you play soccer at your old school?"

"Yes," I answered. "Do you?"

"Yeah." We both smiled. On the way to lunch, she said to me, "Do you want to sit with me at lunch?"

Relieved and happy that I had made a new friend so fast, I smiled. "Sure."

We were immediate friends from then on. Best friends in fact. We spent every waking moment together. Sleepovers, parties, plays, dinners, everything you could imagine—we did it together. She was such a good friend. Always there for me, always understanding, and we always had a good time.

Always. It was that way from third through fifth grade.

Then came dreaded middle school.

We were worried; terrified. "What if we aren't in the same classes?"

Then our schedules came and guess what—we weren't. "We'll stay friends," we promised. "We'll invite each other over every day. And have sleepovers every weekend."

Oh, how wrong we were.

When sixth grade started, Lindsey fell in with the "popular" crowd, and I did not. I wasn't a nerd or unpopular or anything like that, but I just wasn't in that particular crowd.

Then the harassment started. Lindsey endlessly made fun of me and taunted me. "Rat face," she'd say. "You're so ugly. You have no friends. You're such a loser. At least I'm not a freak like you."

I didn't know what to do. I felt so bad. What had I done to turn such a wonderful friend against me? She eventually got all her friends to hate me too. They all trashed me and made fun of me to my face and behind my back.

Now I'm almost out of eighth grade, and Lindsey doesn't make fun of me anymore. At least not to my face. Maybe she still makes fun of me behind my back. But do you know what? I don't care anymore. I have come to realize that there is nothing wrong with me. I didn't do anything to her—she has her own issues, her own insecurities. It has nothing to do with me, and Lindsey is headed for a serious downfall. Throughout sixth, seventh and half of eighth grade, she made me feel bad. What a great way to spend her time. She also smokes, does drugs and skips classes. Where is that going to get her? Nowhere.

And where will I be? Stronger for putting up with it, living through it and doing it all without stooping to her level. And I feel a lot better for it.

Christina Shaw, 14

Sweet Lies

The naked truth is always better than the best-dressed lie.

Ann Landers

I moved from Massachusetts to North Carolina the summer before eighth grade. It didn't take me long to notice that my new classmates were a lot more interested in dating than my old friends had been. Girls on the bus continually talked about who was "going with" who. At first I didn't know what they meant. Having a boyfriend at twelve or thirteen? I was totally not ready for that!

Still, I was all ears when it came to other people's love lives. A boy named Garth was a major subject of gossip. Every other day, the rumors had him going out with a different girl. He was a year behind me, but he rode my bus so I knew who he was. He was blond and cute and very smooth. I thought he was a little too in love with himself, but I could see why he was popular.

Garth never seemed to pay much attention to me. Not that I expected him to—I was a new kid, sort of a nerd and not what most people would call pretty. So I was totally surprised when he called me up at home one day in February. He called to say he liked me. A lot. *Me!*

A day or two later, he took the seat behind me on the bus and started talking in a quiet, serious voice. He talked about himself, about the hard life he'd had.

"We moved a lot when I was a kid," he said. "So I never had a best friend. And maybe because of that, I've always been a loner. I can act friendly on the outside, but I always keep the real, deep parts of me hidden."

He leaned closer to me. "I guess I'm just too sensitive," he said. "I feel things, I take things really hard . . . so, I don't want people to get close."

I got off the bus thinking that I hadn't really been fair to Garth. He wasn't stuck up. That was just a face he put on, so people wouldn't know how sensitive he was. I felt sorry for him. He was so nice—and so unhappy!

A few days after that, Garth came by my house after school. We stood around on my porch talking for a long time. It was cold, but we didn't care. Actually, we didn't notice. We were too involved in our conversation.

"I have to tell you," he said. "I think I'm falling in love with you. You're just so amazing, so perfect—"

"No, I'm not!" I said, blushing.

"You are!" he insisted. "You're beautiful, you have great manners. . . ."

I'm not good with compliments even when I know they're true. But when they're *not* true, and I wish they were . . . "I'm not beautiful," I said. "I'm not even pretty."

"You *are* beautiful," said Garth. He put his arm around me. It felt strange, but I didn't try to stop him. "Look," he said. "I've gone with a lot of girls, and I know. You're special. You really are."

I shook my head, but I didn't try to argue.

"Listen," said Garth. "Tell you what—I'll help you stop

saying bad things about yourself, if you'll help me stop being so sensitive. Okay?"

I smiled at him. "Okay," I said.

He held me closer and bent his head like he was going to kiss me. I didn't know what to do. I turned away suddenly, and his face just brushed my cheek. I felt kind of clumsy, but I was glad he'd missed. I wasn't ready for kissing, and I honestly didn't like him "that way."

I felt all mixed up inside. I was happy and excited and totally flattered, but something still felt wrong. For one thing, I felt like I was pretending to love him when I really didn't. Shouldn't I tell him the truth? But how? And how could he be in love with me, anyway? He hardly knew me!

Just then my mom turned on the outside light, and Garth let go of me fast. He said, "See you tomorrow!" and took off down the road.

The house felt stuffy and warm after all that time outside. I dropped my books in the kitchen and ran up to my bedroom to think.

I really only liked Garth as a friend, but his arm *did* feel nice around me. And it was kind of cool having someone in love with me. I told myself it wasn't like I had to *do* anything about it. What did "going out" with someone mean anyway, besides just spending time together? I could just tell him I wasn't ready for kissing—couldn't I?

The next day on the bus, Garth acted like nothing had happened between us. He acted like we were just friends. I told myself he wanted to play it down so the other kids wouldn't tease us. But his acting seemed a little *too* good.

For the next few days, whenever we were alone, Garth talked about how he loved me. But when other people were around, he acted like we were just friends. Of course, I was just friends with him, but the whole thing was starting to bother me. Was he ashamed of liking me? Or was he lying about it in the first place? Why would he lie?

A week went by, and after that, I hardly saw Garth at all. That was okay. I didn't exactly miss him. I was so confused about him, about what had happened and about what it meant. Then about a month later, I heard something that helped me understand.

I was on the bus when I heard a girl mention Garth's name. "It's disgusting," she said. "They actually brag about how many girls they've kissed! Garth's got the most, of course."

"Yeah," said her friend. "Like every seventh- and eighth-grade girl in the school! I hear he's working on the ninth-graders now."

I felt like I'd been hit in the stomach. I just wanted to crawl under the seat and die. How could I have been so stupid? How could I have believed a single one of his ridiculous lies?

It took me a while, but eventually I got over it. After all, he fooled a lot of girls, not just me. I just wished I'd listened to that voice in my head that said something was wrong. Now I know better. I know that you should always listen to that little warning voice, because it's usually right.

Laura Gene Beck

Okay to Be Me

Each individual woman's body demands to be accepted on its own terms.

Gloria Steinem

"Miss Piggy!" she yelled loud enough for all of our classmates to hear but just out of earshot of the teacher. Unable to think of a quick and clever enough comeback, I simply responded with, "Shut up." Although my birth name was Monica, my own personal elementary school bully had dubbed me with a new title—"Miss Piggy."

The bully made my days in elementary school torturous. I am not sure why I was given the honor of being her daily target, but that was the case most of the time. It wasn't like she would beat me up or anything; as a matter of fact, she never even tried to put her hands on me. She only beat me down with her words, which sometimes hurt more than any blow to the body ever could. Even if she did try to sock me, her fist might have gotten lost in the abyss of flabbiness. Or perhaps it would have bounced back and knocked her out. Weighing in at 140 pounds at the age of eight, I couldn't blame her for her remarks, despite the fact that she was no skinny-mini herself.

After school one day, I came home in tears because of the teasing that I had endured from the bully.

"Oh, Sweetie, you're not fat—you're just big boned," said Mom, in an attempt to make me feel better. I was too worked up from my crying frenzy to respond. But I thought, *Just how big can a bone really be?* I've never seen a human skeleton in any books or on TV that had big bones, only dinosaurs. She led me down the hall so that we could stand in front of the full-length mirror on the bathroom door. She placed me in front of the mirror, stood behind me and said, "Monica, just look at those almond-shaped eyes and that beautiful skin."

I stared . . . and stared . . . and stared some more. I saw nothing. As I continued, a fresh batch of tears began to gather on my bottom lids. The liquid expanded over my eyeballs blurring my vision and morphing my image in the mirror. The more I stared, the more I started to look like . . . Miss Piggy.

Mom would always say that I was pretty. I never saw in myself what she saw in me. She was probably just saying all of this to make me feel better or because I was her daughter. As a matter of fact, several adults commented on how attractive I was *going* to be when I grew up. "Your mom is going to have to build a fence around the house with guard dogs to keep the boys out" is what they would say.

That night I stared in the mirror for hours trying to see those things that they saw—to no avail. I did not—or could not—see the things about me that they saw when I looked in the mirror. What I *did* see was a fat girl.

The next day at school, the assignment in gym class was to run a mile around the playground. I had never even attempted to run a few feet, and now I was expected to run a mile! Ten times around the playground was a mile, and it was timed. When the gym teacher blew the whistle to begin, I took off with all of my might. About forty-five seconds after I began running, I was sweating profusely and gasping for air.

I kept going though. I walked, jogged, ran, trotted, skipped and galloped. I tried any movement that my body could muster to keep pushing forward. I watched my classmates pass by me one by one out of the corner of my eye. And one by one, I watched as students began to finish. I was only on the fifth lap, which meant I was only halfway done. Pretty soon everyone was done except for me, and I still had two laps to go. I didn't let that stop me though. As long I still had a morsel of energy left in my body, I was not going to stop.

The class stood by and watched with an array of mixed emotions plastered across their faces as I completed my mile alone. Some people had a hopeful look in their eyes as if they were trying to will me along with eyesight alone, but most looked on with impatience and disgust. I continued to push on, although I only had enough energy left in my body to produce a staggered walk. Finally, drenched with perspiration, I approached the finish line. I was elated that I had completed the mile, but at the same time I felt defeated and embarrassed. When the teacher opened his mouth to speak, I braced myself because I was sure that he was about to use me as an example of what *not* to do.

The teacher looked at me, then turned to the class and said, "Class, Monica is an excellent example of what it means to try your best and never give up." *Had I heard him correctly?* He then continued on to say, "Even though she was the last one to finish, she never quit until she reached her goal." I somehow stammered a small, "Thanks . . ." as I felt the eyes of my classmates looking at me in admiration.

I may not have been the fastest or the thinnest kid in school, but on that day—at that moment—it felt okay to be me.

Monica Marie Jones

[EDITORS' NOTE: *For more information about developing self-respect and healthy lifestyles through running, log on to* www .girlsontherun.org.]

Ugly Girl

*Not being beautiful was the true blessing . . .
not being beautiful forced me to develop my
inner resources.*

Golda Meir

Every school has an ugly girl. In my elementary school,
it was me.

I had weak ankles. I kind of walked on the inside of my
feet. It's not like I had a career as an ice skater in my
future, but my parents were afraid it would get worse, so
from first grade through fourth, I had to wear clunky,
heavy orthopedic shoes. They seemed gigantic on my
feet, bright white and bubble-toed. The soles were super
sturdy, thick like an overdone pancake and about as
beautiful. They left marks on regular floors—you should
have seen what they did to the gym! Even the laces were
gross; extra wide and decorated in a puke-green and
brown check pattern. What I would have given to wear
slender, lightweight, beautiful shoes just once. I sounded
like an overweight elephant wearing bricks whenever I
took a single step.

"Hey, Bigfoot!"

"Geez, you're going to start an earthquake in those clodhoppers!"

"Frankenstein's coming, can't you hear her?"

Then in sixth grade, I had to start wearing glasses. Would my parents let me choose some stylish frames, something pretty? Not a chance—not if it wasn't on the rack labeled, "Absolute clearance! 75% off!" The optometrist might just have well said, "And, here we have the Pathetic Loser frames" when Mom asked for the least expensive ones. "But, Mom," I pleaded, "I'll look like a dork!"

"We're not spending money on fancy glasses that'll just break the first time you go out to play."

"Mom, these are pink plastic and have stars in the corners," I groaned.

"You're wearing them to see, not to be seen." She wouldn't let me get out of the car each day until I put my glasses on, then she would watch me walk into the school to be sure I didn't try to ditch them. Those frames were so hideous, they practically screamed to one and all, "Make fun of me! Call me names!"

"Four eyes!"

"Does your face hurt, 'cause it's killing me!"

"Couldn't you cover up more of your face? Why stop at the eyes?"

To counteract my newly acquired goofy look, I started competing on the city swim team, thinking that if I got a killer body, nobody would notice my face. Wrong again. I loved being fast and winning ribbons now and then, but now behind my geekoid glasses, I had red, dripping eyes from the chlorine in the pool. I smelled like bleach most of the time, and my hair turned green. I also did not, definitely did *not*, get a killer body. Why did I think that being an athlete in a swimsuit would turn me into someone who could model for *Sports Illustrated?* Instead of becoming a knockout, I looked like a linebacker; shoulders for days, no butt at all—in fact, no body fat anywhere. Not even where I wanted it.

"Flatsy-watsy!"

"Excuse me, little boy, . . . oops!"

"She doesn't wear a training bra, she wears a wishing bra—she wishes she had a chest!"

Eighth grade was supposed to be great. It was the last year of middle school, and there were tons of dances. My one good friend, Janet, showed me how to dance, and I practiced, practiced, practiced. The first dance was a casual after-school thing, and I didn't worry that I spent the whole afternoon leaning against the wall. Hardly any girls got asked to dance, not even Janet. The Holiday Ball was at night and much fancier, so I saved up baby-sitting money to buy a beautiful red velvet dress. I braided pretty silver ribbons into my hair and scooped all the braids up on the back of my head. I wore mascara for the first time. When I put the dress on that night, I gasped when I looked in the mirror. I twirled around like I was on a fashion runway. I smiled so hard my face hurt. The dress was gorgeous, and I glided into the gym confident that I would dance all night. It only took one fast song with a group of girls for me to sweat out the armpits, and the back from collar to waist. Dancing in a velvet dress in the hot gym had helped me go from awesome to awful in less than three minutes.

I stopped going to dances, certain the Hazardous Materials crew would come and hose me down, either for excessive sweating or polluting the gym with the smell of chlorine.

Spring of eighth grade was going to be my season—I was determined. I knew I'd never be popular. I just wanted to walk across the stage at the Culmination

Ceremony and not hear a bunch of giggles and taunts.

My strategy was to do good things for other people, to rack up a lot of points by being unfailingly nice. I became bold and approached the talented basketball player who couldn't write a paragraph and offered my help on a term paper. I sucked up my courage and asked the Holiday Ball Princess if she wanted me to baby-sit her little sister so she could hang out with her friends. When I saw a group of the truly cool girls at the mall, I suggested that they leave all their bags on a bench with me, while they continued shopping. My new program began to work—people who would never have acknowledged my existence before were suddenly seeking me out.

"Hey, Morri, you're strong—will you help me rake the leaves at my house after school?"

"Morri, could you give me some of your good ideas for this essay?"

"Morri, you're good at organizing. Will you come by my house tomorrow and help straighten the garage?"

"Morri, would you be a sweetie and help me address these envelopes?"

The envelopes did it. Up to that point, I'd been feeling pretty good about being seen as the kind of person you could come to, the person who had some skill and talent to offer to others. But when I went to Christine's house for the envelopes, I realized the truth. Going into each envelope was an invitation to Christine's birthday party; a big deal event at a fancy hotel, complete with dinner, the pool rented out just for her, and everyone was going to be picked up in one of the two limos she'd reserved. There was no envelope for me.

"Christine, do you have my address?"

"No, why?"

"Oh." I thought I'd figured it out. "Should I just take one home with me? You know, save you a stamp?"

"Um . . . Morri . . . um," she stammered, "there isn't an invitation for you. I don't have any extras."

My mouth fell open like the Grand Canyon. My eyes were as wide as serving platters. "Morri, it's my birthday. I'm really only inviting my closest friends," Christine explained, licking the twentieth envelope.

I choked a little, blinked a lot, said I understood and walked home. That's what you call Being Used, Being a Sucker, winning the award for Most Clueless.

From that moment through June, I tried to be as inconspicuous as possible. I wanted to escape the hypercritical eyes of middle school and just make it through the summer. High school had to be better, right?

Yes and no. Now that I'm here, I've found out that there are still lots of shallow people who like you or not based on what you're wearing or how cool your hair is. Some kids still think that being popular is the highest goal a person can achieve. But there are also kids who talk to you because they liked your answers in European history or because they thought your art piece was pretty special. Some kids couldn't care less what you wear, as long as you're kind, honest and a good friend.

And there are a whole bunch of kids who want to start making changes in the world now, not waiting until they're all grown up. I volunteer with some of those kids because I like the feeling I get when I am helping people. Jen asked me to join her at a food bank, boxing up groceries for needy families. I went with Hamal when he drove some old people to their doctor's appointments. And I loved it when about twenty of us started hanging out at Children's Hospital, playing games and reading to the sick kids.

This year, eleventh grade, I got braces. Add that to my green hair, drippy red eyes, flat chest and the pervasive smell of chlorine—I'm not getting any modeling contracts.

But you can't tell me I'm not beautiful. Every time I visit the hospital, five-year-old Terry grabs my hand and coos, "Morri, you're so nice. I want to grow up to be just like you."

Morri Spang

Afterword

The road of life is full of bumps,
Potholes, twists and turns.
There are constant battles that you will fight
And lessons you will learn.

How I've been helped along the road,
I didn't realize until now.
There were times when I didn't see the signs,
But there was someone to show me how.

How to grow, how to live,
And even how to love.
We've had our laughs, had our cries,
And even shared some hugs.

Throughout the years with my friends,
We all grew up as one.
But there is still a road ahead.
Our growing up is not done.

Soon the road ahead will split,
And we'll go our separate ways.
We won't forget the road behind,
But we have to grow up someday.

It's time for you to choose your road
And grow up on your own.
I realize now, we're getting older,
And we have to let each other go.

But when you need me, I'll be there.
The one lone little star
Lighting up a path for you,
No matter where you are.

And now we see the path ahead,
With all its twists and turns.
We look forward to who we'll become
Not forgetting the girls we were.

Rachel Punches, 18

Who Is Jack Canfield?

Jack Canfield is one of America's leading experts in the development of human potential and personal effectiveness. He is both a dynamic, entertaining speaker and a highly sought-after trainer.

He is the author and narrator of several bestselling audio and videocassette programs, including *Self-Esteem and Peak Performance, How to Build High Self-Esteem, Self-Esteem in the Classroom* and *Chicken Soup for the Soul—Live.* He is regularly seen on television shows such as *Good Morning America, 20/20* and *NBC Nightly News.* Jack has co-authored numerous books, including the *Chicken Soup for the Soul* series, *Dare to Win* and *The Aladdin Factor* (all with Mark Victor Hansen), *100 Ways to Build Self-Concept in the Classroom* (with Harold C. Wells) *Heart at Work* (with Jacqueline Miller) *The Power of Focus* (with Les Hewitt and Mark Victor Hansen) and *The Success Principles: How to Get from Where You Are to Where You Want to Be.*

Jack is a regularly featured speaker for professional associations, school districts, government agencies, churches, hospitals, sales organizations and corporations. His clients have included the American Dental Association, the American Management Association, AT&T, Campbell's Soup, Clairol, Domino's Pizza, GE, ITT, Hartford Insurance, Johnson & Johnson, the Million Dollar Roundtable, NCR, New England Telephone, Re/Max, Scott Paper, TRW and Virgin Records. Jack is also on the faculty of Income Builders International, a school for entrepreneurs.

Jack conducts an annual seven-day Breakthrough to Success program in the areas of self-esteem and peak performance. The program attracts educators, counselors, parenting trainers, corporate trainers, professional speakers and others from the general public who are interested in creating their ideal life.

Self-Esteem Seminars
P.O. Box 30880 • Santa Barbara, CA 93130
Phone: 805-563-2935 • Fax: 805-563-2945
Website: *www.jackcanfield.com*
E-mail: *info4jack@jackcanfield.com*

Who Is Mark Victor Hansen?

In the area of human potential, no one is more respected than Mark Victor Hansen. For more than thirty years, Mark has focused solely on helping people from all walks of life reshape their personal vision of what's possible. His powerful messages of possibility, opportunity and action have created impressive change in thousands of organizations and millions of individuals worldwide.

He is a highly sought-after keynote speaker, bestselling author and marketing maven. Mark's credentials include a lifetime of entrepreneurial success and an extensive academic background. He is a prolific writer with many bestselling books such as *The One Minute Millionaire, Cracking the Millionaire Code, The Power of Focus, The Aladdin Factor* and *Dare to Win*, in addition to the wildly successful *Chicken Soup for the Soul* series. Mark has made a profound influence through his library of audios, videos and articles in the areas of big thinking, sales achievement, wealth building, publishing success, and personal and professional development.

Mark is the founder of the MEGA Seminar Series, MEGA Book Marketing University and Building Your MEGA Speaking Empire. Both are annual conferences where Mark coaches and teaches new and aspiring authors, speakers and experts on building lucrative publishing and speaking careers. Other MEGA events include MEGA Marketing Magic and My MEGA Life.

He has appeared on television (*Oprah, CNN* and *The Today Show*) in print (*Time, U.S. News & World Report; USA Today, New York Times* and *Entrepreneur*) and on countless radio interviews, assuring our planet's people that "You can easily create the life you deserve."

As a philanthropist and humanitarian, Mark works tirelessly for organizations such as Habitat for Humanity, American Red Cross, March of Dimes, Childhelp and many others. He is the recipient of numerous awards that honor his entrepreneurial spirit, philanthropic heart and business acumen. He is a lifetime member of the Horatio Alger Association of Distinguished Americans, an organization that honored Mark with the prestigious Horatio Alger Award for his extraordinary life achievements.

Mark Victor Hansen is an enthusiastic crusader of what's possible and is driven to make the world a better place.

Mark Victor Hansen & Associates, Inc.
P.O. Box 7665
Newport Beach, CA 92658-7665
Phone: 949-764-2640 x101
Fax: 949-722-6912
www.markvictorhansen.com

Who Is Patty Hansen?

Patty Hansen, with her partner, Irene, authored *Chicken Soup for the Kid's Soul, Chicken Soup for the Preteen Soul, Chicken Soup for the Preteen Soul 2* and *Chicken Soup Christmas Treasury for Kids*—all books that kids ages nine through thirteen love to read and use as guides for everyday life. Patty is also the contributor of some of the most loved stories in the *Chicken Soup for the Soul* series and is coauthor of *Condensed Chicken Soup for the Soul* (Health Communications) and *Out of the Blue: Delight Comes Into Our Lives* (HarperCollins).

Because of her love for preteens, Patty created *Preteenplanet.com*, a Website that gives preteens a fun and safe online experience where they can also become empowered to make their world a better place. Check it out!

Prior to her career as an author, Patty worked for United Airlines as a flight attendant for thirteen years. During that time, she received two commendations for bravery. She received the first one when, as the only flight attendant on board, she prepared forty-four passengers for a successful planned emergency landing. The second was for single-handedly extinguishing a fire on board a mid-Pacific flight, thus averting an emergency situation and saving hundreds of lives.

After "hanging up her wings," Patty became the chief financial officer for M.V. Hansen and Associates, Inc., in Newport Beach, California. Since 1998 Patty has been president of legal and licensing for Chicken Soup for the Soul Enterprises, Inc., and has helped to create an entire line of *Chicken Soup for the Soul* products and licenses.

Patty shares her home life with her two daughters Elisabeth and Melanie; newest addition, grandson Seth (he is SO awesome!); her mother, Shirley; housekeeper and friend, Eva; three rabbits, one peahen, one guinea hen, four horses, three dogs, ten cats, three birds, fifty-five fish, eight pigeons, thirty-four chickens (yes, they all have names), a haven for hummingbirds and a butterfly farm.

If you would like to contact Patty:

Patty Hansen
P.O. Box 10879 • Costa Mesa, CA 92627
Phone: 949-749-9304 ext. 108 • Fax: 949-645-3203
E-mail: *patty@preteenplanet.com*
Website: *www.preteenplanet.com*

Who Is Irene Dunlap?

Irene Dunlap, coauthor of *Chicken Soup for the Kid's Soul, Chicken Soup for the Preteen Soul, Chicken Soup for the Soul Christmas Treasury for Kids* and *Chicken Soup for the Preteen Soul 2*, began her writing career in elementary school, when she discovered her love for creating poetry, a passion she believes she inherited from her paternal grandmother. She went on to express her love for words through writing fictional short stories and lyrics, as a participant in speech competitions, and eventually as a vocalist.

During her college years, Irene traveled around the world as a student of the Semester at Sea program aboard a ship that served as a classroom, as well as home base, for more than 500 college students. After earning a bachelor of arts degree in communications, she became the media director of Irvine Meadows Amphitheatre in Irvine, California, and eventually co-owned an advertising and public relations agency that specialized in entertainment and health care clients.

Irene released her first book in a series titled *TRUE—Real Stories About God Showing Up in the Lives of Teens*, in February 2004, to encourage teens and young adults in their faith. While creating difference-making books, which she sees as a blessing, Irene continues to support her two teens with their interests while carrying on a successful singing career, performing various styles, from jump swing and jazz to contemporary music, at church and at special events.

Irene lives in Newport Beach, California, with her husband, Kent; daughter, Marleigh; son, Weston; and Australian shepherd, Gracie. In her spare time, Irene enjoys horseback riding, gardening, cooking and painting. If you are wondering how she does it all, she will refer you to her favorite Bible passage for her answer—Ephesians 3:20.

If you would like to contact Irene:

Irene Dunlap
P.O. Box 10879
Costa Mesa, CA 92627
Fax: 949-645-3203
E-mail: *irene@lifewriters.com*
Website: *www.lifewriters.com*

What Is *Discovery Girls* Magazine?

If you love connecting with other girls, check out *Discovery Girls*. The magazine by girls, for girls ages eight to twelve, *Discovery Girls* gives you a voice and lets you know you are not alone. Started in 2000, *Discovery Girls* now reaches more than half a million girls with every issue! And they are in touch with their readers like no other magazine—*you* write the articles, model for them (even appear on the cover!), and help decide what goes on the pages. *Discovery Girls* is truly *your* magazine!

So what's inside *Discovery Girls*? Everything you love most!

- Inspiring stories from girls like you about friendships, cliques, family problems and tough times. It's all here!
- Special features that help you deal—with mean girls, the pressures of popularity, demanding teachers, rejection, confusing crushes . . .
- Cool quizzes, exciting contests and fun-to-make crafts . . .
- Hilarious (and mortifying!) embarrassing moments, advice from girls who care, sports tips . . .
- Fabulous fashions, your favorite celebrities, the best in books, CDs and movies . . .
- And much, much more! If you love it—*DG* has it!

To connect with other girls and learn more about yourself and your world, order *Discovery Girls*—your ultimate survival guide—today! You'll find it online at *discovery girls.com*. Don't miss another issue!

Contributors

Jenny Aguilar is a twelve-year-old who dreams of being a singer when she grows up. Her idol is singer, Selena, whom she identifies with. Jenny enjoys going to the beach, cooking, dancing and shopping with her mother. It is her dream to one day meet her relatives in El Salvador.

Laura Andrade is a teacher with a passion for kids, animals and science. She shares her California home with her husband, two cats, two dogs and two horses. Life is good!

Kellyrose Andrews is a student in San Diego, California. She enjoys singing, playing bass guitar, dancing and hanging out at the beach. She dreams of making it as a model or would like to start her own record label for female rockers. Contact her at *dancingkitty697@yahoo.com*.

Lindsey Appleton is an eighth-grader who lives in Hawaii. Her original songs and poems have been enjoyed by many audiences. She hopes to attend a performing arts college to become a professional singer. Lindsey's hobbies include acting, guitar, singing, dancing, horseback riding and team sports.

Carol Ayer received her bachelor's in English from University of California, Berkeley, in 1984. She has been published in *Chicken Soup to Inspire a Woman's Soul, Woman's World Magazine, RunnersWorld.com* and *PoeticVoices.com*. She is currently at work on a children's book and an adult novel.

Laura Gene Beck studied psychology and language at two famous universities. Living in San Francisco, she works as a user-interface designer at various high-tech start-ups and writes children's fiction and poetry. She is married and has two brilliant children and a codependent cat. E-mail Laura at *writing laura@yahoo.com*.

Kathleen Benefiel is a seventeen-year-old who loves writing, journalism and law and who plans to pursue her interests at a university in the fall of 2006. She also plans to write an autobiography about her misadventures in middle and high school.

Robert Berardi was born in New York and educated at University of the Arts, Philadelphia. Robert writes and draws *No Rodeo,* a comic strip about a preteen girl named Desiree. *No Rodeo* can be seen on *PreteenPlanet.com* and will soon be syndicated to daily and Sunday newspapers. Go to *robtberardi@yahoo.com*.

Anna Bittner is a high school senior who lives in Hawaii. She enjoys reading, painting and playing Halo 2. She plans to attend college and major in marine science.

Meredith Brown is attending Indiana University in Bloomington, where she is majoring in journalism. She is a member of the Indiana Field Hockey team and enjoys playing/watching sports, listening to music, and being with her family and friends. She is the fifth of six children and lives in Maryland.

Anne Broyles is a writer and a United Methodist minister. She is the author/coauthor of twelve books, including children's picture books *Shy Mama's Halloween* (Tilbury, 2000) and the upcoming *Priscilla and the Hollyhocks* (Charlesbridge Books, 2007).

Courtney Bullock attends high school in Virginia, where she enjoys reading, running, singing, writing poetry, playing piano, tenor sax, flute, clarinet, guitar and dancing. Courtney is a youth leader at her church and has been a Girl Scout since kindergarten. She plans to major in music, dance and or/literature.

Kelsey Lyn Carone is a thirteen-year-old honor student who enjoys soccer, reading, writing, cooking and being with friends. She has a ten-year-old brother, two dogs, four cats and one fish. Her goals are to graduate from college and pursue a career in writing.

Carrie Joy Carson is a business student at the University of Southern California. Her favorite activities include reading, scrapbooking and driving around Los Angeles. She hopes to someday become a marketing executive and live in New York City.

Cynthia Charlton is an aspiring writer with hopes of helping others heal through the written word, based on her life experiences. She enjoys reading, writing and spending time with her husband, David, and their two miniature dachshunds. E-mail Cindy at *cindy_700@hotmail.com* or visit her Website at *members.shaw.ca/fortheloveofwriting*.

Jennifer Lynn Clay, fifteen, has been published more than thirty times in national and international magazines and in several books, including *Chicken Soup for the Preteen Soul 2*. A state finalist for *Power of the Pen* in 2004, she has appeared on live television and given several radio interviews about her accomplishments as a writer.

Maudie Conrad has been writing since she was in middle school. When given an assignment to write about America's history, her story won an award. She is a wife and mother of four and enjoys spending time with her family, as well as with her extended family at church.

Olga Cossi, the author of "Big Sister," credits being a sister as one of the most important roles in her life. Her list of published books continues to give her the pleasure of sharing her many adventures with young readers, and her avocation as a visiting author keeps her ageless.

Sarah Crunican was born in Perm, Russia. At age four, she was adopted into a family of her new mother and her newly adopted brother. She attends middle school in Seattle and enjoys reading, writing, and playing soccer, basketball, and softball.

Marion Distante, fourteen, likes soccer, writing, drawing and traveling. She hopes to pursue a career in law or possibly to write a novel.

Stephanie Dodson graduated with a degree in English from the University of the Pacific. Currently working for a public television station in northern California, her ultimate goals are to write young adult novels and to learn to surf. E-mail her at *stephd711@hotmail.com.*

Rosephine Fernandes is a thirteen-year-old student from Bahrain. She can't live without shopping, sports, drama, her friends and family. She enjoys all her subjects in school except math. Rosephine makes the most of life and takes every opportunity to make a difference because her teenage years are unlike any other.

Ashleigh Figler-Ehrlich found inspiration for her story in her mother, who continues to be her champion. When Ashleigh was eight, she purchased her first horse, Soxy, and started her own tack-cleaning business. It is her dream to attend UCLA and work for NASA in the space division.

Melinda Fillingim is a middle-aged therapist in Rome, Georgia, who goes around with her husband, David, singing songs and telling stories to anyone who will listen (usually church groups). Her daughter, Hope, who is sixteen, inspires many of these stories as she did when her mom had less wrinkles five years ago.

Hattie Frost is a student at Miami University in Oxford, Ohio, where she is studying to become a special education teacher. She is actively involved in Alpha Phi Omega, a coed service fraternity, as well as many other organizations. In her spare time, she enjoys writing.

Marcela Dario Fuentes attends Pennsylvania State University, where she is a student in the school of music. She enjoys playing her bassoon, traveling, reading, and spending time with friends and family. She plans to move back to her native Honduras and play in an orchestra there. Please e-mail her at *fdw5001@psu.edu.*

Elizabeth Geocaris, age nine, is the African American model on the cover of *Chicken Soup for the Girl's Soul.* She loves to dance and is part of a dance performance and competition team. Elizabeth also enjoys piano and tennis. She plans to attend college and become a dancer and choreographer.

Kacy Gilbert-Gard is a seventh-grader from Fairbanks, Alaska, who enjoys writing fiction stories and poems. She likes playing soccer, downhill skiing, swimming and hanging out with friends. She hopes to work with animals when she grows up.

Cheryl L. Goede has been a police officer in Missouri for more than seven years. She works with teens and is an advisor in her department's Police

Explorer Post. She loves her job, even when she has to respond to calls for someone egging a house.

Paula Goldsmith lives in Norfolk, England, and is a fulltime wife and mum of two sons and one daughter. She is a freelance writer and has recently branched out into photography. Her interests include the countryside, poetry, family outings and crafts. E-mail her at *paula.goldsmith@ntlworld.com*.

Roxanne Gowharrizi is a senior in high school. She loves her family and friends and wants to thank them for being there and making her laugh. She has dreamed of being published in a *Chicken Soup for the Soul* book, and she thanks the publishers for making it come true.

Tonya K. Grant is a teacher and freelance writer living in Lithonia, Georgia. She was eighteen when she wrote the poem "Dreams." Now, at thirty-four, she has been published in various magazines and is a member of The Society of Children's Book Writers and Illustrators.

Alison Gunn received her bachelor of arts degree, with a double major in writing and English, from the University of Victoria in 2004. She loves writing and her many adventures with her husband, Mike Sheehan, and puppy, Nila. Alison can be reached at *alisheehan@yahoo.com*.

Angelica Haggert is fifteen years old and enjoys swimming, playing baseball and doing scouting activities. After high school, she plans to be a teacher or to work with children in some way.

Cynthia M. Hamond has been published numerous times in the *Chicken Soup for the Soul* series and *Multnomah's Stories for the Heart*. Her stories have been in major publications, magazines and King Features Syndication. She has received writing recognitions, and two of her stories have been on TV. E-mail her at *Candbh@aol.com*.

Pamela Hamalainen began writing poems and short stories when she was twelve years old. She resides with her husband in Georgia, where she works as an information specialist. She has two children and three grandchildren and plans to submit her book of inspirational poems for publication.

Penny S. Harmon is a real estate agent in Maine. She enjoys spending time with her two teenaged children and hopes to travel the country while continuing to write.

Kathy Lynn Harris grew up amid the flatlands of south Texas. She now lives along the Continental Divide in Colorado. She has completed two novels and published nonfiction, poetry, short fiction and essays. Discover more of her work at *www.kathylynnharris.com*. She'd love to hear from you via *kathy@kathylynnharris.com*.

Ashleigh E. Heiple is a sophomore in high school, is a member of the swim team and track team, and is a majorette in the marching band. She enjoys performing in school musicals and spending time with her family and friends. She would like to attend the University of Pittsburgh and major in medicine.

Bethany Gail Hicks is attending Texas Tech University in Lubbock, Texas, majoring in English. She enjoys reading, spending time with friends and family, swimming, and listening to music. She plans on becoming a high school English teacher and eventually return to school for a master's degree in library science.

Sarah Hood, thirteen, enjoys reading and writing stories and plans to be an author. She also likes swimming and skiing, and she loves her friends and family.

Tasha R. Howe received her Ph.D. from the University of California, Riverside. She is currently a developmental psychology professor at Humboldt State University in California. Tasha loves reading, writing, exploring nature, traveling and music of all kinds.

Leigh Hughes lives in Texas with her husband and three children and is the editor-in-chief/publisher of the literary journal edifice WRECKED. Her work has appeared in *NFG Magazine, Word Riot, The Glut, Gator Springs Gazette, Underground Voices, Sexy Stranger #5* and *Moondance*, as well as several other online and print venues, and is forthcoming in *BOOM! For Real, Volume 2* and *VOX*. She can be reached at *rleighhughes@yahoo.com*.

Monica Marie Jones received her bachelor of arts with honors in elementary education from Eastern Michigan University and her masters of social work from the University of Michigan. The program director of a nonprofit youth center, Monica enjoys writing, dancing and acting, event planning, traveling, and modeling. She is writing three novels and a poetry book series. E-mail her at *monicamjones@hotmail.com*.

Elizabeth Kay Kidd is in seventh grade and is a cheerleader and a member of her school choir. She enjoys reading and writing and is an avid snowboarder. She loves to be with friends and is a good big sister. Elizabeth loves school and is looking forward to high school.

Katelyn Krieger is fourteen years old and loves writing, singing, dancing and reading. She writes lyrics to her own songs, and in the future, she hopes to write a book.

Kayla K. Kurashige is a freshman in high school on the Big Island of Hawaii. She enjoys writing, playing sports and going to the beach. Kayla dedicates her story in loving memory of her best friend, Ku'ulei Kauhaihao.

Mary Laufer is a freelance writer living in Forest Grove, Oregon. She wrote "The Bust Developer" at forty-six, when she was finally far enough away from the experience to see humor in it. She is currently finishing a children's chapter book about a girl and her crow.

Kathryn Lay has had over 1,000 articles and stories published in magazines and anthologies. Her first children's novel, Crown Me!, is available from

Holiday House books. Check out her Website at *www.kathrynlay.com* to learn about her book, writing classes, speaking and school visits. E-mail *rlay15@aol.com.*

Vivian Ling, thirteen, enjoys Maroon 5, Harry Potter, Vanessa Carlton, and *The Circle of Magic* and *The Circle Opens* series by Tamora Pierce. She is known at her school as vice president, a starter on the volleyball team, concertmaster of the orchestra and someone who falls off of chairs daily.

Laurie Lonsdale of Toronto, Canada, is the author of several women's fiction novels, such as *Neon Nights, Hollywood Blues, Wild Side* and the upcoming *Four of Hearts.* She enjoys music, travel and interior design. To view more of her work, please visit *authorsden.com/laurielonsdale.*

Karin A. Lovold resides in Minnesota with her husband and three daughters. She loves writing, reading and spending time in the beautiful woods of northern Minnesota. She's currently working on two novels and several short stories. E-mail her at *kal3860@chartermi.net.*

Sammi Lupher is an eighth-grader who is involved in cheerleading and is the student council president at her school. Sammi plans to attend college and pursue a career in performing.

Sammie Luther is a freshman in high school and enjoys chatting on the Internet, hanging out with friends and, like any other fifteen-year-old girl, going to the mall. Samantha hopes to major in psychology and become a psychology teacher.

Katherine Anne Magee, a senior in high school, wrote "The Day I Gave My Panties Away" for her ninth-grade English class. Katherine plans to pursue an honors degree in science and hopes to have a career related to mathematics or geriatric medicine.

Zainab Mahmood is an eighth-grade student in Bahrain. She enjoys reading, movies, playing basketball, tennis, acting and, of course, writing. She'd like to say a big "Hey, I'm in a book!" to all her friends and family. Zainab plans to be a journalist or an author. Meanwhile, she enjoys her life just being a normal preteen girl.

Emily Malloy graduated from Michigan State University with an English degree. She was previously a monthly columnist carried by Blue Jean Online and Knight-Ridder/Tribune News Services. Since writing her story, she has been blessed to marry the man who counted to three for her.

Melanie Marks was born and raised in California. She is married to a U.S. Naval officer and blessed with three amazingly terrific kids. She writes for many children and young adult magazines, and her first teen novel is *The Dating Deal.* You can e-mail her at *bymelaniemarks@comcast.net.*

Stephanie Marquez is an eighth-grader who enjoys playing the viola and dancing with Dy.Nam.X Dance Entertainment and teaching fifth- and sixth-grade dance with Kids Edition. She also likes cooking with her father and shopping with her mother, and she loves life!

Nydja K. Minor is a seventh-grade honor student who comes from a large family. She enjoys creative writing, reading and basketball. She has two dogs, Lady and Kika. Nydja plans to become a writer.

Lindsay Oberst is a senior and will be attending the University of Georgia this fall. She enjoys reading books and writing and has been published several times. She also enjoys shopping and having fun with her friends.

Samantha Ott is an eighth-grader who enjoys cheerleading, performing in musicals and dancing. She loves working with children and hopes someday to be an editor for a successful fashion magazine.

Melanie Pastor is a kindergarten teacher in southern California with a masters in education from Pepperdine University. She is publishing a children's book entitled *Wishes for One More Day*, about the death of a grandparent. She loves inline skating, swimming, skiing and traveling. Contact her at *joy@gettingmail.com*.

Satya Pennington is a national Scholastic Arts and Writing Awards winner for poetry who is currently coauthoring a young adult book. Published in several newspapers and magazines, she wants to become a medical broadcast journalist after high school—but until then, she is a teenage advice columnist in the local newspaper.

Michelle Peters, now an adult, vividly remembers the "Hair Horror" that occurred when she was thirteen. She operates her own business, SnomobileWear.com, which manufactures snowsuits designed for those confined to wheelchairs. Michelle was published in the *Cup of Comfort* series and writes a weekly journal for the parenting Website *BabyCenter.com*.

Rachel Punches graduated from Muskegon Catholic Central in 2002 and is now serving our country in the U.S. Army National Guard. Spc. Punches was deployed in October 2004 to Taji, Iraq, with the Transportation Unit. She enjoys reading, writing and watching movies.

Khristine J. Quibilan was born in the Philippines and moved to California when she was five years old. She is pursuing a bachelor of arts in psychology at the University of San Francisco. When she isn't busy with school and extracurricular activities, she enjoys life by working out and spending time with family and friends.

Mina Radman, thirteen, lives with her mother, father and younger brother. She enjoys hanging out with friends, music, movies, TV and surfing the Internet. Mina hopes to be an actress when she grows up.

Barbara J. Ragsdale majored in music education and English in college, plays piano and organ, and has directed children's choirs. She is a certified aerobics instructor for both land and water exercise and works for a company that specializes in custom-made ocular prosthesis for children and adults. Please e-mail her at *barbara@lragsdale.com*.

Paige Rasmussen is a sixth-grade student who is involved in water polo, piano and track. She enjoys reading and being with her family and friends. Paige plans to attend college and play water polo professionally.

Bethany Rogers is a graduate of Middlebury College and Princeton Theological Seminary and has worked as a freelance writer for more than three years. Bethany lives in Denver, Colorado, with her husband and her dog, Duke.

Kim Rogers earned a bachelor's in journalism/public relations from the University of Central Oklahoma in 1993. She resides in Oklahoma with her wonderful husband and two rambunctious boys. She enjoys traveling, kick-boxing and running. She is working on her first novel for teen girls. Please e-mail her at *kkrest1996@yahoo.com*.

Hope Rollins is an eighth-grader who enjoys writing, acting and being with her friends and family.

Gabby Romanello, one of the cover girls, is a fifth-grader who has a passion for dance. She is on a dance performance team and also competes solo. Gabby enjoys acting, singing, writing songs, reading and sewing. She is a straight A student whose goal is to attend the Orange County High School of the Arts, and hopefully one day, Juilliard.

Lauren Alyson Schara, nineteen, lives with her family in Indiana. She enjoys reading and writing—especially poetry. She loves all types of music and attends music festivals every summer with her friends. She loves to travel and be adventurous.

Chloe Scott, a fourteen-year-old from Canada, is a stereotypical bookworm, which has led to her love of writing. She also loves the ocean, dance and golf, and dreams of becoming a successful author.

Christina Shaw, fifteen, a sophomore in high school, plans to attend college, where she will study psychology or education. She enjoys singing, running and dancing.

Lahre Shiflet is a thirteen-year-old cartoonist from northern California. Her work has been featured in other *Chicken Soup for the Soul* books, and she has had her own cartoon strip in the local newspaper for more than a year. Lahre enjoys shopping at the mall and checking out the guys.

Brittany Shope, seventeen, has always dreamed of being a writer who writes something meaningful to others. Aside from writing, she wants to create her own primetime television show. She enjoys her job at a local pizza restaurant, and her favorite hobby is blowing bubbles.

Robin Sokol received her bachelor of arts and masters of communication from the University of Dubuque. She is an IT technician for a quarry company in eastern Iowa. Robin has three children who she enjoys spending time with, and she likes to write mysteries in her spare time. E-mail her at *rsokol@dbq.edu*.

Diane Sonntag is an elementary school teacher and freelance writer. She lives in Indianapolis with her husband and two young children. She can be reached at *Rydeej@sbcglobal.net*.

Morri Spang started writing as soon as she knew the alphabet. But only after retiring from a twenty-five-year teaching career did she devote time to writing pieces she'd let others read. Published in several youth and parent's magazines, Morri is now completing a young adult novel. Reach her at *mospang@aol.com*.

Kirsten Lee Strough is currently a high school sophomore in a small town in Idaho. She has published several poems and has submitted an array of short stories to various publishers. Writing isn't her only creative outlet, however. She is also drawn toward the art of music and filmmaking.

Ariel G. Subrahmanyam is a twelve-year-old Christian girl who is home schooled. She has five sisters and five brothers and loves to baby-sit, read, bicycle, cook and take care of her two birds. Ariel enjoys being part of a big family and wants to someday have lots of children.

Rita M. Tubbs is a stay-at-home mom and a freelance writer from Michigan. Her first nonfiction book for children will be published in 2005. In her spare time, Rita enjoys taking walks in the great outdoors. Please e-mail her at *ritatubbs@hsenet.com*.

Courtney VanDyne is an eighth-grade student living in North Carolina. She is an avid athlete and is a member of the cross-country, basketball, track and soccer teams at her school. She has served as Student Council president for the past two years and is a member of the BETA Club. Her story, "BFF," was originally an entry in her journal—a way to help her deal with very painful feelings. Courtney dedicates this story to Michelle, not to make her cry, but just to think of it as a little love from her and for Michelle to read when she is looking for a sisterly hug.

Katy Van Hoy studies elementary education at the University of North Carolina at Charlotte. She enjoys working with children, cheerleading, gymnastics and painting.

Natalie Ver Woert, a junior in high school, participates in marching band and varsity softball and plays competitive softball in the summer. Natalie plans to attend a state university and major in journalism.

Anna Vier is a junior in high school who enjoys music, drama, writing, shopping, coffee with friends and laughing. She is active in multiple high school clubs and her youth group at church, and she enjoys going on mission trips. Her future plans include attending the University of Georgia or Georgia Tech.

Karen Waldman, Ph.D., loves working as a psychologist. She also enjoys writing, nature, music, acting, dancing, traveling with her husband, Ken, and spending time with her wonderful friends and her children and grandchildren—Lisa, Tom, Lana, Greta and Eric.

Sandra Wallace and her husband, Charles, live in Kansas, where they have two grown sons and a grandson. Her story "Mourning the Loss, Mending the Heart" is in *Chicken Soup for the Romantic Soul.* Sandra centers on God, family and music, spending time with her two-year-old grandson, and working part-time for a recreation facility. E-mail her at *sandykay1@sbcglobal.net.*

Devoreaux Walton is a sophomore in high school. She enjoys hanging out with friends and shopping. She plans to continue writing.

Kristen Weil, fifteen, enjoys writing songs, poems and stories. She loves to sing and dance and be with friends.

Elizabeth White, fifteen, enjoys reading, writing, spending time with friends and family, and attending church. She plans to attend a four-year university and become a journalist or a high school English teacher.

Dallas Nicole Woodburn is a senior in high school. Her magazine credits include *Family Circle, Writer's Digest, Justine, Listen, Encounter* and *Writing.* She has also been published in *So, You Wanna Be a Writer?* and *Chicken Soup for the Teenage Soul.*

Julie Workman is a wife and mom of four children, three of whom are girls. Her story, "Late Bloomer," holds vivid memories of the trials of girlhood, and she looks forward to walking through those trials with her girls. A freelance writer for Christian magazines, she is a contributor to *Chicken Soup for the Sister's Soul.*

Permissions

We would like to acknowledge the following publishers and individuals for permission to reprint the following material. (Note: The stories that were penned anonymously, that are in the public domain, or that were written by Jack Canfield, Mark Victor Hansen, Patty Hansen or Irene Dunlap are not included in this listing.)

Opening poem. Reprinted by permission of Meredith Brown. ©2004 Meredith Brown.

Introduction. Reprinted by permission of Vivian Ling and Cecilia Zhao. ©2004 Vivian Ling.

Introduction. Reprinted by permission of Lindsey Appleton and Maureen A. L. Appleton. ©2002 Lindsey Appleton.

Introduction. Reprinted by permission of Paige Rasmussen and Shani Rasmussen. ©2003 Paige Rasmussen.

Introduction. Reprinted by permission of Devoreaux Walton, Rodd Walton and Athena Walton. ©2004 Devoreaux Walton.

Straight Up Girl Stuff chapter opener. Reprinted by permission of Courtney Bullock and Yvette Benton Bullock. ©2004 Courtney Bullock.

A Perfect Fit. Reprinted by permission of Kathy Lynn Harris. ©2004 Kathy Lynn Harris.

Not Just for Girls Anymore! Reprinted by permission of Diane Sonntag. ©2004 Diane Sonntag.

The Bust Developer. Reprinted by permission of Mary Laufer. ©2003 Mary Laufer.

"One Day You'll Look Back on This . . ." Reprinted by permission of Laurie Lonsdale. ©2004 Laurie Lonsdale.

The Day I Gave My Panties Away. Reprinted by permission of Katherine Magee and Leonard Maxwell Magee. ©2002 Katherine Magee.

Unidentified Floating Object. Reprinted by permission of Sandra Wallace. ©2005 Sandra Wallace.

Girl to Girl opener. Reprinted by permission of Zainab Mahmood and Manzur Mahmood. ©2004 Zainab Mahmood.

Girl to Girl opener. Reprinted by permission of Rosephine Fernandes and Michael John Fernandes. ©2004 Rosephine Fernandes.

Do Girls Belong? Reprinted by permission of Angelica Haggert and Shelley Divnich Haggert. ©2002 Angelica Haggert.

I've Got the Power chapter opener. Reprinted by permission of Kelsey Carone and Melissa Carone. ©2004 Kelsey Carone.

Big Things. Reprinted by permission of Dallas Nicole Woodburn and Woody Woodburn. ©2002 Dallas Woodburn.

Call Me. Reprinted by permission of Cynthia M. Hamond. ©1998 Cynthia Hamond.

The Slam Book. Reprinted by permission of Barbara J. Ragsdale. ©2004 Barbara Ragsdale.

Compassion for a Bully. Reprinted by permission of Melanie Pastor. ©1989 Melanie Pastor.

The Most Important Lesson. Reprinted by permission of Hope Rollins. ©2005 Hope Rollins.

Dreams. Reprinted by permission of Tonya K. Grant. ©1989 Tonya Grant.

Lost and Found Dream. Reprinted by permission of Kathryn Lay. ©2003 Kathryn Lay.

A Cheer of Triumph. Reprinted by permission of Kimberly Rogers. ©2004 Kimberly Rogers.

BFFS chapter opener. Reprinted by permission of Chloe Scott and Elizabeth Scott. ©2004 Chloe Scott.

Soul Sisters. Reprinted by permission of Kayla K. Kurashige and Krysti Kurashige. ©2003 Kayla Kurashige.

The Five Flavors. Reprinted by permission of Roxanne Gowharrizi and Mahvash Gowharrizi. ©2003 Roxanne Gowharrizi.

My Friend. Reprinted by permission of Anna Vier and Chet Vier. ©2002 Anna Vier.

Forget Him. Reprinted by permission of Sarah Hood. ©2004 Sarah Hood.

Do You Remember When? Reprinted by permission of Mina Radman and Parto Radman. ©2004 Mina Radman.

One Is Silver and the Other Is Gold. Reprinted by permission of Karen Waldman. ©2004 Karen Waldman.

A Friend's Secret. Reprinted by permission of Bethany Rogers ©2003 Bethany Rogers.

A Valentine to My Friends. Reprinted by permission of Rachel Punches. ©2001 Rachel Punches.

Family Matters chapter opener. Reprinted by permission of Ashleigh E. Heiple and Donald J. Heiple. ©2005 Ashleigh Heiple.

The Day Our Dad Came Home. Reprinted by permission of Pamela D. Hamalainen. ©2003 Pamela D. Hamalainen.

Chicken Soup for the Soul

Improving Your Life Every Day

Real people sharing real stories — for nineteen years. Now, Chicken Soup for the Soul has gone beyond the bookstore to become a world leader in life improvement. Through books, movies, DVDs, online resources and other partnerships, we bring hope, courage, inspiration and love to hundreds of millions of people around the world. Chicken Soup for the Soul's writers and readers belong to a one-of-a-kind global community, sharing advice, support, guidance, comfort, and knowledge.

Chicken Soup for the Soul stories have been translated into more than 40 languages and can be found in more than one hundred countries. Every day, millions of people experience a Chicken Soup for the Soul story in a book, magazine, newspaper or online. As we share our life experiences through these stories, we offer hope, comfort and inspiration to one another. The stories travel from person to person, and from country to country, helping to improve lives everywhere.

Share with Us

We all have had Chicken Soup for the Soul moments in our lives. If you would like to share your story or poem with millions of people around the world, go to chickensoup.com and click on "Submit Your Story." You may be able to help another reader, and become a published author at the same time. Some of our past contributors have launched writing and speaking careers from the publication of their stories in our books!

Our submission volume has been increasing steadily — the quality and quantity of your submissions has been fabulous. We only accept story submissions via our website. They are no longer accepted via mail or fax.

To contact us regarding other matters, please send us an e-mail through webmaster@chickensoupforthesoul.com, or fax or write us at:

Chicken Soup for the Soul
P.O. Box 700
Cos Cob, CT 06807-0700
Fax: 203-861-7194

One more note from your friends at Chicken Soup for the Soul: Occasionally, we receive an unsolicited book manuscript from one of our readers, and we would like to respectfully inform you that we do not accept unsolicited manuscripts and we must discard the ones that appear.

Being a preteen is harder than it looks! School is more challenging, bodies are changing, relationships with parents are different, and new issues arise with friends. But preteens can find encouragement and inspiration in this collection of stories by other preteens, just like them, about the problems and issues they face every day. Chicken Soup for the Soul: Just for Preteens will help readers as they navigate those tough preteen years from ages 9 to 12 with its stories from others just like them, about the highs and lows of life as a preteen. It's a support group they carry in their backpack!

978-1-935096-73-3

Teenage years are tough, but this book will help teens as they journey through the ups and downs of adolescence. Teens will find support and inspiration in the 101 new stories from teens just like them. Stories in this book serve as a guide on topics about daily pressures of life, school, love, friendships, parents, and much more. This collection will show readers that as tough as things can get, they are not alone!

978-1-935096-72-6

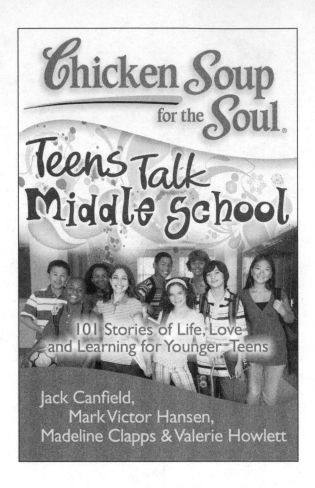

Chicken Soup for the Soul
Teens Talk Middle School

101 Stories of Life, Love and Learning for Younger Teens

Jack Canfield,
Mark Victor Hansen,
Madeline Clapps & Valerie Howlett

Middle school is a tough time. And this "support group in a book" is specifically geared to those younger teens—the ones still worrying about puberty, cliques, discovering the opposite sex, and figuring out who they are. For ages eleven to fourteen, stories cover regrets, lessons learned, love and "like," popularity, friendship, divorce, illness and death, embarrassing moments, bullying, and finding a passion. Great support and inspiration for middle schoolers.

978-1-935096-26-9

Chicken Soup for the Soul
Teens Talk HIGH SCHOOL

101 Stories of Life, Love, and Learning for Older Teens

Jack Canfield,
Mark Victor Hansen,
Amy Newmark & Madeline Clapps

Teens in high school have mainly moved past worrying about puberty and cliques, so this book covers topics of interest to older teens -- sports and clubs, driving, curfews, self-image and self-acceptance, dating and sex, family, friends, divorce, illness, death, pregnancy, drinking, failure, and preparing for life after graduation. High school students will find comfort and inspiration in this book, referring to it through all four years of high school, like a portable support group.

978-1-935096-25-2

Chicken Soup for the Soul®

Our 101 BEST STORIES

Christian Kids

Stories to Inspire,
Amuse, and Warm
the Hearts of
Christian Kids
and Their
Parents

Jack Canfield
& Mark Victor Hansen
edited by Amy Newmark

With 101 great stories from Chicken Soup for the Soul's library, this book was created specifically for Christian parents to read themselves or to share with their children. All of the selected stories are appropriate for children and are about raising Christian kids twelve and under. Christian parents will enjoy reading these heartfelt, inspiring, and often humorous stories about the ups and downs of daily life in today's contemporary Christian families.

978-1-935096-13-9

Chicken Soup for the Soul

CHRISTIAN Teen Talk

Our 101 BEST STORIES

Christian Teens Share Their Stories of Support, Inspiration and Growing Up

Jack Canfield & Mark Victor Hansen
edited by Amy Newmark

Devout Christian teens care about their connection and relationship with God, but they are also experiencing all the normal ups and downs of teenage life. This book provides support to teens who care about their faith and are navigating their teenage years. With 101 heartfelt, true stories from Chicken Soup for the Soul's library about love, compassion, loss, forgiveness, friends, school, faith, and tough issues too, such as substance abuse, teen pregnancy, and divorce.

978-1-935096-12-2

Chicken Soup for the Soul

www.chickensoup.com